Warpath

CHIEF JOSEPH WHITE BULL
(Pte San Hunka)

WARPATH

The True Story of the Fighting Sioux
Told in a Biography of Chief White Bull

BY

STANLEY VESTAL

With Illustrations

Foreword by Raymond J. DeMallie

University of Nebraska Press
Lincoln and London

First Bison Book printing: June 1984
Most recent printing indicated by the first digit below:
4   5   6   7   8   9   10

Library of Congress Cataloging in Publication Data
Vestal, Stanley, 1887–1957.
  Warpath: the true story of the fighting Sioux
told in a biography of Chief White Bull.
  "Bison."
  Reprint. Originally published: Boston: Houghton
Mifflin, 1934.
  Bibliography: p.
  Includes index.
  1. White Bull, Lakota Chief, 1849–1947. 2. Dakota
Indians—Wars. 3. Indians of North America—West (U.S.)—
Wars. 4. Teton Indians—Biography. I. Title.
E99.T34W488 1984   978'.03'0924   84-3557
ISBN 0-8032-4653-6
ISBN 0-8032-9601-0 (pbk.)

FOREWORD
By Raymond J. DeMallie

Warpath is a faithful retelling by Stanley Vestal (Walter S. Camp-bell) of the autobiography of Joseph White Bull (1849–1947), a chief of the Minneconjou Lakotas, one of the groups of Teton or Western Sioux. The collaboration between Vestal—poet, novelist, historian, professor of English—and White Bull—one of the last surviving Lakota warriors—generated a personal narrative that is graphic and direct, the unelaborated life story of a man who prided himself on the exciting and glorious war deeds of his youth. More than any other volume in the vast literature on the Sioux, this one gives the reader an appreciation for the values of plains Indian warfare in practice.[1]

All societies throughout the world are composed of individuals of differing temperament and demeanor. Every culture is represented by both dreamers and doers, philosophers and practical people—what anthropologist Paul Radin characterized as "the thinker" and "the man of action." To the general public, Lakota culture is perhaps best known through the life story of the Oglala holy man–philosopher Black Elk, whose visions provide outsiders with a tantalizing glimpse of another world of thought and understanding. But no society is made up of dreamers alone; not all Lakotas were philosophers. The life story of White Bull exemplifies the Lakota man of action and complements our understanding of the whole of Lakota culture.[2]

Just as the collaboration between Black Elk, the visonary, and John G. Neihardt, the mystic poet who told his story, brought together two men of differing cultures but similar temperament, so did that between White Bull and Vestal. Both had been trained to fight in their youth, the one in the Indian wars, the other in

World War I. Both savored the excitement of war, the courage of the individual fighter tested to the limit. Such a collaboration, of course, results in a composite view—the interpretation by an outsider with literary skills of the insider's life story, complicated by the need to transcend boundaries of history, space, culture, and language. As Vestal wrote, "Good biography, like the good life, is based upon knowledge and inspired by human sympathy."[3] The end product, therefore, always reflects the writer's interest—his "human sympathy"—as well as those of the subject.

For a meaningful evaluation and true appreciation of Vestal's biography of White Bull it is important to understand why and how it was written, to examine its goals and its biases, its strengths and its limitations. Fortunately, Vestal preserved the verbatim transcripts of his interviews with White Bull as well as a large body of related material, now housed in the Western History Collections of the University of Oklahoma Library. From these manuscripts we can reconstruct quite fully the story of this collaboration between the English professor and the Indian chief.

Walter Stanley Vestal was born in Kansas on August 15, 1887. His father died shortly thereafter and when his mother remarried J. R. Campbell in 1896, Walter took his stepfather's name. (Later, as a professional writer, Walter Campbell published his literary work about the West under the pen name of Stanley Vestal.) In 1898 the Campbells moved to Guthrie, Oklahoma Territory, where Walter spent his formative years in the company of the Cheyenne Indians who lived nearby. Indian culture and history became a lifelong passion.[4]

In 1908 Walter Campbell became the first Rhodes Scholar from the new state of Oklahoma. In the fall semester, 1915, he joined the faculty of the University of Oklahoma, Norman. From 1917 to 1919 he served in the army, and although he saw no action, he spent six months in France and was promoted to captain of field artillery. He returned to Oklahoma, where he continued to teach English and professional writing until his death in 1957.

For years young Campbell had tried to coax the Oklahoma Cheyennes to recount the story of their wars, but they told him that their fighting experiences could be shared only with other warriors. When he returned from his own service as a soldier in the European war, the old men accepted him as a fellow warrior, but most of those who could have provided the stories he wanted had died in the influenza epidemic.

In 1926 the fiftieth anniversary commemoration of the Battle of the Little Big Horn—popularly known as Custer's Last Stand—turned Vestal's attention to the northern plains. After completing a biography of Kit Carson, Vestal began to read the literature on Sioux history. By 1928 he decided to write a biography of Sitting Bull, the Sioux chief, to complement his study of the fur trade era. Realizing that the Indians themselves were the only authorities on most of the famous chief's life, he determined to interview as many as possible who had known Sitting Bull— not only his family and tribesmen but members of both allied and enemy tribes as well. During the summers of 1928, 1929, and 1930, Vestal crisscrossed the northern plains in the United States and Canada visiting Sioux, Nez Percés, Cheyennes, Crows, Crees, Assiniboines, and Blackfeet, conducting interviews with more than one hundred individuals, recording reminiscences, and checking historical documents.

Vestal was careful to observe proper protocol when visiting Indian communities, always arranging for an appropriate introduction, offering tobacco to the old men when asking for information, paying respect to the leading men, and earning their confidence. He allowed each man he interviewed to select his own interpreter, although he sometimes hired a second interpreter as a check on the other. He insisted on recording important speeches, prayers, songs, and other historical statements in the Lakota language, to ensure accuracy of translation. In order to allow himself the freedom to devote his full attention to the speaker, to watch carefully the flow of sign language that invariably accompanied the telling, Vestal took with him his cousin, J. Dallas McCoid, Jr., to serve as stenographer. On the day preceding each interview Vestal would suggest the topics on which he wanted information, but he encouraged the old men to tell their stories as they wished. He wrote: "This is preferable to interrupting a story or attempting to direct the talk too closely, for very often the white man's sense of values is quite different from that of the Indian, and it is much wiser to let the old man tell the story in his own way and thus get the Indian emphasis where it belongs."[5]

Crucial to the success of Vestal's project were the two nephews of Sitting Bull, men who had known him intimately and had fought beside him in battles against both Indians and whites— Chief Henry Oscar One Bull and Chief Joseph White Bull. Vestal first met One Bull at the latter's home on the Standing Rock Reservation in 1928 and much of his work that summer and the next centered on One Bull and his people. In 1929 One Bull adopted Vestal as a son, bestowing on him the name of his own father, Makes Room, who had been a leading Minneconjou chief. But even after this honor Vestal hesitated to approach White Bull directly, fearing that the old man might distrust his motives. Later he wrote:

> Sometimes I thought my patience would play out. I was very anxious to gain the confidence and help of Chief Joseph White Bull, the elder nephew of Sitting Bull, who lived on the Cheyenne River Reservation in South Dakota. He was one of the great warriors of his generation, older than his brother One Bull. He had a long string of *coups* and had fought in many a battle. I knew that he was a man of strong, decisive character, and I feared that if I approached him before he had made up his mind to talk he would refuse, and then, perhaps, rather than reverse himself, never offer me any help again. So I took good care not to meet him or to visit his camp. For three long years I waited, making no move in his direction, though feeling sure that he must have heard of my project.[6]

Finally, Vestal's patience was rewarded: White Bull sent him a letter requesting the writer to visit him at his home in the community of Cherry Creek, on the Cheyenne River Reservation. At the same time, Vestal was awarded a Guggenheim Foundation grant for the period June 1930–August 1931 to allow him to complete his research and write the biography of Sitting Bull.

Vestal's 1930 summer trip proved to be the culmination of his field research. He admired White Bull as the man who had been chosen at the fiftieth anniversary of the Custer fight to lead the surviving Sioux and Cheyenne warriors across the battlefield, and he was tantalized by the story he heard at the agency suggesting that White Bull had personally slain George Armstrong Custer. When Vestal and McCoid arrived at Cherry Creek in early June they first camped nearby, making a formal entry into the village on the next morning. Vestal still worried that, like some other old warriors, White Bull might limit the topics he would discuss. "But," he wrote, "once he looked me square in the eye and firmly grasped my hand, my fears evaporated."[7] Vestal struck an immediate rapport with the old chief.

At eighty-one years of age, White Bull was an alert and active man with a lively sense of humor. Eying Vestal's pipe, the old man commented, "Lot like a bucket!"[8] Vestal found White Bull to be a tireless talker, the interviews lasting nine hours a day. These were public events, other old men gathering in the chief's cabin, sitting cross-legged on the dirt floor. They served as witnesses to the validity of the old chief's narrative. White Bull was almost deaf and required a long, flexible ear trumpet to hear the questions asked of him. Sam Eagle Chasing served as interpreter.

For Vestal, the material from White Bull provided exactly the detail needed to flesh out his biography of Sitting Bull. White Bull had participated in seventeen fights with his famous uncle, and related the details of each encounter. The old chief was patient and interested in Vestal's project; he requested that Vestal send him some copies of the published book in order to sell them. Of all his Indian informants, Vestal found White Bull to be the most cooperative in answering questions. From White Bull, he was able to reconstruct a good picture of Sitting Bull as a warrior and a chief.

Delighted with his progress, Vestal wrote to his wife on June 11: "I have sat on the floor of White Bull's cabin so much my buttocks are sore, but he is giving me stuff worth any amount and I can't tear myself away. . . . The old man is fond of me, loves to talk, and is anxious to have me stay on indefinitely. I tell him history connected with his own, and it is pathetic to see his eagerness to listen. How he can tell a story—what pantomime,

White Bull and Stanley Vestal. Courtesy Western History Collections, University of Oklahoma Library.

what mimicry of voice and expression."[9] Vestal had complete confidence in the material dictated by White Bull. The chief said to him, "I will tell you the truth. I am not afraid. The man who lies is a weakling."[10]

Real friendship quickly grew between the two men. White Bull presented Vestal with a Sharps rifle that had been captured in the old days from a buffalo hunter. Vestal reciprocated by giving White Bull a cavalry saber and belt. He wrote:

> This gift aroused the old warriors to such enthusiasm that they immediately started an old-time war dance which the younger men had to sit out. As I sat watching, Chief White Bull came and stood before me, sternly fixed me with his eyes and held the tip of his eagle wing fan against my breast for fully three minutes. I looked him in the eye as a warrior should. Thereupon he invited me to join the dance of the old-timers. It was all in the grand manner of the buffalo days.[11]

Before Vestal left, White Bull announced that, like his brother One Bull, he, too, wished to adopt him as a son. Calling in all the other old men of the community, White Bull said that he was adopting the white man because he was writing the true story of the Lakota people for all to read. Then he named him "Famous," *Ocaśtonka,* literally, "He makes a name by doing something great." Vestal was greatly honored and accepted the name in the spirit in which it was given.

Vestal apparently remained with White Bull about ten days. Then he and McCoid headed north, visiting the Standing Rock Reservation and eventually meeting One Bull in Saskatchewan. Vestal studied documents in the provincial archives in Regina, drove to Ottawa to search through the Dominion archives, then to Washington, D.C., to work in U.S. government records. Taking all his material with him, Vestal and his family sailed in September for France. There they remained for a year, during which Vestal wrote *Sitting Bull, Champion of the Sioux: A Biography.*

Returning to the United States in September 1931, in the midst of the Depression, Vestal was fortunate to obtain an advance of five hundred dollars from his publisher, Houghton Mifflin, for a second volume on the Sioux. He wished to write a book that would exemplify plains Indian warfare; ultimately, he decided that the general theme would be best served by a full-scale biography of a warrior—White Bull.

Once again, in 1932, Vestal undertook a summer trek northward from Oklahoma. The details of this trip are not recorded, but he spent perhaps three weeks at Cherry Creek interviewing White Bull. This time John Little Cloud, an Oglala who was the old man's adopted son, interpreted the talks. Frederick Carder—remarkable for his idiosyncratic spelling—served as Vestal's secretary, recording as closely as possible a verbatim transcript of the proceedings.

During these interviews White Bull told Vestal his entire life story, beginning with early childhood, his first horse, first buffalo hunt, and continuing up through the reservation period to his honoring in 1926 at the Custer battlefield. But most of the interviews were structured around the old chief's war record, a ledger book filled with drawings depicting his more than thirty brave deeds in battle and documenting hunts and other events as well. In 1879 White Bull had learned from missionaries to write in the Lakota language; each drawing was supplemented with inscriptions giving the details of the event. This pictorial autobiography is a record of White Bull's accomplishments as a warrior from age sixteen—when in August 1865 he counted his first coup in a skirmish with U.S. army Indian scouts—to age twenty-seven—when in October 1876 he participated in fights with the army in the Yellowstone country after the Custer battle.[12] As the days passed, White Bull reviewed the ledger book page by page, recalling the context of each event and the participants, and describing minutely his part in each affair. White Bull made copies of these drawings for Vestal, some of which are reproduced in *Warpath*.

White Bull and Vestal were equally pleased with the interviews. For White Bull the occasion provided much-appreciated recognition of his accomplishments and validation of his status as chief. He was happy that white men everywhere would read about his deeds and the story of his people's past. He wrote in Lakota a letter to introduce his story, which, with English translation, is printed in the book (following p. xxxvii). Vestal, for his part, took vicarious pleasure in reliving with White Bull the excitement of the old days. With unashamed romanticism he wrote in the Preface to *Warpath*, "To me, at least, it is no small thing to have known and talked with a man straight out of Homer."

Vestal returned to Oklahoma with more than sufficient material to write the biography of White Bull. He completed the manuscript within a year, submitting it to Houghton Mifflin in fall 1933; the book was published in spring 1934. Vestal was concerned that *Warpath* be understood by readers not as a biography alone, but as a guide for studying the principles of Indian warfare. To this end he prepared an elaborate analytical index covering not only this volume but *Sitting Bull* as well.

To provide further historical context from an Indian viewpoint Vestal included as an appendix to *Warpath* a Minneconjou winter count—a calendar naming an important event for each year, or "winter" (in Lakota, the period from first snow to first snow). This winter count was one that White Bull had bought in 1879 and had subsequently kept up to date himself. As printed in the book (pp. 259–73), the winter count entries are dated from 1781 to 1932; comparison with other winter counts, however, shows that the first event actually corresponds with the year 1762, and the events from then until 1832 are incomplete and garbled in sequence, the last one corresponding with the event on other winter counts for the year 1815. Apparently these confusions occurred at the time that White Bull received the count, since they are repeated in another copy of the winter count that White Bull made in 1931.[13]

Finding that he still had much valuable material from interviews with Indian people and from documentary research, Vestal compiled a third volume to complete his study of the Sioux. Entitled *New Sources of Indian History, 1850–1891: The Ghost Dance—The Prairie Sioux: A Miscellany* (University of Oklahoma Press, 1934), the book is an important collection of primary historical data on many phases of Lakota history. It includes an insightful discussion of the methods Vestal used to interview and record information from Indian informants (pp. 121–30) as well as additional material dictated by White Bull: "Note on the Ways of Warriors" (pp. 141–42), an account of Sitting Bull's ability to control weather (pp. 146–47), "Movements of the Hunkpapa Sioux Camp from the Spring of 1870 until the Custer Fight 1876" (pp. 159–64), "Note on Chief Makes-Room (Kiyu Kanpi)" (pp. 314–17), and "Note on Chief Crazy Horse" (pp. 320–24).

Taken as a whole, Vestal's trilogy—*Sitting Bull, Warpath,* and *New Sources*—marks the beginning of the modern period in Lakota historiography. The work consumed five years of study, travel, and writing, and Vestal was justly proud of his accomplishment. Chief Luther Standing Bear, the Oglala author, wrote to Vestal that he considered *Sitting Bull* "one of the finest books ever written by a white man concerning the Indian." Other important books relating to the Lakotas were also published during this same period, including Standing Bear's *My People the Sioux* (1928) and *Land of the Spotted Eagle* (1933) and John G. Neihardt's *Black Elk Speaks* (1932). But Vestal's books have the distinction of being the first publications on Sioux history to apply critical standards to both oral and documentary sources while attempting to present an Indian point of view. Today they remain classics of American Indian history.[14]

In writing *Warpath,* Vestal followed the 1932 interview notes quite closely, integrating details of hunting, social life, religion, and politics into the chronological sequence of White Bull's life. He chose to write the book in the third person, even though it is in actuality an autobiography. In the Preface he explains that he made this decision in order to incorporate the nonverbal dimensions of White Bull's narrative, which were particularly important since the old man in signs and actions made every episode come alive. This procedure also forestalled the mistaken impression that the book was merely a transcript of what White Bull had dictated. In fact, the written record of the interviews reproduces the interpreter's rendition of White Bull's narrative and is therefore frequently ungrammatical, with incomplete thoughts and no regard for sentence structure. Compounded by sometimes puzzlingly idiosyncratic spelling, the 1932 interview transcripts are somewhat difficult documents to use, requiring extensive interpretation. Nonetheless, in writing the book Vestal only rarely stepped outside the actual content of the interviews, and then only to supply precise dates, names of military commanders, and other pertinent historical material to clarify White Bull's narrative. Overall, the published book is a faithful rendition of the spirit and content of the interviews.

White Bull was, in Vestal's words, "entirely a man of the world and a man of action, to whom a vision is merely a tool or a sanction."[15] While this seems an accurate assessment of White Bull's personality, it must not be interpreted to mean that White Bull was a skeptic, a man lacking in religious conviction. On the contrary, he was deeply involved in the world of the sacred. He experienced his first vision at the age of nine and was given power from the Thunder (*Wakinyan*) (pp. 12–15). Although White Bull's vision lasted only for part of an afternoon, in structure and theme it has strong resemblance to the boyhood vision of Black Elk, for in the dream horseback riders from the four directions give White Bull the power he will need for success in war.[16] He told Vestal that he experienced another vision at age fifteen, perhaps a reaffirmation of the earlier vision, but the old man apparently did not speak about it in detail. He did speak about other visions in later life through which he received power from the elk (pp. 93–94), buffalo bull (pp. 109–11), and buffalo (p. 250). Although White Bull joined the Congregational Church of his own accord in 1879 after learning to read the Bible in Lakota and appreciating its sacredness, he nonetheless continued to believe in traditional Lakota religion. The last vision he mentions, that of the buffalo, occurred in 1907, directing him to use certain herbs to cure an illness from which he had been suffering.

Despite his belief, White Bull was not inclined toward ritual. Following the command of his Thunder vision, he played the role of *Heyoka*, the ceremonial clown, on one occasion, but chose to do so alone rather than join with others in a communal *Heyoka* ritual. He participated in the Sun Dance when he was twenty years old in fulfillment of a vow made on the warpath that if he would count coup on an enemy and survive he would dance for two days. But practicality overcame ritual with White Bull; he admitted to Vestal that in hunting, he had offered prayers only when he had been hungry (p. 111), and when it came to needing eagle feathers, he preferred to shoot the birds than to trap them in the usual ceremonial fashion (p. 184).

During the course of the interviews White Bull told Vestal a good deal about religious beliefs and practices, but he did not elaborate on their meaning and Vestal failed to appreciate much of their significance. For example, before telling about his own vision of the buffalo bull that instructed him how to bring a herd of buffalo to the winter camp (pp. 109–11), White Bull related the story of the bringing of the Sacred Pipe to the Lakota people, the foundation for all their sacred rituals. Vestal omitted the details in *Warpath,* merely mentioning it in the commentary on the winter count entry for 1897, the winter "The Sacred Pipe was Taken by the Agent" (p. 271). The full story as told by White Bull is a significant variant of this important sacred tradition. It illustrates the kind of detail that can still be gleaned from careful study of the transcripts of the interviews.

The old chief began the narrative abruptly, without introduction. In a camp a ceremonial lodge had been erected, composed of the coverings of six tipis, the opening facing in the direction of a butte. A medicine man sent two young men out toward the butte to scout for buffalo, giving them four arrows and medicine to use on their sacred errand. When they found buffalo they were to put down one of the arrows with some medicine; then the buffalo would gather around it. Coming back toward camp the scouts were to lay down the second arrow, thus leading the herd to the people. The third arrow was to be laid down closer to camp, and the fourth arrow was to be placed at the entrance of the ceremonial lodge. There the men of the camp would be able to kill the buffalo.

The interview transcript continues the story:

> They sent two scouts out and they saw a herd of buffalo in a circle and it looked like a band of Indians when there was going to [be something] happen[ing]. While they were watching they saw a [wo]man coming from the herd of buffalo and when it got closer they found out this was a young, beautiful woman. And one of the young men wanted to seduce her but the other

boy would not. He said it was something holy but the other boy said he was going to anyway. So the woman took off some sacred sage [i.e., laid down the bundle she was carrying]. And when they started a cloud covered them and in a few minutes the cloud arose and just the bones of the boy was left and the woman was still there. . . .

This woman told the other boy to go home and tell the good men to come in the big tipi and bring their pipes and pick out the best, honest, clean man and she will give him the bundle. And he was to keep this until he dies and then it was to go to the next good man.

Then she told him to go home and she would follow. So he went straight home. So the boy told them and the men came to the tipi and by that time the woman was at the gate [opening of the lodge], so [s]he came in and laid down the bundle at her side. She told them to pick out the best man and tomorrow you go and kill the buffalo and they would find two men and they were to kill the two men and get one of their ears and tie it on the bundle. Anyone else to do like that boy did on the hill, they would die and be crazy. And the Indians were to live by this bundle. So then she said the gate must be cleared, and the woman turned into a buffalo cow and ran over the hill.

They chose the good man and he was to keep it [the Sacred Pipe bundle] hanging over the door on the outside of the man's house.

Her [the Buffalo Cow Woman's] father and mother had a meeting and sent her there [to the Lakota camp].

The next morning they went to the herd and there was two men there so they killed them and tied the ear on the bundle. Now the ear is like a piece of tanned leather.

The woman said good men could look in this bag [bundle].[17]

White Bull's telling of the story of the bringing of the Sacred Pipe reflects his personality. He emphasized the action of the story, the behavior of the actors, and omitted ritual details. The significance of the bundle, how the people were supposed to live by it, the meaning of the two men whom they were ordered to kill, and the significance of the ear attached to the bundle are all passed over without explanation. The narrative is told as history, not philosophy.

Vestal's interest in Indian warfare, and his own practical nature, led him to emphasize these dominant aspects of White Bull's story. Here was a Lakota who had on occasion gone to war without any sacred *wotawe* (war medicine) to protect him from the enemy; whose visions were eminently practical, meeting the needs of the moment; who once gave away buffalo bull vision power rather than try to use it himself (pp. 109–11). White Bull was a man who lived in the here and now.

Throughout *Warpath,* Vestal tries to make White Bull's motivation clear, to minimize the cultural differences separating the Lakotas from the reader. There is an appealing human reality to the unfolding of the story of White Bull's marital life, of the fifteen women who, at different times, he called wife, and of his persistent but ultimately doomed attempts to establish a harmonious marriage with two women simultaneously, after the custom of Lakota chiefs. On one occasion Rattle Track, White Bull's older wife, in a jealous rage because the junior wife, Holy Lodge, gave birth to White Bull's first son, threw away her husband's protective war medicine (p. 214). The universality of the human emotions transcends differences in cultural expression, bringing the reader closer to White Bull as a person.

The special importance of Vestal's biography of White Bull is that it makes comprehensible the motives and actions of an old-time Lakota warrior. The glory of the fight—clearly romanticized both by Vestal and by White Bull—is the key to the story. White Bull is presented consistently as the reckless daredevil, his uncle Sitting Bull constantly having to prevent the young man from involving himself in unnecessary danger. Consequently, most of the book deals with White Bull's war deeds and the period between 1865 and 1876, ending when he was twenty-seven. Most of his years—the chief was eighty-three when Vestal interviewed him in 1932—are passed over with only brief comment. Today we would like to know much more about White Bull's life on the reservation, his experiences as a chief (appointed to replace his father), Indian policeman, judge of the Court of Indian Offenses, and proponent of Lakota claims to the Black Hills. But for White Bull that was not a story; in the old Lakota way a man was judged by the brave deeds of his youth, and nothing else could substitute for this claim to respect.

After publication of his trilogy of books on Lakota history, Vestal turned to other writing projects. He made only one more trip to South Dakota, during summer 1937, visiting for a last time with White Bull and his brother One Bull. He took the two old chiefs to see Mount Rushmore. They voiced their opinion that a representation of Sitting Bull should join the carved heads of presidents on the mountain.

White Bull died July 21, 1947, at age ninety-eight; One Bull had died June 23 at age ninety-four. For Vestal this was the symbolic end of an era. The last of the old Lakota warriors had taken the Spirit Trail to the beyond. Now only Vestal's books remained as testament to their lives and to the story of their people.[18]

As the years passed and the modern world seemed farther and farther from the frontier of fur trappers and Indians wars, Vestal's perspective on that historical period he had spent so much of his career chronicling seemed to become more and more romanticized. He liked to believe that the men whose life stories he told in his biographical studies—including Sitting Bull and White Bull—had made a difference, that they had shaped the events of history. Concerning White Bull, Vestal cherished the notion that the old chief who had adopted him as a son actually had been the slayer of Custer at the Little Big Horn. In letters he revealed to friends that White Bull had in fact admitted to killing Long Hair, as the Lakotas had called Custer, but that to protect the chief from harm Vestal had vowed not to reveal the truth until the old man was dead.[19]

In 1956 Vestal had the opportunity to revise the historical record when the University of Oklahoma Press decided to reprint *Sitting Bull.* He added a section to the description of the Custer fight in which he presented the story of White Bull killing Custer. The incident is that described in *Warpath* (p. 198) in which White Bull grappled hand-to-hand with a "tall, well-built soldier" whom he finally overcame. In the revised edition of *Sitting Bull,* which appeared in 1957, the description is augmented to read a "tall, well-built soldier with yellow hair and mustache" (p. 170). The revision continues with White Bull visiting the field after the battle (compare with *Warpath*, p.203). In the first edition of *Sitting Bull*, Bad Soup identifies Custer's body (p. 174); in the revision, Vestal added a comment which he attributes to White Bull: "If that is Long Hair, I am the man who killed him" (p. 172).

It is understandable that if White Bull actually admitted to the killing of Custer, Vestal would have wanted to protect him by omitting the identity of the "tall, well-built soldier" in his biography of the chief. But why not set the record straight in the joint obituary of White Bull and One Bull that he prepared soon after their deaths for the *Westerners Brand Book?* The story was a sensational one, and it is puzzling that Vestal would delay nearly a decade in making it public. Its popular appeal was evident in the decision of *American Heritage* to excerpt this section from the forthcoming new edition of *Sitting Bull*. From there the story was picked up by the Associated Press wire service and this publicity was reflected in brisk sales of the book. Vestal received a flood of letters on the subject, leading him to comment, "You would think I was the killer of Custer."[20]

Examination of the transcripts of Vestal's interviews with White Bull fails to provide any evidence to support the claim that White Bull considered himself Custer's killer. It would appear that from Vestal's perspective identifying the dead chief as the man who had vanquished Custer was more a way of honoring him than of setting the historical record straight. Perhaps he reasoned that since no one knew for certain the true identity of Custer's slayer, White Bull might as well be given the honor.

In telling about the struggle with the soldier whom Vestal later identified as Custer, according to the transcript, White Bull did not describe his physical appearance at all. In the section of the interviews in which Bad Soup identifies the body supposed to be Custer's, White Bull commented, "This man had no mustache." There is no mention in the transcript of White Bull's identifying the body as that of the man he had killed. And the lack of mustache suggests that the body could not have been that of George A. Custer in any case. Significantly, Vestal himself once wrote that White Bull had been uncertain that the body was that of Custer, since he had never seen him personally, and told Vestal that such hearsay should not be included in his book.[21]

Campbell himself died December 25, 1957, only a few months after the revised edition of *Sitting Bull* was published. No one questioned the authenticity of his account of White Bull as Custer's slayer.

A decade later the story received apparent verification from an independent source. James H. Howard edited for publication a copy of White Bull's war record that the chief had made in 1931 for Usher L. Burdick. Published in 1968 by the University of Nebraska Press under the somewhat sensational title *The Warrior Who Killed Custer: The Personal Narrative of Chief Joseph White Bull,* the volume includes eight drawings (plates 15–22) with commentary in Lakota by White Bull depicting his role in the Custer fight. The Lakota inscriptions on the drawings identify them as incidents in the Custer fight. Plate 15 refers to *Pehin hanska,* "Long Hair"; plates 16–18 refer to *Pehin hanska akicita,* "Long Hair soldier" (which Howard translated as "Long Hair, the soldier"); plates 19–21 refer to *Pehin hanska ta akicita,* "Long Hair's soldier" (translated by Howard as "one of Long Hair's soldiers"); and plate 22 refers to *Pehi hanska okicize,* "Long Hair fight."[22]

Howard, translating the Lakota inscriptions under the mistaken impression that White Bull was the self-proclaimed killer of Custer, identified the first four drawings as a sequence representing White Bull's struggle with and vanquishment of Custer. However, White Bull's writing style was not polished, and there is nothing to support the interpretation that the chief was attempting in these inscriptions to differentiate between Custer personally and Custer's men. Nor is there any precedent in Lakota warrior art for multiple depictions of a single event. Finally, there is clear correspondence between White Bull's seven coups counted during the Custer fight (*Warpath,* pp. 196–200) and the seven drawings (plates 15–21) that depict coups.

Happily, neither White Bull's reputation as a Lakota warrior and chief nor Vestal's reputation as a historian of the Sioux hinges on the question of the identity of Custer's slayer. If Vestal, in his last years, took liberty in believing that what he had long imagined had actually been so, his motivation was not to deceive, but rather to honor a man whom he had respected in life and whose memory he cherished. But White Bull, always insistent on the truth and the facts only so far as known from personal experience, would surely prefer the record to be set straight.

With the republication of *Warpath* White Bull will again be known to new generations of readers who will keep his name and his story in remembrance. It fulfills the old chief's trust in the man he named "Famous" because of his ability to write and publish, to spread the story of White Bull's life everywhere, for all to read.

NOTES

1. Stanley Vestal, *Warpath: The True Story of the Fighting Sioux Told in a Biography of Chief White Bull* (Boston: Houghton Mifflin, 1934). Surprisingly little has been published on Lakota warfare from Indian viewpoints. Important comparable material is included in Clark Wissler, "Societies and Ceremonial Associations in the Oglala Division of the Teton-Dakota," American Museum of Natural History, *Anthropological Papers* 11, pt. 1 (1912): 1–99; Frances Densmore, *Teton Sioux Music,* Smithsonian Institution, Bureau of American Ethnology, Bulletin 61 (1918), pp. 311–418; and Royal B. Hassrick, *The Sioux: Life and Customs of a Warrior Society* (Norman: University of Oklahoma Press, 1964), pp. 72–94.

2. Paul Radin, *Primitive Man as Philosopher* (1927; enlarged ed. New York: Dover Publications, 1957), pp. 229–30; John G. Neihardt, *Black Elk Speaks: Being the Life Story of a Holy Man of the Ogalala Sioux* (New York: Morrow, 1932; new ed. Lincoln: University of Nebraska Press, 1979); Raymond J. DeMallie, ed., *The Sixth Grandfather: Black Elk's Teachings Given to John G. Neihardt* (Lincoln: University of Nebraska Press, 1984).

3. Stanley Vestal, *Sitting Bull, Champion of the Sioux: A Biography* (Boston: Houghton Mifflin, 1932; new ed. Norman: University of Oklahoma Press, 1957), p. xiii.

4. Biographical details throughout this Foreword are from Ray Tassin, *Stanley Vestal, Champion of the Old West* (Glendale, Calif.: Arthur H. Clark, 1973).

5. Stanley Vestal, *New Sources of Indian History, 1850–1891: The Ghost Dance— The Prairie Sioux: A Miscellany* (Norman: University of Oklahoma Press, 1934), p. 128.

6. Autobiographical data, Campbell Collection, Western History Collections, University of Oklahoma Library, Norman.

7. Ibid.

8. Transcript, interviews with White Bull, notebook 24, p. 1, Campbell Collection.

9. Tassin, *Stanley Vestal*, p. 166.

10. Autobiographical data, Campbell Collection.

11. Ibid.

12. Because the Lakota year ("winter") is measured from first snow to first snow, and individuals counted their age according to "winters," there are discrepancies between White Bull's statements to Vestal concerning his age at a particular time and his chronological age based on calendar years, calculated from his birth in April 1849.

13. James H. Howard, trans. and ed., *The Warrior Who Killed Custer: The Personal Narrative of Chief Joseph White Bull* (Lincoln: University of Nebraska Press, 1968), pp. 5–29.

14. Chief Standing Bear, Huntington Park, California, to Stanley Vestal, December 27, 1932, Campbell Collection; Standing Bear, *My People the Sioux* (Boston: Houghton Mifflin, 1928; reprint ed. Lincoln: University of Nebraska Press, 1975); Standing Bear, *Land of the Spotted Eagle* (Boston: Houghton Mifflin, 1933; reprint ed. Lincoln: University of Nebraska Press, 1978).

15. Vestal, *New Sources of Indian History*, p. 143.

16. For a comparison of the visions of White Bull and Black Elk, see DeMallie, ed., *The Sixth Grandfather*, pp. 84–86.

17. Interview transcript, notebook 23, pp. 186–89, Campbell Collection. I have regularized spelling, added punctuation, and placed editorial additions in brackets. For information on the Sacred Pipe, see Sidney J. Thomas, "A Sioux Medicine Bundle," *American Anthropologist* 43 (1941): 605–9; John L. Smith, "A Short History of the Sacred Calf Pipe of the Teton Dakota," South Dakota University *Museum News* 28 (1967): 1–37.

18. Stanley Vestal, "White Bull and One Bull—an Appreciation," *Westerners Brand Book* (Chicago) 4 (1947): 45, 47–48.

19. Tassin, *Stanley Vestal*, pp. 162–64.

20. Stanley Vestal, "The Man Who Killed Custer," *American Heritage* 8 (1957): 4–9, 90–91; Vestal, "White Bull and One Bull"; Tassin, *Stanley Vestal*, p. 269.

21. Interview transcripts, notebook 23, pp. 147–52, Campbell Collection; Tassin, *Stanley Vestal*, p. 164.

22. See Howard, *The Warrior Who Killed Custer*, pp. 58–59, for discussion of the translation; White Bull wrote the Lakota word meaning "hair" variously as *Pehin* and *Pehi*.

ACKNOWLEDGMENT

I would like to acknowledge gratefully the help of Jack D. Haley and the staff of the Western History Collections, University of Oklahoma Library, in making the Campbell Collection available to me for study.

PREFACE

WAR nowadays is generally regarded with horror and dismay, as a dull, dirty, and dangerous business, bringing intolerable sorrows and burdens upon the world. The Napoleons and the Bismarcks have done their worst, and war has been industrialized, mechanized, and Prussianized, until discipline, efficiency, and Second Lieutenants have made self-preservation the worst bore on earth.

Yet there was a time, only two generations ago, when on the great plains of the West, war was still an affair of personal adventure, individual freedom and daring, to which were cheerfully sacrificed all the modern military 'virtues' of discipline, obedience, and organization — those 'virtues' which have made modern war a vicious, destructive, and dismal hell. That was the warfare in which our Plains Indians delighted to indulge, warfare which was a thrilling occasional pastime rather than a dire necessity, warfare inspired by that classical *gaudium certaminis*, that joy of battle, which animated Achilles and his peers, far on the ringing plains of windy Troy. It was such warfare as the Black Prince reveled in, forming his behavior upon that of King Arthur and his knights-errant. It is this warfare of which old Indians think and talk incessantly to this day. It is this warfare which I have endeavored to present in the pages following.

The Plains Indian was a warrior and a hunter. Hunting was his trade, a drudgery which seldom rose above routine into adventure. War, on the other hand, was his sport, the joy and pride of his life, the thing of which he thought and dreamed, the field in which all his talents and desires were concentrated. To understand the old-time Sioux or Cheyenne, a comprehension of Indian warfare is fundamental.

Therefore, on completing my life of Sitting Bull, I planned to undertake a companion volume dealing with the wars of Sioux Indians within living memory. I wished to display and explain their motives and objectives, their strategy and tactics — matters little understood by white historians. My intention was to tell the stories I had gathered from many Indian eye-witnesses, and to conclude with a chapter of comment and explanation.

But research among Plains Indians inevitably takes the form of collecting the biographies of individual informants. The Redskin fought for his own glory, and always thinks of a fight in terms of his own personal achievements. The individual horseman was the military unit; and a battle was simply a series of single combats. Hence, to narrate stories of battle without taking account of the individual warrior would be as ridiculous as to leave Napoleon out of the history of his campaigns. I accordingly determined to present the life-story of a single great warrior, and, by adding a Topical Index, enable the reader who cares for such things to study Indian strategy and tactics for himself, and so form his own conclusions.

Having made this decision, it only remained for me to choose my man from among the many informants who had given me the story of those wars. That choice was soon made: Chief Joseph White Bull, Sitting Bull's 'fighting nephew,' was the ideal figure for my purpose. I preferred him, not merely because our mutual liking and long friendship had made him utterly frank with me, but because I knew him to have been a participant and eye-witness of

almost every battle which I consider worth narrating. He
was naturally a daredevil, as General Nelson A. Miles has
testified, and was always a ringleader among the fighters of
his generation. His father was Makes-Room, one of the six
hereditary chiefs of the powerful Minniconjou Sioux, his
mother the favorite sister of Sitting Bull, generalissimo of
the warlike Hunkpapa. White Bull divided his time between these two tribes and so was present in nearly every
big fight in which either camp engaged. And as he is now
more than eighty years old, his memory goes farther back
than that of any old chief I know.

Moreover, White Bull learned to write his own language
at the age of twenty-nine (three years after his surrender
in '76), and soon after compiled a written record, not only
of the fights in which he took part, but of all other important
battles of his nation within living memory. Thus his records
date back to the seventies, and are practically contempo-
rary accounts. And though many of the stories he tells
have been narrated to me by other participants, I find his
accounts most detailed and convincing. His own personal
and social standing among the Sioux have given him every
opportunity to gather information from other old cham-
pions, and the high honors which have come to him, not
merely from the Indians but from Presidents, generals, and
other high officials since his surrender, prove beyond a
doubt his eminence among American Indians. Besides, he
is a man of great intelligence and virile character, who
scorns a lie. As he put it, 'The man who lies is a weakling.'

Accordingly, I have taken great pains to give a true
story, presenting every detail exactly as I received it. This
has entailed a considerable problem in presentation. The
stories of old Indians, when given in their own words, are

simple, direct, and as matter-of-fact as such stories can well be. But Chief White Bull, throughout his talks with me, constantly accompanied his matter-of-fact narration with the most vivid pantomime. All day long, as he spoke, his hands and arms, his face, sometimes his whole body, were used in gestures which brought to life in an unforgettable manner the scenes presented so baldly in his spoken words. To omit the color, the movement, the glamor of that pantomime from his story, would be to cheat both the Chief and my readers. I have therefore preferred to write in the third person. I earnestly trust that in this way I have not wholly failed to make the reader feel the glamor and grandeur which were so real to the old warrior himself.

Chief White Bull is one of those men — brave — loyal — generous — fecund — who for countless centuries have been regarded the world over as embodying the permanent type of manly excellence. Today, by contrast, generals die in bed, and the man of action is usually only somebody's hired man. But though industrialism and internationalism may eventually make obsolete that ancient type which White Bull represents, his story must appeal to all who like directness in word and deed. To me, at least, it is no small thing to have known and talked with a man straight out of Homer.

STANLEY VESTAL

ACKNOWLEDGMENTS

I wish to thank the following persons for aid in writing this book: Mr. John Little Cloud, my interpreter; Mr. Frederick Carder, who acted as my amanuensis; Mr. Frank Zahn, for checking certain details; Brigadier General William C. Brown, U.S.A., Retired, for assistance with maps and illustrations; the Secretary, Historical Section, Army War College, for transcripts of military reports; Mr. Lawrence K. Fox, of the South Dakota State Department of History, for certain rare photographs; Mr. John Woodworth; the editors of the *Blue Book Magazine* for permission to republish White Bull's accounts of the Fetterman Fight and the Custer Fight; and the editors of the *Southwest Review* for permission to republish the story of the Ree horserace.

STANLEY VESTAL

CONTENTS

PART III: THE WHITE MAN'S ROAD

ILLUSTRATIONS

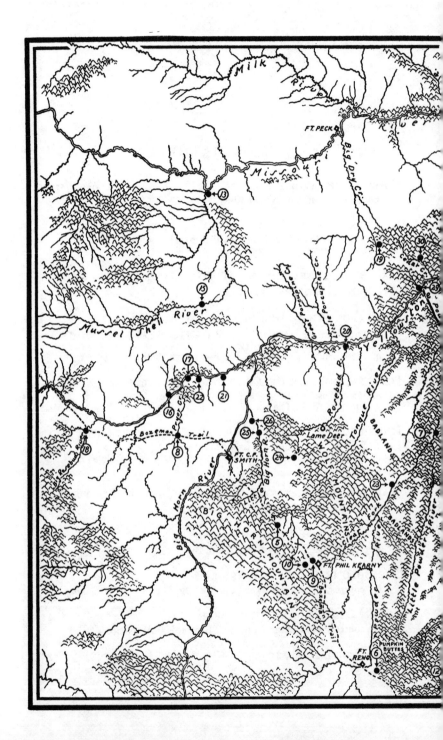

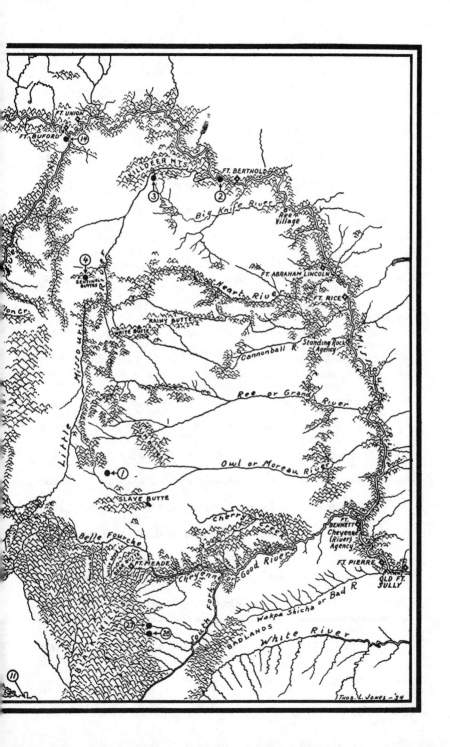

THOS. L. JONES — '34

KEY TO PRECEDING MAP OF BATTLES MENTIONED IN THIS BOOK
(Engagements are indicated by solid circles. Circled numerals alongside indicate the order here following.)

1. On head waters of Owl (Moreau) River, north of Slave (Captive) Butte, 1857. Ten Crows were killed. (Chapter II.)

2. Below the mouth of the Little Missouri on the Missouri River. Ree Horse-Race. (Chapter III.)

3. Battle of Killdeer Mountain, July 25, 1864. (Consult *Sitting Bull*, Chapter VIII.)

4. Battle of the Badlands, August 9, 1864, near Sentinel Buttes. (See *Sitting Bull*, Chapter IX.)

5. Summer of 1865. Attack on the Powder River Expedition, near Big Horn Mountains. (Chapter V.)

6. Engagement near Pumpkin Buttes, August, 1865. (Chapter V.)

7. With Colonel Cole, September 8, 1865, on Powder River. (See *Sitting Bull*, Chapter XII.)

8. Head of Arrow (Pryor) Creek, on Bozeman Trail. Summer, 1865. (Chapter V.)

9. Fetterman 'Massacre' near Fort Phil Kearny, December 21, 1866. (Chapter VI.)

10. Wagon-Box Fight, near Fort Phil Kearny, August 2, 1867. (Chapter VII.)

11. Attack on handcar on railroad on Lodge Pole Creek, Nebraska, 1868. Not shown here, as exact location impossible to determine. (Chapter VIII.)

12. Attack on railroad train on Lodge Pole Creek, Nebraska, 1868. Not shown on map, as exact location impossible to determine. (Chapter VIII.)

13. Battle with the Crows over the White Buffalo Hide at the mouth of the Musselshell River, Montana. (Chapter IX.)

14. Fight with the Hohe at the mouth of the Yellowstone. Summer, 1870. (Chapter IX.)

15. The great fight with the Flatheads on Musselshell River, 1870. (Chapter XI.)

16. Baker's Battle near the mouth of Arrow (Pryor) Creek. August 14, 1872. (Chapter XIII.)

17. With Crow Indians, on the Yellowstone above the Big Horn River, 1872. (Chapter XIV.)

18. At Crow Indian Agency on Big Rosebud River, 1872. (Chapter XIV.)

19. With the Hohe man and woman near Spoonhorn Butte on the Big Dry, 1873. (Chapter XVI.)

20. Mouth of the Rosebud River. Fight with the Slota, 1873. (Chapter XV.)

21. With Crow Indians. On the Yellowstone above the Big Horn River, 1874. (Chapter XVII.)

22. Near Big Bend of the Yellowstone. Fight with white buffalo-hunters in the snow where White Deer was rescued. Winter, 1875-76. (Chapter XXI.)

Kanta sa wi
Canpa Wakpa

MITA KOLAPI, le mita kola Ocastonka kici makin na taku ima-yunge kin hena iyuha owotanla owakiyaka wacin. Ate (Kiyu-kanpi) waonspe makiye kin heon, na Leksi (Tatanka Iyotake) waonspe makiye kin heon. Woowotanla wowicake eceela onmaspe wacin. Ate Wicasayatapa heca, na Leksi akicita itacan tanka heca heon. Lena micaje kin tanka kta cinpi, na mis hecel wacin kin heon. Ate, Leksi ehanna tapi eyas miye anpetu le-hanyan hecel cin waon. Maka wita kin le el Lakota ocaje ota onpi hena, na Tunkasila taoyate hena ob awa-mayankapi. Micaje kin slol-yapi nakun. Maka wita kilel taku tona onki hena Tun-kasila tawa, hena ob tewecirila kta. Heon taku ecamu nao blake kin lena wowicake kta. Wicasayatapa hemaca kinheon. Tona lena wanlakapi hena yuonihanyan nape ciyuzapi. Nahan rci ni waon heon.

PTE SAN HUNKA

Translation

Moon of Ripe Plums
Cherry Creek

MY FRIENDS:

My friend His-Name-is-Everywhere [Stanley Vestal] has ques-tioned me; all that I told him is straight and true. I have acted as I was taught by my own father Makes-Room and my uncle Sitting Bull. My father was a great chief, and my uncle a great leader of warriors. They two wished me to carry their great name through life; I wish the same. My father and uncle died long ago, but I am still keeping what they taught me. There are many Indian tribes on this Island [the United States], and also the Grandfather's people [citizens of the United States] saw me. You all know my name. Everything on this Island belongs to the Grandfather [the President], so we must all love one another. That is why everything I say here is straight and true, and for the reason that I am a chief. I wish I could shake hands with all you who see this. For I am still alive.

(*Signed*) CHIEF JOSEPH WHITE BULL

WARPATH

PART I
THE TRAINING OF A WARRIOR
1849–1865

WARPATH

PART I

THE TRAINING OF A WARRIOR

.·.

CHAPTER I

THE SON OF A CHIEF

Only the finest of men became chiefs.
CHIEF STANDING BEAR, *Land of the Spotted Eagle.*

THIS book is the life-story of a famous warrior, chief, and
hunter of the Sioux, a dare-devil who fought for honor, loot,
and country — and for sheer love of adventure. His people,
the Prairie Sioux, hunted buffalo for a living. And since
a man must eat before he can fight, this story properly
begins with a buffalo hunt.

Behind a grassy ridge near the Black Hills, twenty
hunters, straight of back and bowed of legs, already
mounted on their restless buffalo-ponies, waited impatiently
for the signal to charge upon their shaggy quarry. The
men were eager, clutching their bows. Even the horses
seemed to know what was up, as the chief of the hunters
raised his head to look over the hilltop at the dark mass of
bison on the flats beyond. Suddenly he called out, '*Hopo!*
Let's go!' and laid the lash on his barebacked horse. It shot
away.

In a flash the others, not to be left behind, sped after

him over the hill like a flight of arrows, straight for the buffalo.

It was early in the day and the animals were feeding. Here and there a huge old bull was rolling on the grass, or a column of dust rose up from the scene of some obstinate fight. The wind was favorable, the morning cool, the ground firm and almost level, the herd only three hundred yards away. As the hunters raced down the slope, they saw a sudden movement, a wavering, among the buffalo. The bulls on the outskirts whirled and plunged away, pushing against the bison in their path. In a moment the whole herd was in motion.

Before the racing horses could reach the buffalo, the cows were in the lead, leaving the heavy bulls to bring up the rear. Now and then one of these faced about and stopped, as if wishing to stand and fight, then wheeled and plunged on with swinging head into the dust-cloud behind the herd. With a yell, the hunters broke into that weltering mass, forcing their way at a gallop through the crowding, plunging bulls, which fell over each other in their effort to turn from the hunters, sometimes rolling over and over, hardly seen in the choking dust. Each hunter rode alone, and, singling out a fat cow, rode up on her right side, drew his arrow to the head, let fly, then plunged on to kill another buffalo.

Within a few minutes the herd had disappeared among the hills, leaving the prairie studded with black carcasses over which men were bending with their knives, having tied the lariat of the heaving pony to the cow's convenient horns. Within half an hour all the hunters had butchered, had packed the meat on horses, and were riding home, content with the day's work.

Makes-Room, an hereditary chief of the Minniconjou Sioux,[1] rode after the others, leading a good running-horse laden with the meat of the fat cow he had brought down. He had enough for his wife and small son. And as chief, he was pleased in the thought that all his hunters had been successful. He was singing.

Then he saw a comrade, Crow-Eating, riding along with hanging head; his pack-saddle was empty. Crow-Eating had had no luck. He had killed nothing. The other hunters were sorry he had failed to kill; his downcast looks disturbed them. But all of them had families to feed. None offered to share with Crow-Eating.

Chief Makes-Room thought of his little son at home, a lad of three years. He knew that Crow-Eating also had a small son. The Chief could not bear to see his comrade go home empty-handed to his family. The Chief stopped the man, handed him the lariat of his pack-horse laden with beef, to make him feel better. That was a hard thing to do, hard to beat. That horse laden with meat was one of the best running horses in the tribe. Makes-Room shouted: 'Hear ye, hear ye! I give away this horse and this beef to show my love for my little son, Bull-Standing-with-Cow, just three years old. He was to have eaten of the beef packed on this horse, but for his sake it has been given to the poor.'

That boy, Bull-Standing-with-Cow, was born in April, 1849, between the Spearfish and Whitewood Creek, in the

[1] The Teton or Prairie Sioux (Lakota) during the last century ranged west of the Missouri River, from the South Platte to Milk River, and numbered perhaps 20,000 souls. From south to north the seven sub-tribes of the Teton Sioux were: Ogla'la, Brulé, Minnicon'jou, Sans Arc, Two Kettle, Blackfeet Sioux, and Hunk'papa. The Minniconjou (Those-Who-Plant-by-the-Water) was one of the largest tribes. See Bulletin 30, Bureau of American Ethnology, Washington, D.C., 1905.

Black Hills. His family was remarkable among the Sioux, and has produced more chiefs and head-men than any other Sioux family known to me. His father and grandfather before him were chiefs of the Minniconjou Sioux, and his mother, Good Feather, was Sitting Bull's sister and therefore closely related to Four Horns, Black Moon, Looks-for-Home, One Bull, and other chiefs of the Hunkpapa Sioux. The men of that family were courageous, intelligent, generous, and fecund. They and their women practiced the great virtues admired by their people. They planned to make Bull-Standing-with-Cow a great warrior and a chief, and spared no pains to bring him up to walk in the tracks of his grandfather. His uncle, Sitting Bull, took a great interest in the lad, who spent almost as much time in his uncle's camp as in that of his father, Makes-Room. Together, the two of them trained him for the field of honor.

Bull-Standing-with-Cow was early initiated into the horrors of war. One day, when he was six years old, enemies came to steal horses from the Sioux camp, which was then near the present Ree village. The boy heard the yells and shooting on the frosty air, and, after it was all over, saw some blue beads and a brass armlet, trophies taken from dead enemies and brought into camp. These trophies roused his boyish curiosity. Next morning the child was told that anyone who wished to go and see those dead enemies might go in safety. Bigger boys were going, so Bull-Standing-with-Cow set out on short, sturdy legs, carrying his little bow and blunt-headed arrows. Some of the men went ahead. When the lad arrived, he was startled. His two enemies were standing upright!

Then someone laughed and said, 'Do not fear! They are dead.' The bodies, frozen stiff, had been propped up with sticks. The men egged on the boys to go and strike those gruesome figures. Bull-Standing-with-Cow hung back, but finally ventured to go near enough to shoot at them. He loosed one harmless arrow, then scampered home. Afterward he saw hundreds of men slain in battle, but he never forgot those two grotesque figures propped on the frozen snow....

The boy spent most of his time in active outdoor sports, running races, and hunting small game. He was strong and sturdy, and delighted in coasting down the snowy hills on a sled of buffalo ribs, whipping tops on the ice, or in summer swimming dog-fashion or overhand in the river. His pals in those days were all Minniconjou: Donor, son of Hunt; Chasing-Daytime, son of Eats-with-Bear; and Plenty Hole, son of Goosey (Touchy Loins). They all grew up to be famous warriors.

The boys trapped foxes and coyotes in deadfalls, snared prairie-dogs with a noose laid round the entrance to their holes, shot birds and rabbits. As they grew older, they spent long days on the prairie, summer and winter, from dawn till dark, herding the family horses and keeping a bright lookout for enemy horse-thieves.

All the time his father, Makes-Room, and uncle Sitting Bull, were giving Bull-Standing-with-Cow advice and instruction, which generally ran like this:

'Son, get up early in the morning, take out the horses and water them, herd them, and bring them back in the evening. Break the young geldings and be sure to keep them and teach them to run fast. By doing so you can get fat buffalo, and we shall all have enough good meat.'

'You have a good knife. Keep it sharp and do not lose it. I will make you some arrows, and I want you to keep them and also keep the ropes I gave you.'

'When you go on the warpath, look out for the enemy and do something brave. Do not make me ashamed of you. Study everything you see, look it over carefully and try to understand it. Have good-will toward all your people. Tell no lies; the man who lies is a weakling. He is a coward.'

'Keep an even temper, and *never* be stingy with food. In that way your name will become great.'

The boy's mother also gave him advice. Said she: 'Keep your horses, Son. If you have a mare, keep her until she has a foal, and if the foal will make a good gelding, train him for running. If the foal is a mare, hang on to her; some day your neighbor may need help and you can give her to him. You can help the poor. That is the way to be useful and renowned among your people.' [1]

---

[1] During my talks with the Chief, Indians were constantly coming in to borrow his horses or to ask favors. In giving this information as to his boyhood training, he said: "You see that I have followed the advice of my parents, and so now I am able to help my people." S. V.

CHAPTER II

CAPTIVE BUTTE

Small war-parties on foot leave no trail, are less liable to detection
through being seen, can cross any kind of country, have no care of
animals by night, and for many other reasons find it to their advantage
to go in this way.

W. P. CLARK, *The Indian Sign Language.*

THE winter that Bull-Standing-with-Cow was eight years
old (1857), the Sioux were traveling. They made camp one
night near the Captive (Slave) Butte, on the headwaters
of Owl (Moreau) River. This butte took its name from
something which had happened long before. The Sioux had
captured some Crow women. One woman escaped and ran
away. The Sioux could not find her. After they had given
her up, they saw her sitting on this butte in plain sight and
so recaptured her. She had been gone several days and
still had food with her. The Sioux were astonished to find
her sitting in that conspicuous position. Hence that butte
was ever after known as the Captive Butte. That was long
ago.

But now it was cold and dark. Bull-Standing-with-Cow,
having heard the legend of the butte from his mother, slept
in the snug lodge. Early next morning, Sees-the-Buffalo
left the Sioux camp to look for his horses. He could not find
them, and feared they had been stolen.

Afterward the Sioux learned, from the Crow Indians at
a peace council, what had happened. Twelve Crows had
come on foot to steal horses from the Sioux that night. They
had sent a scout to reconnoiter. The scout had found the
Sioux camp, but was tempted by the ponies he saw there.

Instead of returning to report, as ordered, he rounded up some of the Sioux ponies and took them back with him. This angered the leader of the Crows. He said the scout had done wrong: 'If the Sioux miss those ponies, they will be on their guard. They will kill us all!'

The scout was in the wrong and knew it, but was willing to placate his comrades, if possible. He said: 'Well, if you are afraid to raid the Sioux camp, take for yourselves any of these horses I have captured, and let's go home.'

The Crow leader was armed with a good gun, and angrily replied: 'Keep your horses. I am not going home. I'll steal my own horses!' The others said: 'How, how!'

'Well,' said the scout, 'I am satisfied with the horses I have. I am going home *now*.' He persuaded a small boy in the party to ride with him and help herd the ponies. They started and were soon out of sight. It was still dark, that winter dawn.

When the ten Crows started for the Sioux camp to take horses, Sees-the-Buffalo saw their dark figures coming over the snow. He ran to rouse the camp. Then the ten Crows, all afoot, saw him as well. They knew he would give the alarm. They turned, and began to run.

To the north of Captive Butte, three small buttes stand together. They are of no great elevation, but the top of one is surrounded by large flat stones which form a natural fort. The Crows took refuge there.

Meanwhile the Sioux were scouting around their camp, looking for their enemies. Sees-the-Buffalo did not know where they had gone, for even then it was hardly light. The sun had not risen. The Sioux could not have found them had not the Crows, out of bravado or for comfort's sake, built a fire on their hilltop.

That fire was a beacon to the Sioux. The first Sioux warriors to arrive on the ground built fires here and there around the butte to warm themselves, while waiting for their comrades to come.

When all had arrived, Chasing Hawk said: 'I will find out whether any of these Crows have guns.' He mounted his horse, galloped close to the Crows to let them shoot at him. One gun was fired, only one; then the Sioux rushed to the attack. For some reason these Crows did not put up much of a fight, but cowered behind the rocks, some of them with their eyes tight shut. The Sioux killed them easily; not a man nor a horse was lost.

A number of Bull-Standing-with-Cow's relatives — Long Ghost, Crazy Thunder, Eats-with-Bear, Fast Horse, Flying-Hawk, Bear-Loves — were active in this fight. The Sioux camp was only a mile or so from the butte, and, after the fight was over, the lad Bull-Standing-with-Cow went up to see the dead Crows, where they lay stripped and scalped among the rocks. By the time he got there the bodies were all frozen hard.

The sight of these dead enemies, the lively pantomime of attack and retreat in the victory dances which followed, the constant succession of wild mourning and wild rejoicing, burials and wounds, above all the eternal vigilance of Indians in his camp, made a profound impression upon the boy's mind. He had no doubt as to the path his feet must follow. The warpath must be his trail, the path in which his father, Makes-Room, and his famous uncle, Sitting Bull, had ridden to renown. The men — and the boys who aped them — thought and talked of little else than war. Danger and the love of danger was in the air they breathed, and the very labor by which they fed themselves was one of bloodshed and killing. The tools of their daily trade were deadly weapons.

Every Sioux warrior aspired to have divine assistance in his undertakings, and divine protection. This was usually gained in a vision by those who were fortunate enough to have one. The forms taken by these visions were somewhat conventional as a rule, and the Powers which appeared in them and promised aid might be anything from a small object or creature to great deities like the Sun or the Thunder.[1] Naturally the dream was in consonance with the mind of the dreamer. The Sioux recognized this fact: they did not expect a small boy to dream of the great gods. But Bull-Standing-with-Cow was a lad of strong masculine character and virile intelligence. His vision came at the age of nine, and he dreamed of the Thunder!

One day he was out under the bank of a stream trying to shoot the darting black birds which made their nests in holes in the bank high above his head. Because they lived near water, flew in a darting, zigzag way, and were dark like storm-clouds, these swallows were thought of as belonging to the Thunder. For some time he kept looking up and shooting with his little bow and arrow, but at last, he does not know how, he fell asleep and 'died.' His soul seemed to leave his body, and was in another place.

All at once he saw a man riding a black horse, his face and naked body painted with zigzag lightnings. This man addressed him: 'Boy, you seem to like my birds. Look me over well, so that when you tell about me you will tell the exact truth. When I am facing anything, I do *this*.'

[1] For the Sioux theology, with its sixteen great gods, see J. R. Walker, *The Sun Dance and Other Ceremonies of the Oglala Division of the Teton Dakota, Anthropological Papers of the American Museum of Natural History*, Vol. XVI, Part II, New York, 1917.

Then the man on the black horse rushed with his lance at a man who stood there and pierced him through the heart. Strangely, the dead man was transformed to a plant.

The man on the black horse continued: 'When you have finished dreaming, you must do this.' Then behold! The man on the black horse was holding a club. A cow was standing before him, a painted cow with a white face and horns and legs and tail — one somewhat like a white man's cow. The man on the black horse struck the cow with the club.

Immediately many men appeared on his right hand and women on his left, and between these groups stood a ragged tipi. Two young men stood up and hung a kettle on a pole and put all of the meat of this cow into that small kettle. Bull-Standing-with-Cow watched the young men building up the fire and then suddenly realized that the man on the black horse had vanished.

Thereupon appeared a man painted like the one on the black horse, but riding a roan. He called out: 'None can do what I can do.' He rushed at the kettle with his lance and speared out the meat. Then the young men took it and served it to the crowd.

There were clowns there (Heyoka Dancers), men and women. They would take the meat out of the boiling water barehanded and serve it, the male clowns serving the men and the female clowns serving the women. The man on the roan horse called out: 'This will be the day.' The boy looked around and saw some small birds on the edge of their nest. The man on the roan horse changed into a skeleton lying on the ground, and a Voice called out to the boy: 'If you do not become a clown when the cherries are ripe, you will be lying like this one.'

Then appeared a man on a white horse who called out: 'Do as I tell you, and I will be your friend.' Then appeared a man on a sorrel horse painted in the same manner and shouted: 'Look at me. You may have my power to look in four directions and kill a man in all four.' The black horse had come from the west, the roan horse from the south, the white horse from the north, and the sorrel horse from the east.

They told the boy to get up and go into the tipi, which faced west. There he saw four men in buffalo robes with the fur outside, and a yellow drum. They all entered and said: 'Remain.' They sang four songs, then all left the tipi and faced west. The drummers were leading the men on horseback. Then the four drummers and the four singers started to the north and a man riding a black horse dashed away in that direction. Bull-Standing-with-Cow stood by the tipi watching, yet, strangely, he knew he was also riding that black horse. They returned to the tent in the form of swallows, such as the boy had been trying to shoot.

Next they turned to the east. A man on a white horse led. Bull-Standing-with-Cow was watching, but, strangely, he was also riding that white horse. When they turned back to the tipi, they all were transformed to swallows once more. The third time, they rushed to the south, led by a man on a sorrel horse. The boy stood watching, but knew he was also riding that sorrel horse. This time they returned in the form of a different kind of swallow. The fourth time they started to the west, led by the man on the roan horse, and this time also the boy was in two places at once, standing looking on and also riding that roan horse. Once more they returned, in the form of a fourth kind of swallow. Then they circled the tipi and halted.

Thus Bull-Standing-with-Cow was given the power of victory when riding horses of those four colors. This dream 'made him brave.' After that, he considered himself ready for war, and, somewhat later, fulfilled instructions and acted the part of a Heyoka clown, all alone.[1]

This was the greatest of the Chief's visions. He is not of the visionary type. It is noteworthy that all his other visions came to him when he was starving, or in the delirium of illness, or when knocked on the head.

When he was eleven years old, Bull-Standing-with-Cow was a very happy boy. Not yet quite old enough to have the daily chore of herding the family stock, his time was his own. Moreover, he was well able to ride and possessed a small pony, hardly bigger than a Shetland, of which he was so fond that he thought of little else. Every morning he was up early to look after his pet and ride it to water. He watched to see what grasses the little horse preferred and would never rest until he found a pasture to suit its taste.

In summer they would go for a swim together. The spotted pony would splash into the water, and swim bravely

[1] Though the Chief had promised to tell me the full story of his life, he was somewhat reluctant to relate this vision, and requested that I hear it when there was no one else in the cabin. He explained that, whenever he told this story, a fierce thunder-storm followed, and therefore he told it very seldom. The old man does not see well and is rather deaf. He told the story at four o'clock in the afternoon. He had been sitting with his back to the north wall of the cabin, inside, and the sky was cloudless. We finished the conference at seven o'clock that evening and had supper. By that time ᵗhunder-clouds had piled up in the northwest, and my interpreter pointed out certain features of the clouds which indicated a storm about to break. Immediately after supper, a terrific thunder-storm burst upon us. The cloud was small and swept out of the north directly for my cabin, where the story had been told. No rain fell on the adjacent cabins within a few yards on either side, but the wind was so strong that I had to move my car to keep it from rolling over the bluff. The Chief made no comment on this appalling fulfillment of his prediction. He took the storm for granted.

with uplifted nostrils, while the boy clung to its mane or tail, talking to it as if it had been a human person. Uncle Looks-for-Home, who was an expert saddler, had made a fine rawhide saddle and rope bridle for the boy. Day followed day, and, whether traveling or in camp, Bull Standing-with-Cow was happy with his four-legged playmate.

One day the Minniconjou went into camp on Thick Timber River (the Little Missouri), northwest of Slim Buttes. The people were going to run buffalo. Makes-Room said to the boy: 'Son, I want you to ride with the hunters today. Try to kill a calf.' Though Looks-for-Home still made and used stone arrow-heads, Makes-Room preferred iron ones made from a frying-pan. Accordingly he sharpened ten arrows for his son, strung his bow, and together they rode out to the hunt. They saw buffalo. Makes-Room said: 'Yonder they go. Try to get that calf, and stop when you get him.'

Bull-Standing-with-Cow gripped the sleek sides of his spotted pony with bare legs, and away they went. The calf plunged along, scared and dodging, while the boy drew his first arrow to the head and let it fly. He hit the calf, but did not kill it. The second arrow had no more effect, but the third brought the animal down. The boy dismounted and waited there very proudly until his father came back.

Makes-Room was delighted with his son. He packed the calf on a horse. They set out for home, both very proud and happy.

It was the custom of the Sioux when they had done anything remarkable to make a present to some old man and tell him about it. The old man would then announce the news in a loud voice to the whole camp.

When Makes-Room and his son approached the camp on Thick Timber River, they met Chief Flying-By. Makes-Room, proud and impulsive, called out: 'My son has killed a buffalo. Take this horse and cry the camp.' Then Makes-Room thoughtlessly handed the lariat of the boy's beloved pony to Flying-By. Flying-By went into the camp, shouting the good news at the top of his voice. Makes-Room rode into the camp with the meat.

But the boy Bull-Standing-with-Cow had lost his spotted pony, his dear playmate, saddle and all. His heart was sore. He stood alone on the prairie and cried as if his heart would break.

CHAPTER III

REE HORSE–RACE

Their war tactics are the stealthy approach and sudden onslaught, when, if surprise and numbers sweep everything before them, an heroic display of courage is sometimes made; but a determined or unexpected resistance makes them scatter and retire.

W. P. CLARK, *The Indian Sign Language.*

DURING the late summer of 1862, the Hunkpapa Sioux were traveling, and fell in with some Ree Indians on the Missouri River, not far below the mouth of the Little Missouri. The Rees were on their way home from a tribal hunt up-river, and the two nations made a truce in order to trade. The Hunkpapa had plenty of deerskins and buffalo robes, and they wished to exchange these for the dried squash and Indian corn and beans which the Rees raised in their gardens. The Sioux were always ready to make peace with the farmer Indians when game was scarce. This time the two tribes pitched their camps close together — about five hundred yards apart. As soon as the tents were pitched, the people began to pass back and forth between the camps, carrying their merchandise, and visiting each other in large numbers. Bull-Standing-with-Cow wandered over to the Ree camp with one of his pals.

Such a truce was always interesting. In those small nations, every prominent man was well known to his enemies by name and record, and, when there was a truce, the warriors would get together and discuss last season's battles, checking up on any of their own side whose claims to *coups* might require verification, and giving evidence, when asked, as to the deeds of their enemies. Thus, if a

Hunkpapa had claimed to have wounded a certain Ree,
the Hunkpapa might ask the Ree to show his scar, and
thus make sure of it. In this way, warriors and chiefs became well acquainted between fights, just as rival football
teams might become acquainted and talk over old games.

Sitting Bull was well known to the Rees, for his own
father had had a Ree wife, whose son, Fool Dog, was
Sitting Bull's half-brother. Moreover, the Hunkpapa were
not so fond of fighting the Rees as were some of the agency
Sioux farther down the Missouri. All the same, the two
nations were hereditary enemies, and a truce was a tem-
porary thing at best. However — it was not often that
there were *two* truces in *one* day!

While the women were trading and the warriors talking,
the young men were racing ponies. There was a fine level
space between the camps covered with short buffalo grass
curling against the ground — an ideal turf for a race-course.
There the Indian jockeys walked up and down, leading
their race-horses, trying to match them with those of their
old enemies. It was always difficult for a man to match a
fast horse in his own camp, for all his own people knew the
speed of every pony, and would not bet against a proven
winner. But when two nations got together, there was
always a chance for some good, close races — a good chance
of making a clean sweep of the other nation's stakes. One
of the Hunkpapa young men had a very fast bay horse,
and soon arranged a race with a buckskin pony — the best
horse in the Ree camp. Each nation bet heavily on its
favorite, and excitement ran high. The Hunkpapa threw
down everything they owned in a heap, and the Rees
matched it, piece by piece, in another heap alongside.
Some of the men bet everything, down to their gee-strings.

Meanwhile, a herald was selected to announce the winner, and judges were named. The jockeys, stripped to moccasins and breech-clout, tied up their own hair and the tails of their horses, and, with only a rope bridle and a quirt, were soon trotting off to the start, half a mile away. There the pair of them lined up, the Ree on his wiry buckskin, the Hunkpapa youth on his clean-limbed bay. Both men rode bareback.

'Go!'

Away they went on the jump, the riders crouched low over the flying manes, the swift hooves thudding the grass, the red gee-strings whipping the air, the wooden quirts with the long double lashes flailing the ponies as fast as the riders could jerk their naked arms. On they came, neck and neck, and the excited, yelling men at the finish could not tell who would win. All they could see was that frantic pair looming toward them against a cloud of sunlit dust. Finally, the ponies tore past the judges, and sped away over the prairie, fighting the bridle, unwilling to slow down, turn, and go back to the crowd of excited betters.

There, all was noise and gesticulation. Both riders claimed to have won. The judges themselves could not agree, and every better had his own opinion. Excited talk broke out; the crowd was rapidly becoming angry. The Ree owner proposed to take the stakes laid by the son of the Hunkpapa herald. The Hunkpapa would not have it so, and called the Ree a liar. At once the enraged Ree struck the youth.

Plains Indians do not deal in fistcuffs: when they quarrel, they use weapons, and strike to kill. The Hunkpapa youth immediately struck back. They grappled and struggled together. At once several others joined the brawl;

then the fight became general. Knives flashed from their sheaths, bows and arrows came out of quivers; all was hand-to-hand in the mêlée. The Rees killed several of the Sioux. One of the Rees was shot down, and one of the judges. The two parties separated, began to shoot at each other. It was a regular battle, right between the camps.

In those camps all was confusion for a moment. But when the people saw what was happening, they grabbed the visitors from the other nation, and held them prisoners. The Rees held a lot of Sioux, and the Sioux held just as many Rees — men, women, and children. It was a desperate situation for them all.

Bull-Standing-with-Cow, with another Sioux boy, was then in the Ree camp. They had been watching the horse-racing. Suddenly the boy heard someone call out: 'They are fighting!' At once the two boys began to run for home. When they looked back, they saw people chasing them, but they ran hard and reached the Sioux camp in safety. Bull-Standing-with-Cow ran into his father's lodge and snatched up a gun lying there. Then he ran out with the weapon and, pointing it at the Rees, helped the Sioux capture those in their camp. The Sioux held these Ree visitors prisoners.

Still the fight went on; several were killed on each side. But when the first fury of the quarrel passed, there was a lull in the fighting, and people began to wonder what would happen to their friends and relatives held prisoners in the enemy camp. Nobody knew what to do. Bull-Standing-with-Cow was watching.

While they stood there, the Ree chief walked out between the lines and shouted: 'We want Sitting Bull in the Ree camp right away.'

Sitting Bull mounted his horse and rode out to meet the Ree chief. The warriors stopped shooting, but held themselves in readiness, arrow on bowstring.

The Ree chief took Sitting Bull's horse by the bridle, and led it away through his own party, right into the middle of the Ree camp. There he asked Sitting Bull to get down, and, when he had done so, led him into a tipi. When the Hunkpapa captives saw their leader riding into the Ree camp, they drew a long breath. If anybody could settle this terrible difficulty, he could.

Inside the tipi, the Ree chief helped Sitting Bull undress. Then he brought out several bags of fine clothing, opened them, and took out the garments. He honored Sitting Bull by dressing him in these fine clothes with his own hands. He put on him two fine scarlet trailing breech-cloths, a foot wide, reaching from his belt to the ground, before and behind. He helped him into a pair of handsome leggins of soft, pliant buckskin, decorated with a broad bead stripe down the leg, and having heavy twisted fringes from the hip to ankle. On his feet he placed moccasins with stiff rawhide soles and flexible elkskin uppers covered with designs in dyed porcupine quills. Over Sitting Bull's head the Ree chief slipped a shirt of mountain-sheep's skin, with trailing fringes, decorations of quillwork across the shoulders and chest, and tassels of hair in rows on either side. This shirt he laced up the side, and tied the sleeves to fit, for in those days such shirts, like ponchos, had no seams up the sides and along the arms. Having painted Sitting Bull's face, he then took from a painted cylindrical rawhide case a swagger war-bonnet and put it on his head — a splendid headgear, with an upright crown of glistening plumes from the golden eagle, a beaded brow-band, and a long tail of feathers cascading down the back to his heels. The Ree tied the chin-straps under Sitting Bull's chin, and belted the tail of the bonnet around his waist.

Leading him outside the tent, the Ree made him mount a fine black horse with a bald face. A war-bonnet was tied to the mane of this horse and another tied to the tail, and its back was thick with blankets. When the horse moved, the tails of the war-bonnets dragged the ground. The Ree chief led this horse to the open space between the lines of hostile warriors.

'Now,' said the Ree chief, 'all you Rees bring your Sioux captives, and let the Sioux bring their Ree captives, and let us have peace.'

Sitting Bull commanded the Hunkpapa to do as the Ree chief had suggested. There was no lagging on the part of the captives as they hurried home to their own camps, carrying their gifts and purchases, glad to be alive. Then the dead bodies were exchanged. There was peace again.

The people quickly completed their trading. It did not take long. Both camps were nervous, what with the wailing of the bereaved in their ears all the time and the sight of those dead bodies being prepared for tree-burial. Almost at once both nations broke camp and moved away in opposite directions. Sitting Bull lined up his Strong Hearts on both flanks of the moving camp; they kept a sharp watch on the young men, who might be tempted to slip away and try to kill some Ree. Sitting Bull did not wish to start another fight. And so ended the Day-of-Two-Truces at the Ree encampment.

This adventure made a vivid impression upon the boy Bull-Standing-with-Cow, then just thirteen. Particularly was he impressed by the honors shown to Sitting Bull and by his uncle's influence. The boy began to be conscious of the fact that he belonged to a family of the highest standing and that his father and uncles were great men among their people. He began to look forward to the day when he, too, might be a famous warrior and a chief.

In preparation for that day, he and his comrades formed mimic warrior societies and imitated the dances and insignia of their elders. They kept their eyes open, asked questions, and informed themselves: they soon knew the meaning of the warlike regalia they saw around them.

Thus, at a dance, when a warrior carried a wooden knife with scarlet blade and some horsehair tied to the hilt, they knew he had taken a scalp at some time; if he had his face painted with white spots, he had probably distinguished himself in a snowstorm, or, at any rate, in the winter. A man carrying a spear with a red blade was evidently the hero of a battle with lances, who had slain his foe. And they could tell where a man had been wounded by the wound-marks painted upon his body, horse, or clothing — a straight horizontal line dripping red for an arrow-wound, and a red-dripping disk for a bullet-wound. A man painted with a red hand had been struck by the enemy, that was certain.

Horses, too, were painted up, the lad observed, and all those marks meant something. White paint was used on dark horses, red on light-colored horses. Horse-tracks, the shape of horseshoes, meant captured ponies — one track was used for each horse captured. Stripes on the right leg indicated the number of times the owner had struck enemies on that side, and on the left leg the number of times he had struck enemies on the left side. An imitation scalp tied to the bridle-bit meant that that horse had been used to run down an enemy. Already the boy knew the significance of all these insignia of martial honor.

Naturally, the boy and his pals were keen to learn what deeds gained highest honor, and why some warriors were allowed to walk up and strike the drum at a dance, and how it was that striking an enemy was rated higher than killing him, scalping him, or taking his horse or his weapons. Bull-Standing-with-Cow found all this expressed in the language of feathers — the symbolism of the eagle tail-feathers with which successful fighters adorned their heads.

He was told that these head-feathers were awarded to brave men who had counted *coup* — who had been bold enough to strike an enemy with their hands or with some-thing held in their hands. He learned that four men might count *coup* on the same enemy in the same fight, and ranked on that occasion in the order of their striking him. To strike first was the greatest honor possible, and the man who had done that could wear an eagle feather upright in his back hair. He who struck second wore his feather with an up-ward slant, pointing to the right. The third to count *coup* wore his feather horizontally, projecting to the right over his shoulder, while the fourth man's feather sloped down-ward to the right. Thus, at a glance, the boy could tell what men in camp had been bravest in battle. And he observed that great warriors like Sitting Bull or Crawler, though they had the right to wear many eagle feathers, actually were content to appear, out of modesty — or pride — with only one or two. Then again, they would turn out in glorious war-bonnets, trailing to their heels.

The boys imitated all these deeds and marks of honor in their war-games, counting *coup* upon each other and upon the animals they hunted, in mimic warfare. And among them all Bull-Standing-with-Cow was one of the strongest and most stubborn contenders.[1]

[1] During his lifetime, the following Societies claimed him as a member:
I. Boy Societies:
    (a) Strong Hearts — at six years of age.
    (b) Fox society — at seven years.
    (c) Badger Society — at nine years.
II. Men's Societies:
    (a) Fox Society (Minniconjou) at eleven years.
    (b) Owns Lance Society — at twelve years.
    (c) Fox Society (Sans Arc) — at twenty years.
    (d) Silent Eaters (Hunkpapa) — at twenty-four years.
    (e) Chiefs' Society (Minniconjou) — at thirty-two years.

CHAPTER IV

EIGHT ARE KILLED

Indians possess as much courage as any people, and, when young, sometimes not only scorn the fear of, but really court, death.
W. P. CLARK, *The Indian Sign Language.*

HAVING killed his first buffalo calf, Bull-Standing-with-Cow was anxious to kill a cow, and qualify as a genuine hunter. However, he had to wait a whole year — until he was twelve — before he accomplished his desire.

One day his father said: 'Your cousin and I are going hunting. Get your horse and come along and I will show you a fat buffalo.' Bull-Standing-with-Cow made haste to obey. He had a good bow, and his father sharpened ten iron-headed arrows for the boy. Afterward the three of them mounted and rode out toward the herd.

Makes-Room said to his son: 'The way to know a fat buffalo is to look just above the tail and just below the hair on the neck. If those places are plump and well filled out, the animal is fat. You can tell by the development of the horns whether the animal is young or old. A yearling has short straight horns. When two years old, the buffalo has longer horns. In the third year, the horns are still longer and curved. In the fourth year, the curve is greater, and in the fifth year, the horns are fully curved. In the sixth year, the horns become blunted and slick. All the teeth are there by the fourth year.'

Makes-Room added: 'Ride up on the right side of the cow. Aim for the heart or lungs, through the ribs, or just behind the fore shoulder. Then you can kill her.'

When they reached the herd, the buffalo began to run,

and the three men raced after them. Makes-Room rode knee to knee with his son until they were close to the animals. Then Makes-Room pointed out a buffalo and said, 'There is a fat one, look her over well.' Makes-Room sped away to kill his own meat.

The boy dashed after his quarry. When he was close, he let fly one arrow — without any apparent results. The second time he drew the arrow back as far as he could and let fly. It went into the animal's ribs almost up to the feathers. Still the cow plunged on. A third arrow buried itself in the flesh of the cow without stopping it. Bull-Standing-with-Cow had the fourth arrow on his string when he saw blood flowing from the buffalo's mouth and knew he had killed it. Presently it stopped, and the boy hung around until the animal staggered, fell, and lay with rigid, outstretched legs on the bloody grass.

The boy did not know how to skin a cow, and waited for his father. Finally Makes-Room came up and told the boy what to do, and said that he would be back from his own butchering by the time Bull-Standing-with-Cow had finished. Said Makes-Room, 'I have killed three. Your cousin got two.'

While the boy was laboriously trying to get the skin off the unwieldy cow, an old man came along and offered to help butcher if Bull-Standing-with-Cow would give him the 'center part' (the meat on the ribs, the heart, liver, kidneys, and intestines). Bull-Standing-with-Cow agreed, and the two of them butchered the cow and put the meat on the boy's pack-horses. It was quite an undertaking.

Had the hunters wished to use the cow-hide for making a tent, they would have rolled the animal on its back, propped it so by twisting the head around under the shoulder, and cut the skin along the belly so as to take it off in one piece. But that day they were hunting for meat and robes. Therefore, the boy and the old man laid the dead cow on her belly and stretched out the legs, front and back, to hold her so. They cut from the upper lip up the nose between the horns and along the backbone to the tip of the tail. Each one then set to work to strip off the hide on one side. The boy noticed that the old man did not try to cut all the meat from the hide, but worked rapidly, leaving a layer of meat on the hide of the back and even more on that of the belly. These bits of meat, sticking to the hide, were scraped off by the women before tanning and formed a favorite dish of the Indians. Such dried bits of meat, scraped from a hide with a dubber, looked rather like potato chips, and made excellent soup.

The butchers then cut out the tongue and loosened the outer blanket of flesh from the back and sides of the animal, which was removed in one piece. The front quarters were detached, the hind quarters removed at the hip joints, the fat hump was cut off at the backbone, and the remaining blanket of flesh on the ribs and above the entrails was cut off in two parts. The old man then slit the carcass along the belly, up the shoulder, and along the backbone. He picked up the hind leg of the buffalo, and, using the sharp hoof as a hatchet, broke the ribs from the backbone in the form of a slab on either side. Then the kidneys, liver, fat, and brains were taken out and placed in a pocket-shaped piece of gut to be saved and used in tanning the hide. The paunch he turned wrong-side-out and filled it with the kidneys, heart, and fat. He saved the lower back-bone for the grease which could be boiled out of it.

The hide was then split along the belly. Half of it was

laid on one horse, and on this was placed the large blanket of flesh. The other half of the hide was laid on another horse and covered with the two smaller blankets of flesh. The rest of the meat was divided between the two animals, wrapped up in the hide.

When they started back to camp they left hardly anything for the wolves. Bull-Standing-with-Cow was happy. He had killed a full-grown buffalo. He thought himself a man. But sometimes something happened to remind him that he was still only a boy.

One day, when fourteen years old, Bull-Standing-with-Cow heard of a strange and dreadful event. It had happened when he himself was only one year old. Some Sioux hunters had had a memorable experience.

They were hunting not far from the Good (Cheyenne) River, running buffalo. A Minniconjou named Young Bird shot a cow, and his friend, Nasty Head, a Sans Arc, got off his horse to help butcher. When they opened the belly of the cow, they found there the bag containing the calf. The Sioux considered the unborn calf of the buffalo a great dainty, and Nasty Head at once laid claim to half of it. Young Bird agreed, and they removed the bag and laid it aside on the prairie.

Nasty Head said, 'I will open the bag for you while you work on the cow.' Young Bird assented. Nasty Head ripped open the bag, then started back in astonishment. It was no calf he saw. An old woman with long gray hair and human features sat up and looked at him, then fell over dead. The two hunters were frightened, and began yelling to their comrades to come and see what they had found. All the hunters came running and riding in answer to their calls. They examined the portent carefully, and found that this strange creature had all the parts and characteristics of a human female. It was all very mysterious, *wakan*.

On the advice of older men, the two hunters washed themselves with snow and wiped themselves with sprigs of the sacred sage. They did not touch the cow or the old woman again, but left them on the prairie. This strange event gave its name to that winter, 1849–50, in the Minniconjou Calendar. It is known as the Winter-When-Calf-Woman-Was-Born.

One day soon after the boy heard that story, the herald of the camp announced a buffalo hunt. 'Catch your horses, saddle up!' he shouted. 'We are going to kill buffalo calves.'

Now that the boy had killed a buffalo cow, he felt he was a qualified hunter. He jumped on his fast pony and rode out with the men. When the hunters rushed the herd, the buffalo scattered over the prairie and through the brush along the river. Bull-Standing-with-Cow raced along on the edge of the herd nearest the stream. As his pony dodged through the brush, he saw a calf bouncing along before him at full speed. The boy was very anxious to bring down that calf. He quirted his pony on both flanks, drubbing the animal's ribs with moccasined heels. Before long he came up with it.

That calf proved hard to kill. In his left hand the boy held his bow and five arrows. He shot and shot into that calf until all five arrows were gone. He thought he had never seen such a tough calf. Every arrow had gone through into its vitals, but only the fifth arrow brought it down.

Proud of his success, he reined in his pony, slid from its back, and got out his knife to skin his quarry. Bending over the dead animal, he was startled to see that it had a

long face and jaws armed with sharp teeth. Instead of
hoofs it had claws. The boy was frightened. He remembered how the hunters had found the old woman in the
buffalo's belly. The scared boy wanted company just then.
Not far off he saw a man butchering a buffalo. He ran
over to him, calling out, 'This calf is *different!*'

The butcher, a Sans Arc, stopped his work, straightened
up, and walked back with the boy to inspect his kill. When
the man saw that calf with claws, he broke into a hearty
laugh. 'Son,' he said, 'this is a bear you have killed!'

For all that, Bull-Standing-with-Cow, now going on fifteen, was strong and active for his years. He could ride,
and shoot, and felt it was high time to go on the warpath
and distinguish himself. But so far no opportunity had
offered.

Then one day he learned that some of the men were
going to war. At the time, his father's lodge was pitched
in a large camp of Minniconjou Sioux. In the camp were
also Hunkpapa, Oglala, Sans Arc, and a few Brulé lodges.
It would be a big war-party. Many of his relatives were
going and the boy was eager to join.

Seeing this, his uncle, Chasing-Crow, encouraged the lad
and said: 'Nephew, we are going after enemy horses. Why
don't you come along? It will be a good chance to steal
some fast ponies.'

With Uncle Chasing-Crow's invitation to back him, the
boy went to his father, Makes-Room, and declared he intended to go.

Makes-Room looked at his son in silence, and the boy
thought his father looked unwilling. Perhaps Makes-Room
did not wish to break the boy's spirit or quench his martial
ardor. Perhaps he feared that, if he refused, the boy would

run off and go in spite of him. After a time he said, 'All right, Son, I think I will go too.' Bull-Standing-with-Cow was delighted, and quickly made his preparations for the great adventure.

The war-party set out and rode for two days up the Yellowstone River to an Oglala camp. There other volunteers joined the party, and all fifty of them jogged away toward the country of the Crow Indians. On the second day out, they made camp early and turned their horses loose to graze. They wished their ponies to be in excellent condition in the enemy's country just ahead. Next morning, when it was time to round up the ponies for the start, Makes-Room said to the boy, 'You stay here, Son. I'll go after the ponies.'

Makes-Room went over the hill with the other men and the boy waited in camp for him to come back. Within an hour the first warriors had already come in with their ponies, had packed up and started away. One after another came dropping in and went riding off in the same manner until finally the last of them was gone. Still Makes-Room did not come back with the horses and the boy grew very restless, wondering what had happened, and anxious to be on his way. The morning passed, the afternoon dragged through. All day long he waited for his father. But when at last Makes-Room appeared, near sundown, driving the animals, he said: 'Son, our horses had started for home. I had a hard time finding them. I think the other warriors must be a long way off by this time. It will soon be dark. We can never overtake them now. I suppose we might as well go back home.'

Greatly disappointed, Bull-Standing-with-Cow accepted his father's decision. They rode until midnight, then slept, and on the morning of the second day reached the Oglala camp. Two more days of riding brought them home.

When the war-party returned, the boy learned that they had had a hard time at the Crow camp. The Crows were too many for them and chased them back over the prairie. Some of the Sioux were unhorsed, their ponies played out, and they could not save themselves. Eight were killed. Of the Minniconjou, Walks-with-Arrow-in-his-Body or Red Earring was shot first, then Left-Handed-Buffalo, Bear's Heart, Body, and Whirlwind Hawk; of the Oglala the Crows killed Man-from-Below and Both Legs; of the Brulé Sioux, Elk Rattlesnake. This disaster is remembered by the Sioux as *The Fight Where Eight Were Killed.* A boy would have been in great danger on that warpath.

But the boy, Bull-Standing-with-Cow, thought little of the danger he had escaped, for Uncle Chasing-Crow had been successful. He came back in triumph driving five captured horses. Another uncle brought back three. Nine other horses were brought by other men — seventeen head in all.

Chasing-Crow said to the boy: 'Nephew, what happened to you? If you had gone with me, you might have captured some fine horses.'

Then the boy explained, telling how the ponies had wandered away and how his father had been all day finding them. Uncle Chasing-Crow looked across the lodge-fire at Makes-Room and laughed. Then the boy noticed that his father sat there with hanging head, looking down, and was tapping the ground with his pipe-cleaner, very much embarrassed. The boy saw that there was something hidden there and began to ask questions. Then Makes-Room broke down and admitted with a grin that his horses had not strayed away. He had deliberately delayed bringing them back to keep his son from going to war. 'Son,' he said, 'I thought you were too young for such a warpath. All day long while you were fretting in the camp I was sitting behind the hill, smoking, and holding my ponies.'

The boy did not think this a very good joke. Every time he saw one of the fine horses his uncle had captured, he resented the trick his father had played upon him. He determined that in future he would not be turned from his path by anyone. Twice that summer the boy saw his people fight the troops,[1] and once he himself dashed along their line and let them shoot at him. But still he had done *nothing* to give him the rating of a warrior. He was burning with impatience to be gone on the warpath.

[1] For Bull-Standing-with-Cow's account of the Battle of Killdeer Mountain, July 25, 1864, and of the Battle of the Badlands, August 9, 1864, see *Sitting Bull*, chapters VIII and IX.

PART II
ON THE WARPATH
1865-1876

CHAPTER V

FIRST IN WAR

The Indian... is... the finest natural soldier in the world.
COLONEL RICHARD I. DODGE

DURING the sixties no warrior of all the Minniconjou Sioux was more celebrated for valor and success than High Hump (High Back). He was forever seeking enemy scalps and horses, and was generally lucky as well as brave. For some time past he had been buying eagle feathers, and was having a war-bonnet made. That done, he would be ready to go to war again. And so, when the bonnet was finished, he invited a few friends to dinner, told them he wished to lead a party, and offered them the war-pipe. They smoked with him, thus pledging their word to join, and afterward passed the news privately around camp. High Hump was so favorably known that some fifty men decided to join his party. Among these volunteers were Yellow Shield, High Lodge, Shoots-the-Island, Bear-Loves (Bear-Pities), Runs-Against, Wood-Pile, Iron Lightning, Red Fox, Bull Eagle, Bear-Shedding, Long Bull, Flattening-Iron, Two Man, Two Lance, Big Hail, Turtle, Camp Leader,[1] Stands-Astraddle, and Fast Horse (Makes-Room's half-brother) — all of them Minniconjou Sioux. Two Oglala volunteered also: Hunts-the-Enemy and Spotted Breast or All-Against-Him (At Bay). The moment Bull-Standing-with-Cow learned of this party, he decided to join it.

[1] This name, *Wakicunza*, is the regular title of the official responsible for all movements of a Sioux camp. See Wissler, *Anthropological Papers* of the American Museum of Natural History, vol. XI, Part I, page 8.

Makes-Room saw that *this* time his son would have his own way; there was no stopping him. He therefore gave the boy a fast dapple-gray war-horse called 'Swift Hawk,' and a long wand like a lance without a blade, decorated with a ring of crow feathers (clipped short) near one end, and flaunting a single eagle tail-feather from its tip. It happened that the chief's half-brother, Horse Tail, was a shaman. So Makes-Room gave the shaman a bay pony for a protective war-charm or medicine for his son.

The medicine was in a small leather pouch decorated with an eagle feather. Horse Tail hung it on a thong around 'Swift Hawk's' neck. Then he painted the animal with a red wavy line from the hoof to the backbone on all four legs, and encircled its jaws above the bridle-bit with a red line. He tied a soft eagle-plume in the boy's hair, and around his neck he fastened a thong which supported a whistle made from the wing-bone of an eagle.

'Nephew,' he said, 'this medicine will make your horse strong and long-winded. If you do as I have told you, your pony will never play out.'

High Hump had asked his followers not to advertise the raid, but to get ready for a big parade around the camp. When all preparations had been made, the warriors got together and spent the night singing and dancing. Early next morning they put on their fine war-clothes and rode around the camp circle, singing and shooting. The whole camp turned out to see them start. At sunup they set out. Soon after leaving the camp, Bull-Standing-with-Cow and the others packed their fine war-clothes in their saddle-bags, and, mounting saddle-horses and wearing everyday clothes, jogged away, leading their best mounts in order to spare them for the war ahead.

High Hump was a seasoned partisan. Each day he sent out two scouts in advance of the party, reliable men who knew the country. Every morning, before starting off, these scouts selected the rendezvous for the coming night and announced the time when all should gather at the place appointed. Each day the scouts were changed. It was in July, 1865, when they reached enemy country near the White (Big Horn) Mountains.

The last scout sent out was Bear-Shedding. Late that night he returned and made his report. He told High Hump that an enemy camp was not far ahead. Immediately the party prepared to advance. They put on their war-clothes, painted themselves for battle, and mounted their fast horses. It was midnight.

Bull-Standing-with-Cow was excited, eager to be gone. It seemed to him that the warriors would *never* get started. Bear-Shedding, the scout, was a close friend of his, and of course knew where the enemy camp lay. Bull-Standing-with-Cow pointed out that the first men to arrive there would have the best chance. Bear-Shedding agreed, and the two of them slipped off together ahead of the main party to see if they could capture some horses. After going some distance, they came near a large camp of enemies, dimly seen in the darkness. But, as it was not yet daybreak, these enemies had not yet turned out their horses to graze. While the two men waited impatiently for dawn, High Hump and the others came up. It seemed as though Bull-Standing-with-Cow was to be hindered again.

But Bear-Shedding had reconnoitered that camp thoroughly the day before, and on being questioned, told his friend just where to go to find horses and how to approach the enemy camp. Accordingly, Bull-Standing-with-Cow slipped off and rode 'Swift Hawk' close up to the enemy's camp, taking cover where his friend had advised. The moment it was light enough and the horses were turned loose, the boy dashed into the pony herd alone. Cutting out a bunch of eight head, he started the animals for home. But they were just off the picket-line, and sluggish. He had to blow his bone whistle to scare them into a run.

The scream of that whistle roused the enemy camp. In no time at all ten mounted enemies came rushing out in pursuit of the galloping horse-thief and his swift booty. They came yelling and shooting, hot on his trail. But the boy only blew his whistle the harder, lashing 'Swift Hawk' on both flanks, racing from the camp, pushing the herd ahead of him on the dead run. When he looked back, he could see his enemies gaining, could hear the banging of their guns. He rode hugging his pony's neck to protect himself from flying bullets. For three miles the ten of them kept after him, slowly gaining, shooting as they rode. It seemed that they *must* overtake the boy, but by good luck he ran into his own party advancing. Then his enemies, seeing that great war-party, reined in their panting horses and fell back to their camp.

It was so early in the morning that the boy could not be sure what enemies he was raiding, but, as one of the horses he captured had on a saddle and bridle such as white men use, he decided they must be white men.

Bear-Shedding and one or two other Sioux had also been successful and had captured horses, but most of them had nothing to show for the raid. So far, no Sioux had been killed or wounded, but the enemies were now wide awake and very numerous. It was broad daylight. Most of the Sioux voted to go home.

Bull-Standing-with-Cow was perfectly willing. On this, his first warpath, he was the hero of the day. He had been the first to harm the enemy.

High Hump was not so well pleased with the expedition. As it happened, he had failed to do anything remarkable. This was unusual and exasperating to such a famous warrior, so now he set about organizing a second war-party. At this time (August, 1865) United States soldiers were building forts in the Sioux hunting-grounds on Powder River, and white settlers were swarming up the Bozeman Trail to the goldfields in Montana and Idaho. All this was in violation of the existing treaty, and the Sioux strongly resented it. High Hump therefore decided to lead his party against the soldiers.

At that time the Sioux were in camp on the Yellowstone below the mouth of the Greasy Grass (Little Big Horn) River. More than fifty men started with High Hump. Among them Bull-Standing-with-Cow found a number of his relatives: Shoots-the-Island, Bear-Loves, Yellow Shield, Iron Lightning, Red Horse. The party moved toward the headwaters of Powder River west of the Black Hills, and lay in wait on the trail near the Gourd (Pumpkin) Buttes, not far from Camp Connor (afterward called Fort Reno).

Hiding there, the Sioux soon saw enemies riding south along the trail — seven mounted scouts in blue uniforms, driving four spare horses. When they came near, the Sioux mounted and swept from their covert at a run, whipping their horses on both sides. Bull-Standing-with-Cow was riding his fast gray, 'Swift Hawk.' He got a good start and dashed far ahead of the main party, riding with the foremost. At first the scouts did not see the Sioux coming. When they did, they halted, turned tail, and raced back toward the tents and buildings of their camp with the blood-curdling war-cry of the Sioux loud in their frightened ears.

By the time the foremost Sioux drew near the scouts, the latter had become considerably strung out. They galloped along as fast as they could, with the frightened spare horses plunging through the dust at their sides. Charging-Bear was first to overtake the last of the scouts. He struck the man smartly across the shoulders with his bow, then wheeled away, veering from the threat of the bluecoat's gun. Bull-Standing-with-Cow, plunging through the dust right at his friend's heels, counted the second *coup* on that scout with his lance.

These blows must have frightened the scout, who spurred his horse to desperate speed. For a moment Bull-Standing-with-Cow was left behind. He used that moment to snap an arrow on his bowstring and draw it to the head. The arrow leaped from the string into the back of his luckless enemy. Bull-Standing-with-Cow did not wait to see him tumble, but dashed on to attack the others. He was now the foremost of the Sioux.

As the boy plunged forward, yelling, he raised his lance to strike the blue back before him. But the second scout heard him coming, turned in his saddle and raised his revolver, firing point-blank at the boy behind. *Tchow!* The white smoke almost concealed the scout for an instant. But Bull-Standing-with-Cow did not turn back. The bullet had missed him. He was unhurt, and plunged on. The scout, riding half-turned around, kept threatening his pursuer with the gun. But Bull-Standing-with-Cow was too eager to be scared away. His blood was up, his horse was fast, he was right on the tail of his enemy. At any moment

1. August, 1865. Gourd (Pumpkin) Buttes. White Bull counts the second *coup* upon a U.S. Indian scout and shoots him with an arrow. This was White Bull's first *coup*. (Chapter V.)

2. December 21, 1866. Near Fort Phil Kearny. He shoots a soldier and counts the first *coup* on him with his lance. The two bleeding 'wounds' in his blanket indicate the holes made by the bullet that knocked him off his horse. The black marks behind him represent his comrades; those in front, his enemies. (Chapter VI.)

ITEMS FROM WHITE BULL'S PICTORIAL AUTOBIOGRAPHY

now he might count his first 'first' *coup* and win the coveted right to wear an upright eagle-feather in his hair.

The scout, finding that he could not run away from, or bluff his enemy with the revolver, fired again; but at the same instant the boy stabbed him with his lance in the shoulder, shoving him from his saddle. With a cry he fell from his horse into the dust. The riderless horse plunged on after the others with swinging stirrups. Thus Bull-Standing-with-Cow was the first to strike this enemy. Cloud Man struck second.

Still the boy, never content with his success, rushed on. He had been held back too often to turn back now in the heat of the fight. The third scout, hearing the hoofbeats coming up in his rear, and seeing the dreadful fate of his companions, spurred his horse onward and turned in his saddle to shoot. But he was too excited to take aim, he merely fired into the air above his head. The boy laughed at this, and, charging the foolish scout with outstretched lance, stabbed him in the neck. The scout, though bleeding freely over his blue coat, clung to his saddle, leaning forward, and spurred his horse to desperate speed. In a moment Bull-Standing-with-Cow was racing by his side. The boy seized the bluecoat by the shoulders and with a mighty wrench toward the back and side hurled his screaming enemy from the saddle to the ground. Barefoot struck the second *coup* on this enemy.

All this time the scouts were racing back to their camp, not far off. Now they were near it. The Sioux did not attempt to charge the camp of the enemy, but swept away with the eight horses left behind. Bull-Standing-with-Cow, having done all the harm he could do to the men, now dashed after their horses, heading them back toward his own party. As he came up with each horse, he tapped it with his lance, thus making it his own, before any other Sioux could touch it. He was so far ahead of his comrades that he was able to capture six of the eight horses before any others could arrive.

When the Sioux examined their victims, they found that they were not white men, though they wore soldiers' uniforms. The Sioux thought they must be Omaha Indian scouts and were pleased, for nothing delighted them more than to kill Indians who fought on the side of the whites. These scouts had short hair, therefore the Sioux did not scalp them. Two of the horses captured by Bull-Standing-with-Cow had McClellan saddles and army bridles on them. With these prizes most of the party were ready to start for home.

But High Hump was not content. His horse was slow, he had not come up with the scouts, and had not been able to do anything to distinguish himself. He was unwilling to go home empty-handed, and persuaded ten of his comrades to hang around the enemy with him for two days longer. The scouts were letting their horses run in the breaks and High Hump hoped to capture some of them. He said he would be satisfied if each man got two head apiece. Of course Bull-Standing-with-Cow was one of those who volunteered to remain with High Hump and try again.

High Hump had to be very cautious. His enemies were now on guard and very numerous. He knew that ten Sioux could not hope to stand them off, and that he could hardly run away on his slow mount. But High Hump was as skillful as he was cautious. At the end of two days the party was successful. Each one captured two horses. High Hump got three.

The ten of them turned homeward, jogging along in no hurry toward the point on Powder River where they expected the camp to be about that time. Before leaving home, Bull-Standing-with-Cow had asked his father, the Chief, what movements of the camp were contemplated and what the probable line of march would be. Thus, on any given day the war-party knew where to find their home camp. If, on reaching that spot, they failed to find it, they could easily tell by the sign, or absence of sign, whether the camp had already passed that way. Then they had only to follow the trail if the camp had passed, or, if not, march to meet it. Being victors, the war-party wished to reach home in broad daylight so that the people could see them come in. They managed to arrive about noon.

Bull-Standing-with-Cow came home in great glory. He had struck three enemies in his first fight and two of these *coups* were 'firsts.' Moreover, he had stolen ten head of good horses, of which he gave one to Uncle Sitting Bull, one to his aunt, and one to another relative. He had risen high among his people.

Therefore his father decided to change the boy's name in honor of these great exploits. When he came riding into camp, his parents and other old people sang songs in his honor. Then Makes-Room went to the chiefs and asked them to set up the black pole and hold a Victory Dance. Makes-Room dressed and painted his son for the occasion, mounting him upon a fine horse.

Bull-Standing-with-Cow was pleased, but he was well aware of his father's trait of heedless generosity and knew how likely he was to be reckless in giving away his son's property. The boy had not forgotten the loss of his pony on the day he killed his first calf. He knew also that by custom his people had the right to strip off a hero's moccasins and clothing as he rode to the dance held in his honor. Bull-Standing-with-Cow did not wish to lose his best suit. He therefore stripped to the gee-string and put on an old pair of moccasins.

Then four of the six head chiefs, Scalp-Shirt Men of the Minniconjou Sioux — Flying-By, Lame Deer, Black Shield, Makes-Room — put the boy on his horse and led it to the dance. Sure enough, on the way to the dance, an old woman came running and jerked off the boy's moccasins, leaving him barefoot.

When they reached the black pole, they found the people assembled. Uncle Black Moon then announced that he was going to give the boy a new name. He called out: 'From this day Bull-Standing-with-Cow will lay down his boy name. From this time he shall be called by the name of his grandfather, White Bull.'[1]

Makes-Room then gave the horse his son was riding to one Little Tail, and all the boy's relatives made presents to the women of the camp. Bull-Standing-with-Cow did not sing or dance himself, but walked about offering a filled pipe to the old men. His heart was big that night. He was now a full-fledged warrior with a name earned on the warpath.

Fired by these honors, White Bull went to war a third time that summer. He joined a party of thirty men under Brave Bear and Little Bear, and rode to the headwaters of Arrow (Pryor) Creek. There the scouts found a hundred infantrymen in tents not far from Bag Butte. The soldiers were traveling the Bozeman Trail. A skirmish followed.

[1] *Pte San' Hunka.* This name has no exact English equivalent, the element Hunka being the same used in the Hunka ceremony or Calumet Dance. Here it appears to connote some such meaning as venerable, honorable, or friendly. The modern Sioux sometimes translate the name 'Lazy White Bull.'

Runs-Against captured one horse from the soldiers, Bull Eagle took seven. It was not much of a fight.

Again, early in September, the young man rode out with Sitting Bull and saw the Sioux attack the soldiers on Powder River.[1]

Whenever a war-party set out, he was ready to go.

[1] For White Bull's account of the fight with Colonel Nelson Cole on Powder River, September 8, 1865, see *Sitting Bull*, Chapter XII.

CHAPTER VI

ONE–HUNDRED–WHITE–MEN–KILLED

However absurd it may appear, it is nevertheless certain, that five hundred Indians have it more in their power to annoy the inhabitants, than ten times their number of regulars. For besides the advantageous way they have of fighting in the woods, their cunning and craft are not to be equalled, neither their activity and indefatigable sufferings. ... Indians are the only match for Indians.

GEORGE WASHINGTON

SINCE the founding of the United States, American arms have suffered two great disasters which no soldier survived. The first of these was the so-called Fetterman Fight, or Fort Phil Kearny 'Massacre,' when the Sioux and Cheyennes destroyed the entire force of Captain W. J. Fetterman, December 21, 1866. The second was the fight on the Little Big Horn River, in which General George Armstrong Custer and five troops of the Seventh Cavalry were wiped out by the same Indians, June 25, 1876. Only the celebrated affair at the Alamo can compare with these disasters. On the monument which commemorates the heroic combat of the Texans against the Mexicans under Santa Anna is this inscription: '*Thermopylæ had her messenger of defeat; the Alamo had none.*' This inscription might serve equally well on the monuments on Massacre Hill, Wyoming, and on the Custer Battlefield.

Few Indians now survive who can tell of even the more recent of these two battles, and naturally the white men's histories have little to relate concerning them.

But there is one man living who has the distinction of having taken part in *both* the Fetterman and Custer fights. Not only that. He took a leading part in both. That man is Chief Joseph White Bull. Here we have his account of the first one, known to the Indians as One-Hundred-White-Men-Killed.

The Sioux fought for glory. To strike an enemy, to capture a weapon or a horse, or to be hit in battle were all rated as war honors, and in each of these battles White Bull won them all.

The Minniconjou Sioux were governed by six hereditary chiefs or Scalp-Shirt Men. In 1866 these were Brave Bear, Makes-Room, White-Hollow-Horn, Black Shield, One Horn, and White Swan. Lame Deer and Fire Thunder were then vice-chiefs. Of these, White Swan in particular hated the whites, and thought he had good reason to. He had fought them often. It is said that some drunken soldiers once looted his home in his absence, and before they left, defiled it. This insult he could not forget nor forgive. When his time had come to die, White Swan had himself dressed up in his war-clothes, had his face painted ready for burial, and then summoned his head men and comrades-in-arms to the bedside. When they had assembled, he uttered his last request.

'Friends,' he said, 'you must look out for yourselves and protect your people. Try to kill white men, for the white men have come here to kill you. I am about to die. I can kill no more. Therefore I look to you. Carry on.'

White Swan died, but the Minniconjou did not forget his last words. The head men decided to organize a great war-party to carry out his wish. Accordingly they summoned the Oglala under Crazy Horse to join them. Early in December, 1866, the Minniconjou, a large number of Oglala, and some Cheyennes were in camp on Tongue River near the White (Big Horn) Mountains. The Cheyennes were

about to go against the Shoshoni Indians, as they considered themselves at peace with the white men. But when the
Sioux asked them to join the expedition, they could not
refuse. The Sioux and Cheyennes had always been allies.
Moreover, recently the troops had fired at some Cheyenne
young men passing a fort.

The chiefs decided to organize a great party and attack
the troops at Fort Phil Kearny.

War-parties were organized in different ways. Sometimes
an individual would call in his friends and ask them to join.
Again a large party might be organized by some Warrior
Society, which would hold a feast to elect officers on the
understanding that next morning the officers-elect would
lead the Society in battle. In this camp, however, the warriors were so numerous that two Societies held elections the
same day. First the Mandan (Miwatani) Society elected
officers, and afterward the Fox Soldiers.

White Bull had so distinguished himself on the warpath
that the herald of the Fox Soldiers called out his name first
of all and invited him to come and feast with the members
of the Society. After him, the herald summoned Little
Soldier, Thunder Hoop, Bear-Grabs, Thunder Hawk, Bear-
Loves, Lazy Ghost, these seven. White Bull led the way
into the lodge of the Society and was shown a seat at the
right end of the place of honor opposite the door.

Each of the seven men was then given the insignia of his
new office. Two were given whips; these acted as dance
leaders. Two were given war-bonnets covered with crow
feathers, two were given lances, and White Bull, as the first
one summoned, was given a big drum painted red, with four
ornamented sticks on which to hang it when in use, and six
drumsticks. The man who owned the drum was always

head chief of this Society. Each of the new officers was given an eagle-bone whistle. They were expected to distinguish themselves and lead the way in the fight, but not, of course, to direct the movements of the war-party. That was the duty of the regular chiefs.

Seeing their son so honored, Makes-Room and Good Feather came to the lodge leading two horses. At that time the Sioux were — for a wonder — at peace with the Crow Indians, and as several Crows stood there looking on, White Bull's parents gave the horses to these visitors.

Before the meeting broke up, the former leader of the Fox Society made a speech. Said he: 'I have been the leader of this Society. The members appointed me to this post. Now these young men here are to be the leaders and we must all stand together with them. We are all supposed to look after each other on the warpath and to consider the wishes of our people. It is not likely that these new leaders just appointed will be living long. Probably they will soon be killed. We all live but once. Friends, love each other. If you do this, I will love you. Help the poor and the old folks with donations. Of all things between heaven and earth, food is the most important. If you are eating, and someone comes into your lodge, share with him. If you wish to amuse yourselves, bring in some food, and two or three couples, and dance. If you see someone about to do something wrong, bring him into our Society lodge, get him to smoke the peace-pipe, and quiet him down. That is my advice.'

Next day the whole camp moved up Tongue River toward the fort. The Minniconjou and the Cheyennes were more than a thousand men, and besides these were the numerous Oglala. They moved along by easy stages, White

Bull riding with a group of his friends, among them young White Swan, Standing Bull, Thunder Hawk, Runs-Against, Feather Earring, Little Bull, Little Bear, Long Forelock, and the famous High Hump. Crazy Horse was the leader of the Oglala detachment and rode with his friends Long Man and He Dog, leading his brother's pony, which he had borrowed, a bald-faced bay with white stockings, very fast.

Black Shield was the principal chief leading the Minniconjou. They rode first, followed by the Oglala and Cheyennes.

It was cold weather and there was snow in places. White Bull had put on a pair of buffalo-fur moccasins with high tops which his mother had made for him. He was wearing plain leggins of dark woolen cloth and a red flannel gee-string, but no shirt. Some of his comrades wore buckskin shirts with the hair outside. But White Bull preferred to wear his buffalo robe with the hair turned in, belted around him. He wore no mittens and no cloth on his head; he left such protections to old men.

Like the others, he was riding his laden pack-horse and leading his war-horse by the lariat. His saddle he had made himself; it had only one cinch. On his saddle he carried some pemmican and a wooden cup, and a war-bag containing his dress clothes. He had a four-point Nor'west blanket, red as blood, strapped to the cantle. In his belt on the left side he carried his knife in a sheath, but had no whetstone. His weapons consisted of a quiver containing his bow and forty arrows, and a lance. His father had made the iron points of those arrows from a frying-pan.

As he moved along with his comrades, he sometimes joined a group which turned aside to kill buffalo or deer, and would take as much meat as he could carry on the saddle.

Early each day eight scouts were sent out with instructions to return if they saw nothing, but if they saw enemies to signal back with hand-mirrors from the highest hilltop. They all started about sunup every day and halted for an hour about noon to rest their horses. They always chose a trail through the coulies and gulches, avoiding the hilltops. At sundown they would make camp. Each of the three tribes camped separately in a circle in the creek bottom, the three circles in the brush extending more than a quarter of a mile.

When making camp, White Bull and his comrades planted poles or willow shoots in the ground in a circle, covering them part way up with saddle blankets all around and building a fire in the center of this windbreak. Ten men slept with White Bull in his shelter. He used his buffalo robe and his red blanket for bedding. At night, guards were used. These guards did not walk a post, but generally sat in a group and kept their ears open. It was the custom for anyone who waked during the night to get up and walk around the camp to see that everything was all right. Indian warriors could determine in advance their hour of rising by regulating the amount of water drunk before going to bed. Of course every warrior had his weapons ready, and in enemy country the men never undressed. White Bull kept his face painted red as a protection against the weather.

This large party was full of patriotic spirit. White Bull's relatives were very proud because of the honor done him by the Fox Soldiers. Uncle Flying-Hawk accordingly called these relatives to council — Long Ghost, Crazy Thunder, Fast Horse, Runs-Against, and Powerful. He told them they ought to make a donation and confer another title upon their brave nephew. They agreed, and each man present contributed two arrows, making twelve in all. They decided upon the name of a distinguished ancestor for the young man. Then Flying Hawk called over two singers, men with good voices, Two Herd and Wrinkled Leg. Flying Hawk explained what he wished announced and gave each of them six arrows. They walked out into the camp and called aloud: 'Hear ye, hear ye, Bull-Standing-with-Cow is going to leave that name here. From this day you will call him Big-in-the-Center.'

This announcement was a complete surprise to White Bull, who was still commonly known as Bull-Standing-with-Cow. Even his father had said nothing of any change. No sooner had his name been changed than he heard someone calling from another camp. It was Long Forelock, who belonged to the Don't-Eat-Dog Band. He was calling: 'Big-in-the-Center, my friend, you have a good name. So I am inviting you to come and feast with me.' White Bull was pleased to go, for Long Forelock was one of the best fighters in the whole tribe.

When that great war-party reached a point some ten miles northwest of the fort, the Indians halted and made camp. There the chiefs held council. They knew that Indians armed only with bows and lances could not hope to capture the fort by assault. They therefore decided to lure the troops out of the fort and along the Trail into the rough country to the north. In the forks of Peno Creek, five miles from the fort, was a long narrow ridge, high and steep. The Trail passed along the top of this ridge. The plan was to lie in wait on each side of this ridge and send a few young men on fast horses to tempt the troops out of the fort and lead them into the trap. By means of this ambush the chiefs hoped to kill all the soldiers and afterward burn the fort.

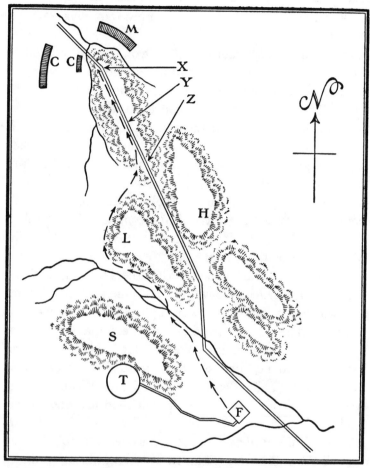

MAP OF THE FETTERMAN 'MASSACRE' NEAR FORT PHIL KEARNY,
DECEMBER 21, 1866, KNOWN TO THE INDIANS AS ONE-
HUNDRED-WHITE-MEN-KILLED

F. Fort Phil Kearny
T. Wood-Train Corraled for Defense
L. Lodge Trail Ridge
C. Cheyennes and Oglala Sioux in Am-
   bush
M. Minniconjou Sioux in Ambush
X. Where the Fight Began
Y. Where the Infantry were Killed

Z. Massacre Hill, Where the Cavalry were
   Wiped Out. (Site of Monument)
H. Hill from Which Captain Ten Eyck
   Viewed the Battlefield
S. Sullivant Hills
→ → → Fetterman's Route
═════Bozeman (Montana) Trail

Six young Sioux and several Cheyennes were chosen to act as decoys.

At daybreak next morning these young men rode off to the fort to make an attack, and at sunrise all the warriors saddled up, mounted, and followed Peno Creek up to the forks. There they halted to conceal themselves. As the Cheyennes were guests of the Sioux, they were given their choice of positions. They and the Oglala chose the west side of the ridge. Some who were on foot stopped near the lower (north) end of the ridge, close to the stream. Those on horseback went on higher and took position almost a mile distant from the Trail. The Minniconjou hid themselves behind a ridge to the east of the road within half a mile. White Bull was with them.

Young White Bull stood with the others behind the ridge, armed with a lance, a bow, and forty arrows, holding his gray war-horse and eagerly waiting for a chance to show his valor. He had his four-point Nor'west blanket, red as blood, and because of the cold he folded this blanket and fastened it around him like a short coat. He had two eagle feathers in his hair. Beside him stood Fine Weather, Long Forelock, Little Bear, Thunder-with-Horns, and Runs-Against.

When White Bull peeped out of his covert he could see no one; all the Indians were hidden. Straight ahead of him to the west were the grassy flats and the shallow stream from which the road climbed up the ridge to his left and disappeared in the direction of the fort five miles away. The Indians stood quiet, waiting to spring their trap.

At Fort Phil Kearny that morning there were less than four hundred soldiers. The commanding officer, Colonel Henry B. Carrington, well knew the dangers which surrounded the little post, and felt a heavy responsibility for the women and children there. He knew how numerous and brave the Sioux and Cheyenne warriors were.

Some of his officers, however, knew nothing of Indian warfare and were eager, overconfident, and impatient of Colonel Carrington's cautious methods. Captain F. H. Brown was so anxious for a fight that he slept in his uniform with his spurs fastened in the buttonholes of his coat and sidearms handy, ready day and night. He had orders to go to Fort Laramie and said he 'must have one scalp' before leaving the post. Captain (Brevet Lieutenant-Colonel) W. J. Fetterman, who had never fought Indians, talked of 'taking Red Cloud's scalp,' and boasted that 'with eighty men I can ride through the whole Sioux Nation.' He led just that number of men into the ambush, and none of them ever came out of it.

At about eleven o'clock the morning of December 21, the lookout on Pilot Hill signaled 'many Indians,' and orders were given to send a detachment to the relief of the wood-train then corralled some distance west of the fort. At his own request Captain Fetterman took command of the detachment, which Captain Brown joined without orders. The little force consisted of three commissioned officers, seventy-six enlisted men, and two civilians. As they moved out, Colonel Carrington gave orders 'to relieve the wood-train, but under no circumstances to go beyond Lodge Trail Ridge.' It was with great anxiety that Carrington saw Fetterman's command moving straight for Lodge Trail Ridge instead of going toward the wood-train as ordered.

All this time White Bull and his comrades had been waiting in their concealment. Suddenly far away to the southeast White Bull heard on the frosty air a faint sound of firing. It lasted only a few minutes. After a silence he heard it again. It seemed nearer, but did not last long. After a time came a third burst of shooting, not far off this time. Within a few minutes he saw the decoys at the top of the ridge riding back and forth across the Trail in their retreat, and shooting as if trying to stand off the soldiers and save someone behind them. Immediately after, the blue-coated soldiers came into sight and the Sioux began to get ready, grasping their weapons and pinching the nostrils of their ponies to keep them from whinnying to the troop horses. They were all waiting for the signal to charge.

Down the Trail along the ridge came the soldiers, almost a hundred of them, in two bodies, half of them afoot, half mounted, the cavalry in the lead. They were in no hurry, they kept on coming slowly down the ridge, firing at the decoys until the cavalry reached the flat near the forks of Peno Creek and the infantry behind them were already well within the trap. Then the decoys forded the little stream at the end of the ridge and divided into two parties. These two parties separated and rode in opposite directions, then turned and crossed each other. When White Bull saw this signal, he cried out, 'Come on! We must start!' The Indians on both sides jumped on their horses and rushed yelling out of the ambush. The Minniconjou, being nearer the Trail than most of the Oglala and Cheyennes, reached the soldiers first. Thunder Hawk was in the lead. He was first to strike a soldier.

When the soldiers saw them coming, they halted, but when the Indians came close and arrows began to fly and one or two of the soldiers were shot down, the infantry quickly fell back up the hill to some large rocks which lay on the slope. They flung themselves down behind these rocks and began to shoot. The cavalry did not join the infantry, but moved back and took a position on the hillside about a hundred yards above the infantry.

This left the infantry between the Indians and the cavalry, and the Indians therefore spent their first fury upon the infantry among the rocks. The Oglala and Cheyennes swept around the infantry to the north and east, the Minniconjou circled to the south and west, and for a short time there was hot fighting in which the cavalry took little part. The infantrymen defended themselves bravely, firing their muzzle-loading rifles at the circling Sioux. The Indians greatly outnumbered the whites, but their advantage in numbers was balanced by their lack of firearms. It took courage for a man armed only with a bow or lance to charge in the face of forty rifles, especially as the two civilians with the troops had up-to-date Henry rifles. Nevertheless one brave Minniconjou, Eats-Meat, rode his horse right through the infantry. They shot him down after he had passed. He was the first Indian killed.

The Indians kept riding around, hanging on the sides of their horses, loosing arrows at the infantry, and there were so many of them that the fight with the infantry did not last long. But it lasted long enough to kill and wound a number of Indians and their horses.

The Sioux always carried off their wounded and dead, if possible. But when Bull Eagle was shot, the fire of the soldiers was so hot that no one dared go to his rescue. After most of the infantry had been killed, three of the survivors jumped up and ran up the slope to join the cavalry. When the Sioux saw these three men running past, they all rushed them. Bull Eagle, on foot, was in the lead. He ran forward with raised bow, ready to strike his victim.

He ran right up within two paces of the foremost soldier. One of them fired and dropped him. He lay on the prairie, shot through the right thigh, unable to move. When his comrades saw him lying there, they ran to cover. No one went to his rescue.

Then young White Bull remembered his duty as Drum Keeper of the Fox Soldiers. When he saw his friend lying there helpless, he jumped off his horse, ran out to him under fire. Bull Eagle was bleeding freely and groaning — but like a wounded bear, to show that he still had a strong heart. A white man would have cursed for the same reason. White Bull seized Bull Eagle by the wrists and dragged him away over the edge of the ridge to safety. There the wounded man's uncle took charge of him. Then White Bull ran back to his horse, mounted, and joined in the charge. The Sioux were killing the infantry one by one with their arrows; the rifle fire was steadily lessening; the white smoke drifted away. Suddenly, as White Bull dashed along, circling the rocks, he was shot from his horse. He fell with a thud on his shoulder, but managed to keep hold on the lariat tied about the horse's neck. A bullet had passed through the red blanket behind his left shoulder and had knocked him off his horse without touching him. There were two holes through the blanket.

White Bull ran to his horse and remounted. Being knocked off his horse that way made him angry instead of afraid. Soon after, the Indians killed the last of the infantry. When they had wiped out the doughboys, they turned their attention to the cavalry farther up the ridge.

Up to this time the cavalry had held their ground about a hundred yards south of the infantry, but now, as the Indians rushed them from all sides, the troopers began to fall back toward the fort, slowly fighting their way up the ridge. They moved in a compact body, shooting all the time. They were half-hidden in the powder smoke. Some of them were on foot leading their horses. Others, whose horses had been shot, would stop, and kneel, and fire, then go on. In the rear White Bull saw one trooper on foot, facing the Indians, running backward, and yelling at the top of his voice. He carried a carbine, threatening the Indians, pointing it first one way and then another.

Young White Bull thought he saw a chance to distinguish himself. He made up his mind to charge that man. Quirting his pony on both flanks, he raced forward ahead of all the Sioux, holding an arrow on his bowstring, expecting the soldier to shoot. When within ten feet of the trooper, he drew his arrow to the head. The trooper seemed too much excited to resist. He did not try to shoot until White Bull was almost on top of him. White Bull let his arrow go, shot the man in front, through the heart. As he fell on his back, White Bull cracked him across the head with his lance, knocking the man's cap off. Thus he was first to strike that soldier. He counted a first *coup*.

White Bull's charge put heart into his comrades, and after this soldier was killed the Indians swarmed up the icy slopes more and more, while the cavalry made more and more haste up the ridge. Almost every minute White Bull shot an arrow at the troops. In that way he killed a troop horse. All the Indians were shooting, arrows were flying in every direction. Indeed, even some of the Indians were hit by arrows, among them Thunder Hump and King. The ground was so covered with arrows that a warrior did not have to use his own, he could pick one up almost anywhere.

Under this hail of arrows many of the troop-horses were

hit, became frightened, and broke away. Finally the soldiers reached the upper end of the long ridge and all at once let all their horses go. The Indians were all eager to capture a cavalry horse. They stopped shooting then, and raced after these animals. This gave the soldiers time to breathe. They ran up and flung themselves down behind some boulders which lay close together at the top (south end) of the ridge. White Bull took after the horses also, though the ground was very steep and icy, and his own horse was slow. He caught none, the other Indians outrode him. When all the horses had been captured, the Indians came back to the fight.

The ridge on which the troopers had flung themselves down was high and narrow, only about forty feet wide, just where the monument stands now. On every side but the south the ridge fell away very steeply into the bottoms far below. That was no place for horsemanship, more especially as the slopes were covered with snow and ice, and the weather had now become so cold that blood froze as it flowed from a wound. The chiefs called out, ordering the Indians to leave their horses in the ravines and to fight on foot.

Up to this time White Bull had been fighting to the north and west of the troops, but now he crossed the ridge and joined the warriors who were creeping up the eastern slope. The fight with the infantry had occupied only a few minutes, but the destruction of the cavalrymen among the rocks on the steep ridge was a longer business. The cavalrymen were armed with single-shot breech-loading carbines, using percussion caps: they could fire more rapidly than the infantry had done. For all that, the Indians kept advancing, swarming up the slopes and shooting back and forth across the ridge. The air was full of arrows. All this time the Indians kept encouraging each other, and advancing foot by foot toward the doomed troopers. White Bull moved forward side by side with his friend Charging-Crow, a Minniconjou Sioux. He says that the Minniconjou braves did most of the fighting at this end of the field.

When the Indians were already crowded close up to the top of the ridge on both sides, Long Fox, leader of the Minniconjou on the west side, stood up and yelled, '*Hopo!* Let's go!'

Then all the Indians jumped up and rushed forward. White Bull and Charging-Crow reached the top of the ridge at the same moment. An instant later Charging-Crow tumbled at the boy's feet, shot dead. This man's death frightened the boy for a moment; he dropped to the ground. Immediately after, his uncle Flying Hawk fell dead there, shot through the right breast. The other Indians rushed on — right in among the rocks. They fought hand-to-hand with the troopers, stabbing and scuffling there in the smoke and dust. It was a dreadful mixup, the kind of fight which the Sioux call 'Stirring Gravy.' That charge ended the battle, killed the last white man. Because of his delay when Charging-Crow fell, young White Bull got there just as the last soldier was killed. But he was in time to capture a carbine.

After that the Indians stripped the soldiers, and White Bull took two pairs of trousers. He cut off the legs so that his father could use them for leggins, and threw the seat of the pants away. In the pockets of the troopers, he and other Indians found paper money and silver coins. They knew the value of the silver, but paper money was unknown to them. They saved only the new bills; they thought the children at home might like to play with them. White Bull also got one overcoat from the troops and some cartridges. He says that less than half the ammunition carried by the soldiers had been used in the fight. He himself had shot away twenty of his forty arrows. The length of the fight, estimated by those in the fort by the duration of the firing, was hardly more than forty minutes. If each of the other two thousand Indians present shot as many arrows as White Bull, one can imagine how the ground was littered with those feathered shafts. White Bull picked up many of these arrows and filled his quiver with them, for arrows were valuable and hard to make. Others did the same. They left only the broken or blunted arrows.

All the troopers were killed in the battle, fighting, with weapons in their hands and ammunition in their possession. It was therefore no 'massacre,' as it has been called. It was all over about noon.

When Colonel Carrington at the fort heard all that heavy firing, he knew that a desperate fight was going on beyond Lodge Trail Ridge. Within twelve minutes Captain T. Ten Eyck was dispatched from the fort with infantry and cavalry, two wagons, ambulances, and two surgeons. He went on the run, but just as he reached the hillside overlooking the battlefield, all firing ceased. He saw the Peno Valley full of circling Indians. At first they beckoned him to come down, but he stood his ground until they left the battlefield, soon after.

Then he advanced and found Captain Fetterman, Captain Brown, and more than half the command lying in a space about forty feet in diameter. A few cavalry horses lay dead not far off, all with their heads toward the fort. Following the road down the ridge he found the naked bodies of the infantrymen, the two civilians, and Lieutenant G. W. Grummond, surrounded by ten dead Indian ponies and sixty-five pools of dark and clotted blood. Only six of the command showed gun-shot wounds. Captain Fetterman and Captain Brown were found shot through the temple, with powder burns around the wounds. These officers had declared that they would not be taken alive by Indians; they feared torture. It was supposed that they had committed suicide. The dead soldiers had been stripped, cut to pieces by the Indians, scalped, and shot full of arrows. One man had more than a hundred arrows in his body. All the bodies lay along, or near, the road on the ridge.

White Bull was only a boy of seventeen at this time, but he thinks the Indians cut these enemies to pieces because they had put up such a good fight and had killed so many Indians. Of the Sioux the soldiers killed or mortally wounded Bear Ears, Little Crow, Yellow-White-Man, Lone Bear, Clown Horse, Male Eagle, He Dog, Eats-Meat, Fine Weather, Charging-Crow, Eagle-Stays-in-Air, Broken Hand, Eats-Pemmican, and Flying Hawk. Flying Hawk was White Bull's uncle, the brother of his father, Makes-Room. The dead man's two brothers, Long Ghost and Crazy Thunder, took his weapons and horse home with them. The Indians laid away their dead a few miles from the battlefield, wrapped up well in blankets and covered with rocks to keep the wolves away.

When Captain Ten Eyck returned to Fort Phil Kearny with forty-nine dead bodies and the dreadful news of the disaster, those in the fort were terrified. Guards were doubled, and every man slept in his clothes with loaded weapons at hand. The officers did not sleep at all, expecting an immediate attack. The women and children were placed in the powder magazine, which had been stocked with water, crackers, and other supplies. There an officer was on duty pledged not to allow the women to be taken alive, if the Indians should get over the stockade. Colonel Carrington then set out to bring in the remaining bodies left on the field.

All these precautions were unnecessary. The Indians were satisfied with their victory. They knew they could not take the fort. Had they wished more fighting, they might have attacked Captain Ten Eyck. Instead, they rode home to the camp on Tongue River. There, four days later, they danced the Victory Dance.

This Victory Dance was the first occasion on which White Bull began to pay attention to the girls. He was only a boy, seventeen years old. The girls must have been friendly toward him, however, when he came home with a captured carbine, a 'wound,' and a *coup* to his credit.

The monument on the battlefield gives Chief Red Cloud of the Oglala Sioux credit for leading the Indians in this battle, but all the Indian testimony, both Sioux and Cheyenne, is unanimous in stating that Red Cloud was not present, and took no part in the fight, or in planning it. Crazy Horse was the leader of the Oglala, Black Shield of the Minniconjou. Many of the chiefs besides Red Cloud led their warriors against the white men in that year of '66. Every wagon train which passed over the Bozeman Trail was attacked. More than a thousand head of horses and mules were captured and about two hundred whites were killed and wounded. It was the most sustained warfare the whites had ever encountered from the Sioux. But the biggest battle of all was only the fulfillment of the wish of a dying man, Chief White Swan.

Of all the warriors who took part in this fight, few showed more courage or won more honor than young White Bull, now also called Big-in-the-Center.

White Bull was surprised to learn recently that Captain Fetterman committed suicide. He says he never knew an Indian to do such a thing, in a fight. As to torture of captives, he is unable to recall any instance among the Prairie Sioux, though he does remember an instance or two of assault upon Indians of enemy tribes when visiting the Sioux camp. The Plains Sioux, he says, killed their enemies in the fight, or else adopted them, or turned them loose. That was the custom.

I knew, of course, that stories of Indian atrocities had been hugely exaggerated on the frontier — often for very base motives. Still, I thought he might remember *some* atrocity, if pressed, and so continued to question him on this point. And to make it easy for him, I told how white men sometimes burned Negroes at the stake. The chief turned upon me in horror, and cried: 'Would *you* burn a Negro?' I hastily explained that I personally would not, but that many whites had been guilty of such cruelty. The chief was so upset by this news that he could not go on with the talk for some little time. Had I confessed to such a crime, I am certain that he would have broken off our friendship then and there.

No man knows the Plains Indians better than George Bird Grinnell, and he writes: 'There was practically no torture of captives by the Western Indians.' Atrocities do occur, of course, in all wars; but the Plains Sioux had no deliberate policy of frightfulness. The fact is that the white men brought with them from the East a ready-made notion of Indians, which did not fit the Plains tribes at all.

CHAPTER VII

THE WAGON–BOX FIGHT

I have seen our friendly Indians, riding at full speed, shoot and kill a
wolf, also on the run, while it is a rare thing that our troops can hit an
Indian on horseback, though the soldier may be on his feet at the time.

GENERAL GEORGE CROOK,
Report of the Secretary of War, 1876–77.

OF ALL the Indian battles on the Northern Plains, none,
except Custer's last stand, has received more attention than
the Wagon-Box Fight near Fort Phil Kearny, August 2,
1867. Several of the white participants have left vivid
accounts of their experiences in this desperate encounter,[1]
and their stories have been repeatedly enlarged upon by
imaginative writers. The large number of Indians (variously estimated as from sixty to fifteen hundred) said to
have been killed in this fight, and the many controversial
points raised by these varying accounts, have attracted
much attention to the combat. However, no history of
this battle by an Indian participant has ever appeared,
and the Indians whose authority is given by the various
white historians in support of their statements are generally
unnamed. George Bird Grinnell makes no mention of the
Wagon-Box Fight in his history of Cheyenne warfare, and
most other white historians seem to have been more
anxious to seek confirmation for their preconceived ideas
than to ascertain the facts as Indians knew them. Therefore White Bull's account of this fight is of more than
usual interest. It is the *only* Indian account.

[1] These have been collected in *The Bozeman Trail*, by Dr. Grace Raymond
Hebard and E. A. Brininstool, Cleveland, 1922, a most excellent compilation
on which I have drawn for certain details.

His statements are corroborated by those of the follow-ing living Indian survivors: of the Minniconjou, White Horse, Kills-Crow-Man, Black Bull, Chasing-Eagle, Gray Eagle, and Little or Chasing-Crow; of the Sans Arc, Brave, Hatchet, Crazy Horse No. 2; of the Oglala, Little Shield. There can be no reason to doubt that White Bull's story is straight and true — the accepted Indian version.

His account is the more interesting and complete be-cause he was, for the most part, a spectator, and therefore saw what happened with a certain detachment. In obtain-ing his account no leading questions were asked and no attempt was made to influence his statements. He, of course, had no knowledge of the stories told by white participants. Moreover, his story is, in part, corroborated by the researches among the Oglala of Mr. T. J. Gatchell, who obtained information also from Frank Grouard, a close friend of Crazy Horse and Red Cloud.

In July, 1867, a large camp of Sioux and Cheyennes was on the Rosebud River, and the Indians were making pre-parations to attack the forts on the Bozeman Trail. Some disagreement arose as to whether the Indians should attack Fort C. F. Smith or Fort Phil Kearny. Finally two parties were formed. One of these went west to Fort C. F. Smith and made the attack known to history as 'The Hayfield Fight,' August 1, 1867. The other party, led by the Oglala chief Crazy Horse, High Hump the Minniconjou, and the Sans Arc Thunder Hawk, moved southwest to attack Fort Phil Kearny. Chief Ice led the Cheyennes. Red Cloud, chief of the Oglala Bad Faces, went along, but he was not the leader. Flying-By was the principal chief in the party.

Nearly one thousand Indians rode out with Crazy Horse, including White Bull's relatives Flattening Iron, Bear-

Chasing, Dog-with-Horns, White-Hollow-Horn, Long
Ghost, Crazy Thunder, Little Bull, Wood-Pile, With-
Horn, Fast Horse, Feather Earring, Bear-Loves, Shot-by-
White-Man, White Deer, Between-Legs, Strong, Standing
Rock, Shell Necklace, Red Fox, Brave Thunder, Carries-
Chicken, Charging Eagle, Front, and Runs-Against.
On August 1, they made camp in the rough country a few
miles north of Fort Phil Kearny. The ambush of the previous winter (in which Captain Fetterman was killed) had
been so successful that the chiefs decided to repeat those
tactics. They therefore selected seven scouts to ride forward next morning and if possible decoy the troops from
the fort. Among the decoys were High Hump, Lone Bear,
and Thunder Hawk of the Minniconjou Sioux; Eats-Meat
(Oglala and Brulé), and Red Bear, a Cheyenne. Very early
in the morning the seven set out on their fast horses to the
fort, leaving the main party hidden in the hills to northward.

After the destruction of Captain Fetterman's command,
the commanding officer of Fort Phil Kearny had given
strict orders against pursuing small parties of Indians away
from the fort. For months no one had left the stockade
except under the most urgent necessity. But in the last
days of July, 1867, wood-trains, accompanied by armed
escorts, were sent out to cut timber and fuel for the post.
Though the woodcutters' camp was only about five miles
west of the fort, elaborate precautions were taken to prevent disaster and surprise. The woodcutters' camp was
in the pine woods south of the creek called Little Piney,
where an officer and twelve men were constantly on duty.
Some two hundred and fifty yards north of the Little
Piney on the highest point of the open second bench, some

fourteen wagon-boxes of the wagons used by the wood-cutters were placed on the ground end to end to form an oval corral into which the animals could be driven at night for protection. Outside this wagon-box corral, a number of tents were pitched for sleeping-quarters. Twenty-six men and an officer made their headquarters there.

The wagon-box corral was somewhat more than a mile from the woodcutters' camp across the creek. On the stream between the two a picket or lookout was established to guard against surprise.

About nine o'clock on the morning of August 2, the seven mounted Indian decoys were seen by the picket guard coming in single file on the dead run over the divide from the north. Sergeant Gibson adjusted the sights of his new breech-loading fifty-caliber Springfield rifle to seven hundred yards, and, with a rest, fired at the Indian in advance. The bullet struck a stone in front of the Indian, ricocheted and wounded the foremost pony. The rider, thrown off, immediately mounted behind one of his comrades. The decoys kept on coming.

Meanwhile White Bull and his comrades had been waiting impatiently for the return of the scouts. When this shot was heard, they waited no longer, but came swarming over the foothills north of Big Piney Creek. Not wishing to attack the wagon-box corral, they circled it, and while some two hundred of them swept down on the grazing herd belonging to the fort, the main party, led by Crazy Horse, rushed the woodcutters' camp south of the Little Piney. Most of the men there fled toward the mountains. One of the civilian herders fled to the picket camp. White Bull followed Crazy Horse, riding with his friends Red Bear (Sans Arc), With-Horn (Minniconjou), Eagle Thunder and Painted-Brown (Oglala). When he reached the tents of the woodcutters, he found two white men lying dead shot full of arrows, but was too late to count a *coup*. The Indians stopped to ransack and burn the camp. White Bull's share of the loot was only some hard bread and molasses.

While he was eating these, the other party of Indians had run off the Government herd, and the white men from the picket post on the Little Piney were running for their lives across the prairie toward the wagon-box corral. Gulping down the last of the crackers, White Bull joined the mounted Indians who swarmed across the Little Piney in pursuit of the three fugitives — Gibson, Deming, and the herder. A great horde of mounted Indians took after these fugitives — High Hump, Bear-Shedding, Long Bull, Charging-Bear, and Fast Thunder among them. But the white men, halting at intervals to fire, kept them off, and White Bull saw them shoot Paints-Yellow, an Oglala, from his horse. This casualty kept the Indians at a distance until the three whites reached the corral. Paints-Yellow was, apparently, the man said to have been dropped by Sergeant Gibson. He was hit in the chest, near the right nipple. The Indian was rescued by his comrades and carried from the field.

There were now thirty men under command of Captain (Brevet Major) James Powell and First Lieutenant John C. Jennes in the corral. They had recently been armed with new breech-loading rifles and had in the corral seven thousand rounds of ammunition. They stationed themselves in the wooden wagon-boxes all around. Some romancers would have it that these wagon-boxes were lined with iron and provided with loopholes, but the best authorities deny this. The wagon-boxes provided no protection against bullets, other than concealment. However, they were high as a man's shoulder, so that, unless firing over the top, a soldier was completely hidden from the Indians and entirely safe from arrows. Some of these men of the Twenty-Seventh Infantry had seen the mutilated bodies of Captain Fetterman's men brought into the post the winter before, and they were prepared to die fighting, though outnumbered more than thirty to one. Several of them immediately made preparations to commit suicide rather than be taken; they prepared shoestrings with a loop at either end, one to go round the foot, the other over the trigger of the rifle.

Meanwhile, the mounted Indians gathered and continued to circle the corral at a run, brandishing their war-clubs, firing, and loosing arrows at their hidden foes. The first attack was pushed from the banks of the Little Piney to the south and west. In the front of the charge, Hairy Hand (a Minniconjou sometimes known as Sitting Eagle) rushed toward the corral. White Bull was watching. Suddenly Hairy Hand fell from his horse a hundred yards south of the corral and lay motionless. Up to this time no Indians had been killed.

When White Bull saw his friend lying on the prairie under fire, he left his horse by the creek and ran forward afoot to save the wounded man. White Bull was armed only with his lance and quiver. When he reached Hairy Hand, he found him shot in the right breast and bleeding from the nose and mouth. The bullet had not gone through. Hairy Hand had fainted. White Bull seized him by the wrists and dragged him back to a low place out of danger. Hairy Hand's relatives took charge of him. He pulled through and lived many years.

Not long after Hairy Hand was rescued, a Sans Arc named Crazy Horse (not the chief) was shot from his horse in a charge from the Little Piney. He was shot in the right leg, just above the knee, but not seriously injured. Two of his friends ran out and saved him. He is living now near Rapid City, South Dakota.

All this while the men in the wagon-boxes kept up a furious firing at the circling Indians, who made no attempt to ride into the corral through the openings at either end. But now that so many Indians were being wounded, the chiefs put an end to the mounted charges and the Indians withdrew and left their ponies in the brush and along the creek bottom out of range. There was no cover to the south and west, but on the north and east of the corral, at a distance of about a hundred yards, a ravine ran down to the Little Piney. Many of the Indians, now afoot, took cover in this ravine and fired at the soldiers from there. White Bull was with them.

Meanwhile, the soldiers had run out and jerked down the tents so as to have a clear field of fire. They fired so constantly that the corral was hidden in smoke much of the time. Nevertheless the Indians in the ravine made repeated efforts to reach the corral, rushing forward in their usual zigzag, erratic fashion and throwing themselves down in any slight depression they could find between rushes. Though the thirty-two men in the corral had succeeded in hitting only three of the eight hundred mounted Indians circling them, they did much better in firing at the smaller numbers on foot.

The first Indian dropped was Only Man. Only Man rushed forward almost to the corral before they dropped him. He was so close, in fact, that the Indians could not recover his body. He lay to the north of the corral. He was the only Oglala killed. All the other Sioux killed in this fight were Minniconjou.

After Only Man fell, some of the Indians became more cautious. But Jipala,[1] stripped for battle, led a charge from the east. He was a very tall Indian and came out 'slowly but grandly with his big buffalo shield in front of him, brandishing his spear and chanting a war song. Then he would hold his shield on one side and run forward, alternating this movement by dodging to one side.'[2] The soldiers admired 'his superb courage.' They fired at him a number of times without effect, but as he came near they determined to get him. From time to time he jumped into the air, loosing his arrow from the apex of the leap. At last one of them dropped him. He fell to the north of the corral, close in. White Bull cannot say where Jipala was hit, as his body could not be recovered.

Each time an Indian was killed there would be a lull in the fighting, when the chiefs harangued the warriors, telling them to be brave and careful, and time hung heavy on the hands of the anxious soldiers in the corral. By this time Lieutenant Jennes and Privates Haggerty and Doyle had been killed. Lieutenant Jennes lay at the west end of the corral, the two privates on the north side.

The Indians launched a third charge from the ravine, in which Muskrat-Stands-on-His-Lodge was shot dead. No one could get to him, the firing was so heavy. Soon after, Packs-His-Leg (otherwise known as Dog Tongue) advanced from the north and was hit in the leg. His

[1] Jipala was a Sioux, but his name is not a Sioux name and cannot be translated.

[2] See *The Bozeman Trail*.

comrades tried to reach him, but dared not. The soldiers shot him dead. He could not be saved. Finding that the attack from the north was unsuccessful, the Indians gathered in the ravine to attempt a rush on the east side of the corral.

Young Duck led this attack. He ran right out into the open northeast of the corral and was shot down there. Three of his pals, Bear-Loves, Liar, and Pack-on-Him, ran out to drag Young Duck away. They reached his body, picked him up, and started back, but before they could reach cover all three were wounded. Bear-Loves was hit above the left knee; Liar's knee-cap was grazed by a bullet; Pack-on-Him was hit below his right knee. They were all hit at the same time. That startled them. They dropped Young Duck and ran back into the ravine. Casualties had been so heavy that the Indians made no further attempts to approach the corral from the ravine. White Bull and others mounted, and, circling the corral to the northward out of range, reached the shelter of the trees on the Little Piney southwest of the corral. Here a charge was made on horseback and a Cheyenne (name unknown) was hit on the left side and fell from his horse. He was so far from the corral that his comrades could approach him. Two Cheyennes rode in and carried off his dead body.

It was now about noon. Six Indians had been killed and six had been wounded. Scouts reported a relief column moving out of Fort Phil Kearny, and soon after the howitzer began to boom. About that time White Bull heard the leaders, Crazy Horse, High Hump, and Thunder Hawk, calling to their men that the fight was over. Red Bear called off the Cheyennes also, and all the Indians fell back, mounted their ponies and made off to the northward, leaving five dead comrades on the field. The Wagon-Box Fight was over. They all rode back to their camp on the Rosebud.

The white men's estimates of the number of Indians killed in this fight vary greatly. Captain Powell reported that sixty Indians 'must have' been killed, while some of the enlisted men put the figure as high as fifteen hundred, and estimated the number of their assailants as three thousand or more. The judicious have long since discounted these extravagant stories, but inasmuch as the casual reader may be inclined to accept them, some of the reasons for a more cautious estimate may be summarized here.

To begin with, the soldiers in the corral labored under great practical difficulties. As Private Frederick Claus puts it: 'We had to contend with a rifle with which we were not acquainted. They were breech-loaders, and we had received them only about two weeks previously ... the air was so full of smoke from our guns that it was seldom we could see further than a few rods and we had to be very careful in putting our heads above the wagon-boxes in order to shoot.' Colonel Richard I. Dodge reports: 'Some of the men were poor shots and fired wildly'; and the gun-barrels are said to have become overheated from rapid firing. Moreover, for a great part of the time the Indians were out of range or under cover, and one of the survivors reports that time hung heavy on the hands of the anxious soldiers during these lulls. The whole fight lasted only about three hours and a half. No one who knows the tactics of Indians at war can believe for a moment that they would keep on coming after suffering a loss of anything like fifty per cent. And if three thousand Indians had suffered a loss of fifteen hundred or anything like that number, it is dif-

ficult to see how they could have carried away their dead
and wounded. No instance in the whole history of warfare
can show such a feat under fire within such a short space of
time.

As a matter of fact, three thousand warriors is the top
estimate of the effective man-power of the Western Sioux
when all together (as when Custer fell), and half the Sioux
were then fully a hundred miles away near Fort C. F.
Smith, resting after the Hayfield Fight of the day before
(August 1). The Northern Cheyennes were never numerous.
It is therefore certain that not more than a thousand warriors were at the Wagon-Box Fight. Indian losses rarely
ran to more than one or two per cent. The highest casualty
list in all Sioux history (1869 — when the Thirty Crows
were killed) was only fifteen per cent! Even Captain
Powell's estimate is therefore fantastic.

There is another reason also why the estimates of the
white survivors are to be taken with a grain of salt. By
all accounts they were frightened. Their preparations for
suicide at the beginning of the fight show this. Repeatedly
we are told that they talked in 'hoarse whispers,' though
why anyone should whisper in such an action is not very
clear. They had to tear down the tents during the fight
in order to see to shoot, and Captain Powell repeatedly had
to caution his men to keep their heads down. When the
relief column arrived, the surgeon issued whiskey to steady
their nerves, and Sergeant Littman states that 'the battle
could not possibly have lasted half an hour longer than it
did, for we were almost completely exhausted....' In
fact, when the relief arrived, the men all jumped to their
feet and yelled, threw their caps into the air, hugged each
other, laughed, cried and sobbed like children in the delir-

ium of their delight. The awful strain was over. Brady [1] states that even 'when Powell's men reached the post they were literally crazed with excitement and the nervous strain of the fight. The health of many of them was completely broken. Powell himself never fully recovered from the strain of that awful day, his wife informs me.' Men in such a state of nerves were hardly in a condition to form accurate estimates of enemy losses.

Doane Robinson [2] quotes William Garnett as to the number of these casualties:

> There is a great deal of genuine 'bull' in that account of the Wagon Box Fight, for there was no particular Indian chief in charge of the Indians at that time, they simply having gathered there at that time and had the fight.... This book says there were several hundred Indians killed there, some estimates being as high as 1500. This is very much exaggerated, for there were not 1500 Indians killed by soldiers (that is, Sioux and Cheyenne Indians) during the ten years from 1860 to 1870. I am told by Red Feather, who was in this fight, that there were actually only five Indians killed there and that it was not much of a fight. In addition to this there were five wounded.

Red Feather, being a Sioux, naturally mentioned only the five Sioux Indians killed and said nothing of the dead Cheyenne. And Liar's wound was trifling.

Certainly, whatever may be thought of these estimates, the white survivors were utterly wrong as to certain other points of facts mentioned in their accounts. Some of them speak of 'continuous charges,' others of 'lulls' in the fighting. They tell us that the Indians supported their gun-barrels on crossed sticks which could be seen above the edge of the ravine, though what they probably saw were eagle feathers. They tell us that the Indians were 'mad-

[1] C. T. Brady, *Indian Fights and Fighters.* New York, 1904.
[2] South Dakota Historical Collections, volume XII, page 171.

dened' by their losses, though losses commonly produced a very different feeling in the Indian warrior's heart. They tell us that 'couriers' rode furiously about the field, that Red Cloud sat in majesty on the hill 'directing operations,' and they overestimate the number of Indians present by at least two thousand. Their stories that fire arrows were shot into the corral arouses inextinguishable laughter when called to the attention of warriors who were present.[1]

Red Cloud was present, but he was not the leader of the Oglala. That credit belongs to Crazy Horse, as it does for the Fetterman Fight.

One other error in the popular account of this fight is that the Indians withdrew in amazement at the rapidity of the firing of the new breech-loaders. This, on the face of it, is a mistake. The Indians had no idea how many men were concealed in the corral and therefore could not have felt any such amazement, though they were undoubtedly impressed by the volume of fire, which made it impossible for them to carry off their dead.

Red Feather's opinion that the Wagon-Box Fight 'was not much of a fight' is borne out by Chief White Bull's neglect of this fracas in telling me the story of his life. Though he mentioned it briefly, he at first neglected to draw the picture showing his rescue of Hairy Hand, and quickly passed over the incident as one of slight importance. I had to pump the story out of him, and it was only when he learned that the white men took great interest in the battle and that his participation would add to his fame that he became really interested and went into details. In his opinion the wagon-boxes saved the whites that day.

[1] W. P. Clark, in *The Indian Sign Language* (Philadelphia, 1885, page 415), states that 'These [fire arrows] are rarely used at present and the stories in regard to them have, I think, been exaggerated.'

Had the Indians known how few their enemies were or how many whites were being killed in their concealment, the Indians might have rushed the corral successfully. Though the battle was a draw until the relief column appeared, most of the men on both sides behaved like heroes. Six white men were killed. The site of the corral is now marked by a tablet....

Young White Bull was too self-sufficient and aggressive to seek out friends for himself, and though he naturally ran with the most enterprising and courageous members of his generation, all his closest pals were men who frankly sought his friendship. His first close friend of this sort was a lad named Standing Bull (Standing Buffalo), the son of a Sans Arc warrior also named Standing Bull. One evening young Standing Bull invited White Bull to dinner, and after he had eaten, the father said that he wished the two boys to be close friends. White Bull made no reply at that time, but on going home consulted his father. Makes-Room considered and said, 'Standing Bull's father is a good man. He has taken good care of his son. I think it will be all right.'

Standing Bull was proud to have White Bull for his friend, now that White Bull had distinguished himself. White Bull was willing to be friends, for young Standing Bull was tall and well built, with a dark complexion, a lad not given to talking, but who was always laughing and joking. He was younger than White Bull and not so strong or daring, but he was a good warrior and went on the warpath with White Bull three times. He counted *coup* on the Crows, captured horses, and remained White Bull's close friend for six years until he was killed in the great battle with the Flatheads.

CHAPTER VIII

SUN DANCE

The Sioux is a cavalry soldier from the time he has intelligence enough to ride a horse or fire a gun. If he wishes to dismount, his hardy pony, educated by long usage, will graze around near where he has been left, ready when his master wants to mount either to move forward or escape.
GENERAL GEORGE CROOK,
Report of the Secretary of War, 1876–77.

THE winter of 1867 was a cold winter. It had been snowing. Then the clouds departed and the wind began to blow. It was so cold that all the Indians remained in their lodges as much as possible. White Bull, naked to the waist, sat by the lodge-fire talking with his father. Meanwhile, the cold wind brought some buffalo drifting by; they passed within a quarter of a mile to the west of the camp. This was a great temptation to the hunters, for buffalo seldom came so near the village. White Bull heard one of the head men calling out, 'Somebody ought to go around and head those animals off, and kill them.'

White Bull jumped up and looked out. Seeing the herd so near, and being in a hurry, he did not stop to put on his shirt. He belted a buffalo robe about him, snatched up his bow and arrows, and ran out. Two other hunters joined him, and the three managed to get on the other side of the herd. They whipped up their horses and rushed the buffalo. White Bull was in the lead, bow in hand. He had no mittens, though the cold was terrible. After a short chase he came up with the cows, and, riding up on the right side of a fat one, he shot and dropped her. Dashing on, he tried to fit another arrow to the string. To his surprise he found he could not. The fingers of his right hand were too stiff with cold; he could not bend them to grasp the arrow or pull the string. The arrow slipped from his fingers to the ground.

He got off his horse to get the arrow, and then discovered that his left hand was frozen around the bow. This frightened him: he called out, and his comrades turned back from the chase to see what ailed him. Both dismounted. But neither of them could help him: their hands, too, were stiff with cold. Just then an old man came running to help butcher. When he saw what had happened, he stopped to aid White Bull, and rubbed his fingers energetically with snow. He tried hard, but could do nothing: the fingers holding the bow would not unbend. Then the old man worked the bow free from the palm of White Bull's hand. Still the fingers would not bend. The old man had to remove the bow-string, and then slip the bow out, pulling it through White Bull's closed fingers.

The old man kept up his rubbing with snow until the fingers softened a little. Then he gathered some sage and wrapped White Bull's hands in the leaves.

White Bull tucked his hands into his naked armpits for warmth, and when the old man had butchered the buffalo, they all went home. By that time White Bull's hands pained him terribly. He was so cold all over that he hurried into the lodge to warm himself. In the warm air, the pain increased; he was in such agony that he kept his hands behind him, away from the fire. Next morning his hands were covered with blisters, and his chest and forehead were also blistered as if they had been burned. But the father of the other hunter whose hands had been frozen came in, opened the blisters with an awl, and wrapped White Bull's hands in soft buffalo wool. This treatment cured him: he did not lose his fingers....

Soon after, White Bull went snowblind. Very early the next spring, in the Moon-of-Sore-Eyes, when the country was still covered with snow, the people were short of food. There was not a mouthful of meat in the camp. White Bull, two of his uncles, and another man set out to kill meat for the village. They traveled all day without finding game. Near sundown one of them shot a rabbit; that was all the four had to eat that night. At daybreak they went on, and soon after White Bull dropped a white-bellied deer (pronghorn antelope). By that time the sun was bright on the snow; White Bull's two uncles were snowblind and helpless to hunt. Nevertheless the young man kept on. He shot two black-tailed deer, the fourth man killed another. They slept that night where they had killed the deer, and next morning started home. On their way back they saw fresh buffalo tracks, and followed these over the hill to the valley where the herd had taken shelter.

White Bull and his companion were about to shoot, but their eyes were so inflamed they could hardly take aim. Then White Bull's uncle said, 'Nephew, wait a minute.' Placing some gunpowder in the palm of his hand, he spat in it and mixed it into a paste. This he smeared on White Bull's eyeballs. The gunpowder smarted so that White Bull smeared the rest only on his eyelids and around his eyes. Afterward the fourth man said he could see a little better, and the two of them approached the herd.

White Bull raised his head to look. The moment the buffalo saw him, they whirled and dashed away out of the hollow. He fired and dropped one. They butchered the animal and packed the meat on their horses. By that time the third man had gone blind. White Bull was the only one who could see at all. He went first to make trail and guide his blind companions. The other three drove the pack-horses.

All the way in, White Bull's eyes pained him more and more, and just as he reached the camp it seemed to him that grains of sand came into his eyes. He went blind himself.

They led White Bull into his father's tent and called a doctor. The doctor came, and, putting his lips to White Bull's eyes, sucked them. Then he spread a black cloth down and blew upon it from his mouth the things he had sucked out of his patient's eyes — sand and the sharp points of grass blades. This doctor then treated the other hunters in the same manner. They all suffered intensely.

White Bull had saved the camp from famine, but there were so many mouths to feed that after all his hardships he was given only one small morsel of meat....

The four great virtues admired by the Sioux and taught in the Sun Dance were Bravery, Generosity, Fortitude, and Fecundity. White Bull had exhibited the first three of these, as we have seen, and after tne Hundred-White-Men-Were-Killed, began to take an interest in the girls. Like other young men, he strolled about muffled in his blanket, with only his eyes showing, watching his chance to talk with some young woman. A Victory Dance always gave opportunity for courtship, and often the young man would wait on the trail to the river in order to stop a girl when she came down to get water. If the girl halted when addressed, White Bull would throw his arm and blanket around her and they would stand and talk for as long as she chose. If they liked each other, they might caress and kiss. Sometimes the young man waited in a queue of suitors at the door of the lodge of some popular girl, taking his turn in talking with her.

In his nineteenth year White Bull decided to marry, and persuaded a girl to go home with him. She remained with White Bull seven nights. Then he tired of her and sent her home to her folks. White Bull says: 'Of course her family said lots of mean things about me, but I didn't care. This happened a long time ago. I have even forgotten the girl's name and the name of her father. Perhaps we should not count this girl as one of my fifteen wives.'

A month later, White Bull stole another girl. Her name was Eagle Shawl. He stole her in the daytime. They met at an issue of Government rations at Fort Bennett and set a date for eloping. White Bull brought her home. She walked into the lodge while he waited outside. When Makes-Room saw her come in and learned what had happened, he went out and announced: 'Whoever is out here has won this horse.' He gave away a pony in honor of his son's marriage.

Two days later, two men came in with a filled pipe. They laid it before him and talked with the Chief. Makes-Room granted their request: he lit the pipe and smoked it. Much pleased, the two men returned home and put two tipis together to make a big lodge. They sang and beat the drum and came with their party to the lodge of Makes-Room, carrying two calumets decorated with horse-hair and feathers. One man led a horse to the tent door. They led Makes-Room's whole family out to their big lodge. White Bull rode ahead wearing a war-bonnet. There the whole family was dressed in fine clothing by their hosts. By means of this ceremony the two families were united. They all danced together in the double lodge. Afterward Makes-Room and his wife brought twelve head of horses and presented them to the herald, who announced the alliance to the whole camp. This was the greatest thing that Makes-Room ever did to honor his son White Bull. Thus Eagle Shawl and White Bull were publicly united.

In that society, harlotry was rare, celibacy was unknown, and divorce was easy. At the end of five months Eagle Shawl went home to her parents.

White Bull went to war.

It was the early spring of White Bull's nineteenth year, 1868. The Sans Arc and the Minniconjou Sioux were encamped on the headwaters of the stream Where-the-Woman-Broke-Her-Leg (O'Fallon Creek). Crazy Heart, Black Shield, and Thunder Hoop (all Minniconjou) organized a war-party to go south. Some thirty men, including White Bull, went with them.

At this time, White Bull had no war-charm, no medicine. He had had to give back the charm he had been using to make his horse long-winded. But he was so eager to join this party that he decided to go without any such protection.

They moved southward, west of the Black Hills, and crossed the Shell River (the North Platte) without finding enemies. Following the Platte down toward the forks, they crossed it and reached Lodge-Pole Creek.

There they found a strange thing. Two long pieces of iron stretched side by side across the prairie, and under these irons were logs. While they watched there, they saw something come bobbing along the track, up and down, up and down, in curious fashion. It stopped within sight, and White Bull then saw that men were on it. The men got down and built a fire and were cooking something. Then the Indians mounted their horses and rushed, yelling, at the white men. They expected an easy victory, for the white men were all afoot, and the odds were almost ten to one in favor of the Sioux.

But when the white men saw the Sioux charging them, they dropped their frying-pans and ran back to the thing from which they had come. Jumping upon it, they began to move their arms and bodies up and down, up and down, and the thing began to move, at first slowly, then faster and faster. The mounted Sioux sped down the railroad track after the white men, but the handcar was too swift for their ponies. The white men escaped them and disappeared over the skyline.

While the Indians waited, eating the food left behind by the white men, they saw something large and black coming, making a great noise, from the direction in which the handcar had disappeared. This thing seemed alive, and great clouds of smoke came from the top of it. They all drew back a little and watched. Then they discovered that this thing was not an animal, for men came out of it and started shooting. For a while the Indians shot back, until the white men climbed aboard and the train pulled out.

Up to this time, White Bull had never seen a wheeled vehicle of any sort. He says he thought the train was alive. Now, of course, he knows better. He has traveled on trains and wagons, and at his own request has even gone up in an airplane within recent years, but he still likes to laugh at and mimic the curious antics of the men on the handcar.

Following up Lodge-Pole Creek, the Indians came to a camp which White Bull supposed to be a camp of white men. There were houses, and near one end of it several Indian tipis. Crazy Heart, the leader, kept the warriors behind the hill, out of sight, while he peeped over to reconnoiter.

He said: 'I see two enemies down by the creek, this side of the camp, and some horses. Get ready to charge.'

White Bull had a black horse and carried a bow and a knife. He had no other weapons. When the Sioux rushed over the hilltop to capture the horses, White Bull and Crazy Heart separated from the main party and took after the two enemies down by the creek. The moment these two men saw White Bull and Crazy Heart coming, they turned and ran over the prairie as hard as they could toward the camp, though both of them had arms in their hands. White Bull lashed his horse to top speed, but before he could reach the nearest enemy, a great many people came running out of the houses and tents and began to shoot. He could see the smoke and hear the banging of their guns. Crazy Heart, who was chasing the other enemy, gave it up then and turned back, for the men from the houses were mounting their horses and charging back at the Sioux.

White Bull, however, kept after his man. He was all alone, facing all those enemies, and he had no medicine.

So, in that moment of danger, he rode praying. He vowed that, if he should strike an enemy and be spared, he would dance the Sun Dance for two days and make an offering of five buffalo robes. His enemy did not look back or resist, though in his left hand he held a bow and arrows and in his right a gun, which he fired in the air. As White Bull came close, he saw that his foe was an Indian with long hair, unbraided, wearing Indian clothes. He thought he might be a scout for the soldiers.

As soon as White Bull was near enough, he raised his bow and struck the man a heavy blow on the head, knocking him down.

The men from the houses were getting quite close now, and White Bull was in a great hurry. He jumped from his horse, but had not time to kill his enemy. He was in a hurry. He grasped the man's hair with his left hand, pulled out his knife quickly, cut the skin of his head all around, and jerked off the scalp. The man was still alive, and after White Bull had mounted his horse again, this wounded enemy got up and staggered away. 'Perhaps he died later,' says White Bull.

The other Sioux had turned back. All they had accomplished was to capture two of the five horses grazing there. They were now in full retreat, with the enemy charging on their trail. White Bull was one of those in the rear, nearest to the enemies. It seemed that they would surely catch him, for his horse was slow, and at this moment — of all times — his horse played out and stopped, heaving and gasping. White Bull jumped off and ran on afoot, with the sound of the firing and the thudding of hoofs coming up behind in his ears. But Thunder Bull, seeing White Bull's danger, dashed past him, offered a hand, and White Bull swung himself up behind his friend and was saved.

The enemies still kept on coming, however. Before long, Thunder Bull said: 'Friend, you had better get down. I am afraid my horse cannot save us both.' White Bull jumped to the ground, ran on afoot, until Bull Head, who had a better horse than Thunder Bull, took him up behind.

That was a close shave for White Bull. He says: 'If I had had my medicine along, my horse would never have played out.'

Once more White Bull was the only one in the party to strike an enemy. He had the only scalp taken on that warpath.

On the way home from this expedition to Lodge-Pole
Creek, White Bull became separated from his party and
traveled on alone. He found great difficulty in feeding
himself. There was no game to be found anywhere. For
six days he had nothing to eat but Cheyenne turnips. On
the sixth day he reached an oak grove west of Bear Butte
and heard something moving in the brush. He turned
aside to see what it was. Under the trees he saw an elk
standing. In his faint condition it seemed to White Bull
that the elk spoke to him.

The elk said: 'Friend, you are having a hard time traveling, but by tomorrow you will see your people. I wish to be
your friend and show you my power. Look me over well,
friend.'

The elk, standing in the checkered shadows of the trees,
turned to show his left side to White Bull. On the left
shoulder of the animal appeared a painted black ring or
circle, and in the center of it, a yellow leaf. On the left
cheek or jaw was also a yellow circle. Then the elk turned
to show his right side. On the right shoulder, White Bull
saw a red circle with a leaf in the center. On the right cheek,
a red circle containing a yellow leaf.

The elk declared, 'Friend, when I am painted like this,
all the women are crazy about me.' White Bull had observed that elk are very amorous.

The elk showed White Bull a hoop with a leaf in the
center. On the four sides of the hoop were four marks,
white for the willow, red for the cherry, yellow for the oak,
and blue for the cottonwood. The elk said, 'Friend, I
went to war carrying this.'

In front of the elk was a pool of water. Said the elk:
'This is for you. Men and women will come here and wish

to drink from this.' Then the pool was transformed to a cup. The elk continued, 'Friend, if you do not obey me, if you let a man or woman drink from this cup, you will wear a red leaf.[1] You must get those leaves I have shown you, tie them up in a leather pouch. They are medicine. If you do so, I will give you my power. Stop here overnight, and tomorrow morning you will meet your people.' Thus the elk gave White Bull a medicine for war and power over women.[2]

White Bull obeyed his friend, the elk. He camped there that night, and next morning, sure enough, his people found him. When his family saw him they began to cry; he looked so bad, and they had almost given up hope of seeing him again. They gave him soup and a little lean meat. He rested at home for six days. Afterward he prepared the medicine and carried a wooden cup from which he allowed no one else to drink. He followed the elk's instructions.... [3]

[1] Apparently a threat that White Bull would be wounded and lose blood.

[2] It is noteworthy that this vision came to White Bull in the year he first began to look at the girls.

[3] Three years later, White Bull had a chance to test the power given him by this elk. He tried it out.

There was a competition among those gifted with mysterious power in which he took part. White Bull, Boat-Upper-Lip, and Woman-Who-Lived-with-Wolves all attempted to outdo each other in the camp. This Woman-Who-Lived-with-Wolves was supposed to have great power. She it was who abandoned her family and lived a whole winter in a wolf-den, running with the wolves. This den is still pointed out by the Sioux and, though the woman is now dead, her family still tell the story.

The three of them tried to 'kill' each other. They 'shot' grasshoppers, bumble-bees, and rolled-up buffalo-hairs from their hands at each other, but were unable to overcome White Bull. Their best missiles failed to overthrow him.

But when White Bull 'shot' them with the worms which came out of the forehead of an elk, he hit them both. They could not repel his power. They both fell unconscious. White Bull had to revive them and draw out these worms. This convinced everyone that the elk was a true friend to White Bull....

When White Bull reached home from that warpath, he fastened the scalp he had taken to a pole ready for the Victory Dance, and gave it to his mother. She painted the scalp red on the flesh side and carried it in the dance. What she did with it afterwards, White Bull cannot say. As a rule, the Sioux did not keep scalps long.

Not long after, the young man informed his family that he had vowed the Sun Dance, and asked their help. Accordingly they made ready his costume for the ceremony, gave him an eagle-bone whistle, five calf-robes, a hundred small pouches of tobacco, a peace-pipe decorated with porcupine quills, and the small, pointed, decorated sticks to be worn in his hair and to be used for scratching himself, since dancers were not permitted to touch their bodies with their hands. The following summer, when the people had assembled for the ceremony, the chief of the dancers, Iron-White-Man, and some fifty others who had vowed the sacrifice, got together and practiced the songs for three nights. The fourth night they sang and danced all night. On the following day the Sun Pole was brought in and the lodge erected.

When all was ready, the dancers — White Bull, Bear-Loves, Big Hail, Wood-Pile, Hawk Man, Council Bear, Catch-the-Bear, Soaring Eagle, Bets-His-Ears, Thunder Horn, and others — entered the lodge and began the dance. White Bull was wearing a war-bonnet. From three o'clock that afternoon until the next day at noon, the dancers remained on their feet, facing the sun, to test out their hearts. He found it very hard, and three of his comrades fell to the ground.

At this time there came in a man named Nape-of-the-Neck, carrying a stick with a large eagle-feather fastened to it. He walked along the line of dancers staring into the eyes of each one, as if looking for someone. On his head he had the stuffed skin of a yellowhammer, and when he would touch the head of this bird, the bird would sing. This shaman stopped in front of White Bull and swung his feather in front of White Bull's face until White Bull fainted and fell forward.[1] They carried him into the shade and laid him on his back. He was not breathing. Some thought he was dead. At last he awakened to find they were putting something in his mouth that was sweet and cool. When he opened his eyes they gave him more medicine, and brought him a pipe to smoke. When he was himself again, Nape-of-the-Neck sat down beside White Bull and smoked with him. He said: 'Young man, you are the only young man I approve. That is why I did this. You shall be the first to strike a Crow.'

White Bull went back to the dancing, during which Nape-of-the-Neck held his hands to the sun, then rubbed his palms together, and behold, there was black paint covering both his palms. This was an omen of victory.

It was now time for White Bull to make the sacrifice of his flesh and blood. There were several ways in which a Sioux could sacrifice in the Sun Dance. Sometimes a man was suspended (by thongs attached to skewers the size of lead pencils, pushed through slits in the skin of his chest or back) until he could tear himself loose. But White Bull felt that this sacrifice was too severe. He had seen one dancer dreadfully torn in that way. He therefore decided to offer a hundred pieces of skin from each arm. He went forward and sat down with his back to the Sun Pole. Sit-

[1] It is interesting to remember that trances were induced in the Ghost Dance (1890) in the same way. S. V.

ting Bull did the cutting on his left arm, and Pacing-Hermaphrodite on the right. They both worked at the same time, grouping the cuts in horizontal rows of ten, just below the shoulder. They would thrust in an awl, lift the skin clear of the flesh, and then with a thin knife, cut out a bit of skin the size of the head of a match. Then the awl would be withdrawn and inserted in a new place. The cuts were close together in rows, all hundred of them occupied a space no larger than a pack of cigarettes. When healed, the puckered scars of such torture show on the skin like ruching.

White Bull says that Sitting Bull's hand was swift and sure, that he did not hurt him much, but the other fellow kept sawing away in a clumsy and very painful fashion. Before the cutting began, they painted the skin with red paint, and afterward put pine ashes on the wounds to stop the bleeding. White Bull says he did not bleed much, and that it did not hurt him much afterwards, though his shoulders were swollen. Thus he fulfilled his vow and went on his next warpath confident that he would be the first to strike a Crow because of the promise made by Nape-of-the-Neck.

CHAPTER IX

FETCHES–THE–WOMAN IS PUNISHED

Many of the most daring adventures were made by braves who, un-accompanied, penetrated the enemy's country and watched opportunity to inflict some signal stroke of surprise.

W. P. CLARK, *The Indian Sign Language.*

AFTER the Sun Dance was over, the Sioux went on a tribal buffalo hunt. Fetches-the-Woman was in command of the 'soldiers' whose duty it was to keep the hunters in a body until the word was given to rush the herd. When the hunters came near the herd, they were halted, and Fetches-the-Woman crept up to the hilltop to look over. As White Bull was one of the soldiers, he went forward also. This angered Fetches-the-Woman. He threatened White Bull with his quirt, but could not intimidate him. The blow was never struck. All the same, this threat made White Bull very angry. He determined to give Fetches-the-Woman a beating and so 'make his father and mother feel good.'

After that hunt on the headwaters of Tongue River, a war-party of forty men started off to attack the Crows (1868). They rode up the Yellowstone to the mouth of the Musselshell River. Though White Bull had no war-charm at the time, he went along, relying upon the promise of the shaman Nape-of-the-Neck that he should be the first to strike a Crow.

When they reached the Musselshell, their scouts reported they could see across the river a camp of enemies. All prepared for battle. White Bull was the first one mounted. He had painted his face, and held his bow and some arrows in the same hand with his bridle reins. The lariat tied around his horse's neck was coiled and tucked under his belt on the right side so that, if thrown or shot off his horse, he could catch the animal again as the rope uncoiled. White Bull laughs at the pictures made by white artists showing Sioux Indians riding with dragging lariats. He says they never dragged their ropes in hunting or on the warpath; it would have been dangerous.

White Bull soon became impatient. He was ready to start, and with his usual impetuosity rode forward to look over the hilltop.

Fetches-the-Woman was leader of the war-party. He tried to make White Bull stand back. He raised his heavy quirt with its long double lash and struck White Bull a stinging blow on the bare shoulders. This blow enraged White Bull. Without a word he rode over the hill, leaving the party behind him. He was mad 'to do something first again,' to distinguish himself and put Fetches-the-Woman in his place. Of course, when he advanced, the others all followed, not wishing to be left behind.

The river was up, and the warriors stripped and swam their ponies over. It was early in the morning, but the Crows were wide awake. They came to meet the Sioux on foot, very many of them. Before long they were driving the Sioux back. There was much charging back and forth between the lines. White Bull kept out in front as usual, standing off the Crows, keeping his horse in motion to avoid bullets, and shooting at his enemies. Suddenly he saw that his rope bridle was coming loose. The rope, lashed around his pony's lower jaw, had come untied; he could not guide his horse. White Bull jumped to the ground to fix his bridle. As he stood there motionless, he offered a tempting target to the Crows.

The horse was restless, and it took some time to fasten the rope. While White Bull was knotting it, he heard Sitting Bull's adopted brother, Jumping Bull, yell a sudden warning. 'Look out,' he yelled, 'that enemy will shoot you!' At his cry White Bull turned (thereby probably saving his life) and saw a Crow crouching close by with a rifle aimed at his head. Just as he turned his head, the Crow fired at White Bull. Then everything went black.

When White Bull came to, he found himself in the rear. They told him that Jumping Bull had carried him back and saved him from the Crows. When White Bull realized what had happened, he searched his body for wounds, but could find none. He could not understand it. Finally he discovered that his hair, which hung in two braids, had been cut just below his right ear. The bullet had struck his braid on that side, and the shock of it, jerking at his head, had knocked him senseless.

Finding his hair cut, and resenting the injury of being knocked out by the enemy, White Bull became very angry. He said to himself, 'I'll get even with them.' He jumped on his horse and galloped back into the battle. The ground was rough, and cut up by gullies and ravines, but White Bull went plunging across them to meet the Crows, who were lined up opposite his comrades. In his left hand he held his bow and three arrows and the reins of his horse. In his right hand he brandished the saber Dog Eagle had given him, for he meant to strike the Crows.

Out in front of the line of Crow footmen he saw one brave Crow coming to meet him, with a bundle of some kind tied upon his back. White Bull supposed it was a medicine bundle, but he was too angry just then to fear the power of the Crow gods. He plunged forward over the

3. Late summer, 1868. Mouth of the Musselshell River. Battle-over-the-White-Buffalo-Hide. White Bull is first to strike the Crow who carried the bundle containing the White Buffalo Hide. The bundle is shown lying on the ground, where its owner dropped it in his flight. The Crows are shooting. Horse-tracks indicate the circle made by White Bull's pony. Bullets fly through the air. (Chapter IX.)

4. 1870. Musselshell River. The Fight with the Flatheads. He strikes a Flathead armed with a rifle. This is reckoned White Bull's bravest deed. A first *coup*. Smoke from rifles is seen on both sides, indicating a general engagement. (Chapter XI.)

ITEMS FROM WHITE BULL'S PICTORIAL AUTOBIOGRAPHY

rough ground, circling towards the enemy line, making straight for the leader. He rode the man down.

When the Sioux saw the Crow leader tumble, they charged on White Bull's trail. Enemy-Chaser was the second Sioux to strike this fallen Crow; next Catch-the-Bear struck him, running up on foot. Little-Half-Woman (Little Hermaphrodite) was the fourth to strike.

By that time the Crows were charging White Bull, and the man knocked down was on his feet and running. White Bull wheeled and hit him again with the saber. The Crow was eager to escape; he let his bundle fall. One of the Sioux picked it up and opened it. Inside he found a white buffalo-hide, a thing held sacred by the Sioux. When he unrolled the hide, he found some bones. Then he was afraid and dropped it, but another Sioux picked it up and brought it home. Ever since, this battle with the Crows on the Musselshell has been known as the Fight-Over-the-White-Buffalo-Hide.

Now the Crows were pressing the Sioux back, trying to recapture their bundle. White Bull, having knocked his man down, turned to retreat. In his path he found two deep ravines or ditches. His horse jumped the first one safely, but the second was wide. The horse was afraid, refused the jump, stopped suddenly on the brink, and bucked White Bull off. He got a hard fall, and lost his hold on the lariat. The horse galloped away to the enemy's ranks, leaving White Bull afoot and surrounded by his foes. He was in a tight place. But his brave comrades rallied and stood off the Crows until he could make his getaway.

When the fight was over, the Sioux started home, victorious. White Bull had distinguished himself. He had been the first to strike that Crow, as the shaman Nape-of-the-Neck had promised, but all the way home he kept thinking of the way Fetches-the-Woman had struck him. He could not put it out of his mind. He was looking for a chance to get even.

It happened that, when they reached the spot where they expected to find their home camp, they found only the trail of that camp. The village had already passed — only a few hours before.

The trail was quite fresh, and some of the young men were eager to hurry home and begin the celebration of their victory. Fetches-the-Woman was one of those who wished to hurry on. Said he, 'We can get in tonight.' White Bull and most of the others preferred to go home in a body in broad daylight and so make a better showing. The party finally agreed to go in a body — all but one.

Fetches-the-Woman was obstinate. He would not wait. He started on horseback. The others knew that if he went in alone he would tell what they had done on the warpath, and by the time they got in the people would have lost interest in the news. The young men sent Bear Hail after Fetches-the-Woman to order him back. Fetches-the-Woman paid no attention to Bear Hail and continued to ride on, followed by the straggling party, some of whom argued with him. White Bull saw the commotion and said, 'Who is that up there?'

Someone answered: 'The rebel is Fetches-the-Woman.'

Then White Bull quirted his pony on both flanks and raced forward to the head of the party. There was Fetches-the-Woman, who had lashed White Bull for disregarding orders, and now he was doing the same thing himself. He had played right into White Bull's hands.

White Bull pushed up to him, horseback, and raising his saber, struck furiously at the man's head. Fetches-the-Woman jerked his buffalo robe over his head and ducked as he saw the blow falling. The saber struck the folds of the buffalo-robe across the neck of Fetches-the-Woman. He fell from his horse, unconscious. White Bull laughed.

After that no one attempted to go ahead of the party. They all rode together and halted within a quarter of a mile of the home camp. There they made camp for the night in plain sight of their people, and for fear some one of them might try to slip away and go home during the night, all the warriors danced until morning.

Next morning, before the main camp moved, the parents of the young men in this war-party brought supplies of food to them. Then the young men invited the old people to come and eat. In this way, by keeping their party separate from the main camp, they let everyone see who it was that had been successful. They made a good showing. Late in the afternoon they rode home in triumph. That raid was over.

Immediately after this exploit, White Bull married a Minniconjou girl, Sits-with-Hail. But at the end of three months a woman named Twin met the young man at a dance and said, 'Don't you think I'm pretty?' White Bull agreed. Said she, 'Then send your wife home, and I'll marry you.' White Bull suggested that his wife go home on some errand, and took Twin to his lodge. Sits-with-Hail was offended and did not come back. However, White Bull visited her from time to time.

Polygamy was common in the Sioux camps, where women greatly outnumbered men. White Bull soon became interested in a young woman named Eagle Lodge, daughter of Paints-His-Ears-Red. Twin and Eagle Lodge were close friends, but when the wife learned that White Bull was wooing her chum, she broke off the friendship and deserted him. She told the aunt of Eagle Lodge what was going on, and one day, when White Bull was courting Eagle Lodge, standing with his blanket about her, the aunt, in a high temper, came and pulled the girl from his embrace. She took Eagle Lodge home, and this marriage was quickly broken off.

Not long after White Bull punished Fetches-the-Woman, the young man went to visit his uncle, Sitting Bull, who camped with the Hunkpapa on the Yellowstone. There he met a young warrior with gray hair, King Man. King Man was older than White Bull and took a liking to him. Several times he invited White Bull to dinner. One day he said to White Bull, 'I know all the young men, but of them all I would rather have you for my friend.' White Bull was pleased. He made friends with King Man, and for many years they ran together. King Man fought beside White Bull in eight battles, capturing horses, killing soldiers, counting *coups*, rescuing comrades. He was wounded three times. King Man liked to bluff and taunt his comrades. He still lives on the Rosebud Reservation.

One day he said to White Bull: 'I wish to go on a raid against the Hohe. They are camped at the mouth of the Yellowstone.' White Bull and some forty others joined the party. Though White Bull had no war-charm at the time, he was not afraid. He rode down the river with the others.

The Sioux found the Hohe (Assiniboin) camped across the river. They had to strip and swim to reach them. White Bull was scouting ahead of the party and saw five enemies coming. They had an ox-cart and some horses with them.

All the Sioux rushed these enemies, but the Hohe ran into the timber and shot at the Sioux from behind the trees. The sound of this shooting brought seventy or eighty Hohe and a whole company of white soldiers from the camp and fort near-by. The Sioux were outnumbered three to one. They turned back.

White Bull wanted some horses. He remained, and Dry Eyes stayed with him. They dashed into the herd of Hohe horses and each cut out a bunch and ran it off. White Bull got five head. The Hohe pursued.

White Bull found one of these horses hard to drive. The animal kept turning back, and White Bull had to head it off time after time. This slowed him up, and all the time his enemies were coming horseback, hot on his trail, yelling and shooting.

The troublesome horse was a good animal. White Bull saw he could not run it off, yet was unwilling to leave it to his enemies. Fitting an arrow to his bow-string, he let fly. The arrow pierced the horse in the ribs on the right side. The animal stopped, and, coughing out its life, fell to the ground. It lay on its left side, so that the feathered end of the arrow stuck up.

White Bull's enemies were coming, whooping and shooting at him, but when he saw that the arrow was on top of the horse, out of bravado he rode back to the dead pony and pulled his shaft from the wound. In this way he saved his arrow, added insult to injury, and made a perfect grandstand play.

Dry Eyes had a hard time too. The Hohe pressed him so closely that he had to abandon the horses he had captured, and felt lucky to escape with a whole skin. The Hohe pushed the Sioux hard. They shot a horse under

Catch-the-Bear and killed White Head. Not one of the Hohe was killed.

When the Sioux got home, White Bull gave one of his captured horses to Sitting Bull, one to his sister, one to his mother. The fourth horse he kept for himself. He was the only one who had anything to show for that warpath.

After his return, the Sans Arc, Hunkpapa, and Minniconjou camped in adjoining circles. It was in the spring, and the people were talking of going to fight the Flatheads. One day White Bull heard the herald of the Minniconjou chapter of the Fox Soldiers calling his name, saying: 'White Bull, the Minniconjou Fox Soldiers want you to come and feast with them.' Immediately after, Strong Foot, herald of the Sans Arc chapter of Fox Soldiers, was heard calling the name of White Bull, saying: 'White Bull, the Sans Arc Fox Soldiers invite you to eat with them.'

White Bull was in a dilemma. He did not know what to do. He appealed to his father, for he could not accept both invitations. His father said: 'Son, I advise you to go to the Sans Arc feast. You are a Minniconjou. It is a greater honor to be invited by the chapter of another tribe than by your own people.'

White Bull, therefore, went over to the lodge of the Fox Soldiers in the Sans Arc camp and feasted with them. The chief of the Society at that time was Charging-Bear. The boy's father, Makes-Room, went along with him, leading a horse which he gave to the herald who had invited his son. White Bull was pleased with the double compliment done him that day.

Not long after, he was in Sitting Bull's camp, and was invited to join the Fox Society there.

Not all White Bull's expeditions were successful, of

course. Once, when the Sioux were in camp on the Yellowstone, it was announced that next day the men would go out to run buffalo. The horses were turned out to graze so as to be in good condition for the hunt. When White Bull went out to catch his pony next morning, he could not find it, but he found tracks of ponies going west from the camp. Following that trail, he came upon a bull-roarer or twirler, a flat stick attached to a string, which would make a loud, humming noise when whirled round and round by anyone holding the end of the string. White Bull knew that this stick had been used by the Crows to frighten horses. He knew at once that the Crows had stolen his animals.

He hurried back to warn the camp. All the men mounted and rode up the river past the mouth of the Little Big Horn. After nightfall they saw a light ahead. Creeping up to the camp-fire, they expected to find the horse-thieves, but the Crows were gone. From the sign, they knew there were many Crows, who had left only a short time before. The ten Sioux talked the matter over, and decided to turn back.

White Bull, however, went on alone, hoping to get back his ponies. He came in sight of the Crow camp. When he got near, he heard dogs barking. This frightened his horse. White Bull knew he had no chance of approaching a camp where there were dogs. Reluctantly he turned back. He rode hard for two days. It was dark when he saw the tents of his people just ahead. The other Sioux had reported White Bull missing. Therefore, when he rode in, his father gladly announced to the camp, 'My son has come home.'

The Crows had stolen White Bull's best horse, a well-known black. White Bull was in low spirits because of this for some time.

CHAPTER X

THE BULL IN THE SNOW

If the war-party had been unfortunate and suffered loss, its return was quiet, and gave rise to dejection and unrestrained lamentation on the part of friends of the lost.

W. P. CLARK, *The Indian Sign Language.*

IT WAS now the time of the year when the leaves turn yellow, in the last phase of the moon. White Bull and his brother set out from a large camp of their people to shoot elk. They started at sunrise and rode all day. At sundown they saw a bull elk coming from the west straight toward them. An east wind was blowing, but they concealed themselves behind some rocks and pines.

The bull passed them within fifteen yards. The hunters had agreed that White Bull should shoot first. They both fired almost together: the bull ran on. As soon as they saw this, the hunters looked at the muzzles of their rifles to learn whether or not they had killed the elk. It was well known that, when a man shot an elk in the heart, there would be minute red spots, like drops of blood, on the muzzle of his rifle-barrel. Both guns showed these red spots.

Full of confidence, the men took up the trail of the wounded elk. The bull soon slowed down, and, when he reached the bottoms along the creek, fell dead.

The hunters mounted, rode down there, and butchered the elk. They took everything.

As they approached Thick Timber River (the Little Missouri), where their people were camped, they saw a man. Fearing this might be an enemy, they avoided him and kept on until midnight before making camp. They did not sleep in the light of their cooking fire, but moved on and made camp in the darkness. On reaching home next afternoon, they learned that enemies had been seen in the neighborhood on Tongue River.

This was one of the longest rides White Bull ever made. He had been in the saddle almost thirty-six hours. But he was soon on horseback again.

The Minniconjou moved camp to the mouth of Tongue River, the Sans Arcs camped not far off, and the Hunkpapa farther away in the same direction. White Bull, now twenty-one, decided to ride up to the Hunkpapa camp and visit his uncle, Sitting Bull. Though it was winter, the weather was pleasant when he started. The first night he spent at the Sans Arc camp, visiting friends. That night a snowstorm came, and next morning the snow was still falling heavily. But White Bull was not easily discouraged; he rode on through the breaks along the river. As he rode along hour after hour, it grew steadily colder. Soon he was hungry and crying with the cold, wailing for pity: 'God help me and save me and give me some good thing.'

He was riding up a dry creek-bed, his horse could hardly go against the wind and the cold, and he himself held his head down, wailing and crying. Suddenly his horse stopped, snorting, with rigid ears, staring at something ahead. White Bull looked up and saw a big buffalo bull facing him. The bull was singing:

'My mother and father said so.'

White Bull stared at the buffalo in amazement. The great bull said: 'Friend, look at me. I am going to a good people. My father and mother are taking my trail. They want something.'

After the bull said this he rolled in the snow, and when he got up, one side of his body seemed covered with white paint. The other side was red. Tied to his horn on the white side was a white shell, and tied to his horn on the red side was a streamer of red flannel.

The buffalo said to White Bull: 'My friend, I want you to be my friend, and I will show you what to do. Look me over well.' Then the buffalo turned and turned, so that White Bull could see first one side of him, then the other. Sometimes the bull would paw and kick.

The bull said: 'Now I have shown you what I want and what I wish you would show the people. And this is all I wish to show you. Go now on your way and you will be saved.'

White Bull kicked the ribs of his pony and pushed on through the whirling snow. Soon after, it stopped snowing, the skies cleared, and White Bull's pony carried him on in a daze, and stopped at Sitting Bull's tipi.

White Bull remained in Sitting Bull's lodge for a day or two, but told no one of his strange communication from the bull in the snow. On his return he stopped at the Sans Arc camp, and there, in the big council tipi, White Bull advised the head men — Black Eagle the elder, Big-Shell-Necklace, Short Lance, Iron-White-Man — to decorate the buffalo as he had seen it. The headmen had faith in White Bull's vision and said it was undoubtedly connected with the Sacred Pipe brought long ago to the Sioux by the White Buffalo Maiden. Immediately they set out on the hunt.

White Bull did not go with them, but afterward they told him about it. They met a lone bull, killed it, painted it red and white, and decorated it with red flannel and a white shell, just as White Bull had been instructed in his vision. Soon after, buffalo herds came on the trail of the slain bull right up to the Sans Arc camp, as the bull had promised. The people had plenty of meat. From that day, the Sans Arc held White Bull in honor because of this divine revelation.

That winter the Minniconjou were not so fortunate as the Sans Arc. They went hungry.

When game was scarce the hunters habitually offered a prayer to the animals they hunted. When approaching an antelope or a lone buffalo, the hunter would say in a whisper: 'I need you. Please go into my lodge. If you do, I will give you red paint.' If successful, the hunter would paint the head of the slain animal with red, in fulfillment of his promise. Of course, such methods were not in use when running a herd of buffalo. When meat was as plenty as that, such prayers seemed quite unnecessary. White Bull says, 'I prayed only when I was hungry or starving.'

White Bull was by habit a horseman. Never once did he go to war on foot, and it was very seldom that he hunted on foot. But once, when twenty-one years old, he did so.

The heralds had announced that the camp would move, and the morning after, the people were packing up and getting ready to start. There was snow on the ground. White Bull asked his father where the people were going to camp that night. The chief replied, 'We shall camp on this same stream at the end of that big belt of timber.' With this information White Bull set out on his hunt.

After going some distance he climbed a hill, and with his father's telescope saw several herds of buffalo. Selecting one herd which he could approach unseen, he crept and crawled until he was within easy range. A young bull, the one lying nearest him, appeared to be the fattest. White Bull fired and killed him.

When there was fresh meat to be had, the Sioux were always eager to share it, and so, when the sound of White Bull's gun was heard, two men came hurrying up to help butcher. One of these men was the son of Chief Lame Deer, a young man named Crazy Heart, better known by his nickname, 'Said-it-Wrong.' They cut up the meat and made packs, which they wrapped in pieces of the hide. Part of the hide they cut into ropes or strips to tie the bundles of meat with, and the men made other strips into a sort of harness, with which to drag the packs, for they had no horses along. Some of the meat they also carried on their backs.

About noon they started for the place where they expected to find the camp. White Bull went first, instructing the others to follow his tracks. It was dark before White Bull, well in advance, reached the first camp of his people. As he approached, he heard Chief Lame Deer calling to his son: 'Said-it-Wrong, we are camped over here.' When the hunters were out late, it was the custom for their relatives to call aloud at intervals all night to guide them to the camp.

White Bull went to the chief to let him know that the boy would soon be home. In the darkness Lame Deer saw him come, and called out, 'How, Son.' White Bull replied, 'I am Big-in-the-Center.'

White Bull advised the chief to send some horses to meet the young men and bring in the meat. As White Bull went on toward his own camp, he could hear his brother, One Bull, calling: 'We are camped over here, Big-in-the-Center.' It was pleasant to hear the voice of his brother calling him home in the darkness.

Had it been warm weather the men would have brought

in only the heart, kidneys, and part of the intestines of the buffalo, leaving the rest until the family could send horses. In such cases, there was always danger that the wolves would devour the meat as soon as the hunters had gone. But White Bull knew how to keep them away. He would wrap the meat in the hide and leave it in a pile. Tearing a few strips of cloth from his blanket, he would rub these with wet gunpowder and tie them to three or four sticks set up all about the meat. Then he would walk around the meat a dozen times so as to leave a strong human scent there. The waving of the blanket strips, the smell of the gunpowder and of the tracks would keep the wolves away until he could get back with his pack-horses.

The next spring the Minniconjou and Hunkpapa were encamped east of Powder River. With-Horn set out with thirty men toward the Black Hills. On the way down they met a smaller party of Hunkpapa and joined forces, making fifty men altogether. When they came near to the houses of the white men (where Rapid City is now), they waited overnight, planning to attack next day.

Some of the young men, however, could not wait to attack. White Bull and Wood-Pile slipped off in the darkness, and at daylight saw seven head of horses grazing on the prairie. About this time they met Gray Eagle and another man who had slipped off from the main party. The four of them rounded up the seven horses and started back. White men came out and shot at them. They fired back and dropped one of the whites. As they galloped away, one of the captured horses, a sorrel, which was dragging a long rope, suddenly stopped. White Bull saw that the knot on the end of the rope was caught in a crack between two rocks. Going back, he whipped out his knife, cut the rope, and drove the horse along. By touching this rope he made the horse his property.

As the Sioux retreated, White Bull saw two more horses and picked them up. Nobody fired at him that time. They found their people in a large camp (four tribes of Sioux and some Cheyennes). White Bull brought home six horses. He presented two of them to his partner, Wood-Pile, and one each to his mother, father, and sister.

White Bull was twenty years old when he got back from this warpath.

Soon after, Little Bull and Bear-Loves organized a party to look for enemies beyond the Yellowstone River. It was cold. They struck the Yellowstone below the mouth of Rosebud River. The ice was out, but the water was full of slush ice coming down.

They halted on the bank of that gray, rushing water, and tried it with their hands. The water seemed very cold, but, after talking it over, the high-hearted young men decided they might as well try to cross and go ahead on the warpath. White Bull volunteered to cross first.

He stripped to his breech-cloth and tied his moccasins and fire-making equipment in a cloth on his head. Then he mounted his horse, urging it into the water. The horse stepped gingerly, snorting, into the icy water. Step by step the water grew deeper until finally the horse had to swim. White Bull clung to the mane with his left hand, holding the reins in his teeth, and paddling with his right arm to help the horse along.

It was a long swim through the swift current, and both horse and naked man were chilled to the bone when they reached the other side. The horse had a hard time clambering out of the water. White Bull suffered acutely from the cold. He got off his horse and immediately fell down; again he tried to stand, but found he could not. He fell down and had to crawl up the steep bank to the flat bottoms. There he exercised his limbs until he could stand and stagger about. He put on his moccasins. Then, dancing, and running up and down, he limbered his joints and hurried over to the timber some distance back from the bank.

Once in the timber, he gathered fuel for a fire. Taking an old dry rag from the bundle on his head, he spread it on the palm of his hand, placed a percussion cap upon it and poured a little gunpowder over the cap, twisting the cloth so that it held the powder and cap tightly in a ball. He then struck this ball with the hilt of his skinning-knife. The blow set off the cap, ignited the powder, and the rag began to burn and smoulder. Blowing on this, he soon was able to set fire to a handful of dry grass. Adding twigs and larger sticks, it was not long before he had a good fire going at the edge of the timber. Thoroughly warmed by the fire, he trotted back to the river bank and called out to his comrades: 'You can come on across now. The water is very cold. It will freeze you, especially your privates. Tighten up your breech-cloths and try to keep them warm.'

Bear-Loves, Little Bull, and the others had meanwhile made a raft of driftwood. They put their guns, saddles, and clothing upon it, and started across. Three men swam in the lead, holding in their teeth the ends of lariats attached to the raft. Three others swam behind, pushing, while the last man swam horseback, herding the horses. It was very cold, but they managed to cross without mishap. White Bull almost died laughing, watching the antics of his half-frozen comrades, as they crawled and staggered about when they came out of the water. When all were warm and dry and clothed again, they set out to the north, but could find no enemies. On the way home the party stopped and visited at the Hunkpapa camp on the north bank of the river. Soon after they got home they all joined the great war-party which was starting against the Flatheads.

CHAPTER XI

THE FIGHT WITH THE FLATHEADS

'Of all the Indians I have fought, Chief White Bull was the greatest
dare-devil.'

GENERAL NELSON A. MILES.

ON THEIR return, the young men found the Sioux in camp
on the Yellowstone at Big Bottom below the mouth of
Rosebud River. Hunkpapa, Oglala, Minniconjou, and
Sans Arc were there, almost a thousand lodges. They had
made a good hunt. The young men were ready for war.

Long Forelock and Big Crow, both Minniconjou, organized a great war-party to go against the Narrow Heads.
These Narrow Heads, or, as the white men call them, Flatheads, had been coming into Sioux country to hunt for
some years past because white gold-seekers had overrun
their own hunting-grounds west of the mountains. Almost
four hundred warriors joined this party, among them Chiefs
Sitting Bull and Flying-By.

Before their preparations were complete, a party of
Oglala, led by Mole, reached the camp, bound west for the
same objective. This caused some argument. It was evident that, if two separate parties attacked the Flatheads,
one of them would be at a disadvantage. Yet the leaders of
neither party wished to yield precedence. Finally the two
parties combined and rode up the Yellowstone in a body.
As a result of this dispute, Hunts-the-Enemy was in a bad
humor. He said: 'I feel bad; some of you have done me
wrong. I shall not come back from this warpath.'

They crossed the Yellowstone at the mouth of Arrow
(Pryor) Creek. There they sent out six scouts. These

scouts reported many Flathead hunters coming. The scouts had not seen the camp of these enemies. Therefore it was decided to push on that night up the Musselshell River.

During the night White Bull and Gray Eagle gave the Indian soldiers the slip, and riding ahead, saw the fire-lit tipis of the Flathead camp. Before long the two were joined by Sitting-Snug. The three of them kept watch the rest of the night, but the Flatheads were feasting after their hunt, they were wide awake. The three young men had no chance to steal horses.

Shortly before daybreak the scout, Bear-Shedding, turned up. He had been sent out to locate the Flathead camp. Having done this, he dutifully returned to the main party and came back with a detail of picked young men on fast horses. These forty men, led by Mole and Herald, had been sent as decoys. They intended to attack the Flatheads, then retreat, and so lead the enemy into an ambush where the main party was concealed — some two miles west of the camp. White Bull's friends joined this party, who climbed a high hill overlooking the Flathead camp. The leader warned them to be cautious. Said he: 'I am sure the Flatheads have glasses.' But White Bull paid no attention. *He* was not hiding from the enemy. He rode right up to the hilltop to look over.

Bull Eagle raised his quirt and struck White Bull's horse across the face. He was angry. He said: 'Get back there, get out of sight; the Flatheads will see you and kill us.'

White Bull was contemptuous: 'Well, we came here to fight; that is what we are here for.' He would not budge.

Mole said: 'White Bull, if you will come back here, we will all start together and attack these enemies.' Then White Bull drew back.

As the young men advanced they could see the Flathead tipis, about a hundred of them, sharply outlined against the brightening east. They kept a sharp lookout, not making much noise. They saw one of the Flatheads driving seven ponies out upon the prairie; he was heading south from the camp. As soon as the Sioux saw him, they rushed him. He was half a mile from his camp before he saw them coming. At once he let his horses go, and raced for his life, back to his friends among the tipis. The Sioux were after him, yelling and lashing their horses. But he had a start, he rode hard, he got back to camp. The Flatheads swarmed out of their tents like hornets. Then the Sioux rounded up the lone Flathead's seven ponies and turned back, as if they had got what they wanted. Iron Lightning captured five of the ponies.

Away went the young Sioux, running off with their capture, back toward the four hundred warriors in the ambush. After them, pell-mell, came a hundred mounted enemies riding like mad. The Flatheads were well armed with guns and pistols, they were shooting all the time.

It was two miles back to the ambush. The young Sioux raced for that place. But White Bull wished to distinguish himself and keep the enemy coming. He held his horse down. The Flatheads were gaining and coming nearer at every jump. He kept charging back at them, as if trying to hold them so that his comrades could get away. He rode last of all the Sioux young men.

The Flatheads came so close that White Bull called out, 'We must do something.' He gave two yelps, turned his horse back, and charged his enemies. All alone he charged them, chased them back alone. One of the Flatheads in the rear waited for White Bull. White Bull struck at him with his lance three times. The Flathead fired his revolver at White Bull, but missed. White Bull jerked out his own revolver, pumped three bullets into his enemy's horse, and wheeled away. The man's horse dropped. It fell on the Flathead's leg and held him down. When White Bull saw this, he thought he had him. He dashed back to finish him, but the Flathead, now afoot, ran in among the tents and White Bull could not touch him.

White Bull followed his comrades, and once more the Flatheads pursued. Again White Bull chased them back a little, firing at them with his revolver, but failed to kill any-one. As he fell back, the Flatheads came after him again. It was back and forth that day.

The third time he chased them they nearly caught him. Two of them took after him. He raced away, hugging his pony's neck, to escape them. They were close upon him, but the other Sioux stopped and waited for him and he reached them safely. His comrades kept saying, 'Come on, we must hurry.' But after the Sioux had gained a little ground they all dismounted and began to shoot. The Flat-heads got off their horses, and they had a good fight.

One of the Flatheads was very brave and kept advancing; he jumped off his horse to shoot. White Bull shouted, 'Now is the time to strike the enemy!' White Bull mounted and charged him with lowered lance.

The Flathead did not run, however, as White Bull ex-pected, but stood his ground, with rifle raised ready to shoot. Nevertheless White Bull, though all alone, wished to do as chiefs and chiefs' sons do; his father was a chief, he was Sitting Bull's nephew. He had started after this Flat-head, and, if he failed to strike him, he knew people would say he was a coward and a woman. So he went right ahead, lance against rifle. White Bull struck the man on the head with his lance. The Flathead ducked under the blow, and fired at the same instant. The blow spoiled his aim. He missed White Bull. The bullet broke the lance shaft and cut away one of the eagle-feathers with which it was decorated. This deed is reckoned the bravest of all White Bull's *coups*. Owns-Swayback struck second.

By this time the Sioux reserves had come whooping out of their ambush. The fight became general, and a hot fight it was. The Flatheads were well armed, they fought on foot, they hit a number of Sioux.

White Bull dashed back to his party. He looked over his shoulder and saw the man he had struck still coming. That Flathead was brave.

White Bull stopped, and fired, and dropped the Flathead, hitting him in the breast. Pretty-Voiced-Eagle (Good-Voiced-Eagle) rushed the fallen man. The Flathead jumped up. When Pretty-Voiced-Eagle saw that, he turned and mounted his horse. Then the Flathead shot the Sioux's horse. Immediately after, someone behind White Bull fired and killed this Flathead. Pretty-Voiced-Eagle struck the dead man first, White Bull counted the second *coup*.

One of the Flatheads was very brave. He was out in front. The Sioux were all around him. Standing Bull, White Bull's bosom friend, was on horseback; he rushed this Flathead. The Flathead raised his gun, and Standing Bull wheeled away. Just then the Flathead fired. Down went Standing Bull, shot through the head.

White Bull jumped from his horse and ran to his friend. He was already dead, blood streaming from his left temple under the gay beaded browband of his war-bonnet. White Bull took him in his arms and wailed and cried at his great loss, but Standing Bull lay limp and unresponsive.

Then White Bull held his friend's hand and promised to avenge him. He carried the body back out of reach of the Flatheads, then came running forward with his carbine. Meanwhile, Bluff-in-the-Face (Daunts-Him-by-Blow-in-the-Face) counted the first *coup* on this enemy. Red Shield ran up to count the second. The Flathead shot Red Shield in the leg and brought him down. Then Bull Head rushed up, covered by his shield. The Flathead had dropped his gun, and now had an arrow on his bow-string. He let fly. His arrow pierced Bull Head's shield, the point penetrated Bull Head's flesh an inch deep.

But White Bull, with tear-wet cheeks and raging heart, did not stop. He came running on foot at the man who had killed his friend. He raised his gun and pulled the trigger. The carbine jammed! And at the same moment the Flathead loosed his arrow!

Tchk! It went by — a miss. White Bull raised his gun, struck the Flathead on the forehead, knocked him out, jumped on him, whipped out his knife and cut him about the face and throat. The Flathead was apparently dead. White Bull began to scalp him.

It was White Bull's custom to scalp only one side of an enemy's head. While he was busy with his knife, Struck-by-Eagle or White Tail called out, 'Friend, let me have the other half.' White Bull answered, 'Sure.'

While White Bull was ripping off the Flathead's hair, the man grunted and came to. He jumped up and ran dizzily around a few steps before he fell dead. White Bull was the fourth man to strike this enemy. There were beads tied in the hair of the scalp he took.

By this time the Sioux had suffered losses. Hunts-the-Enemy was dead, his premonition was fulfilled, and Crow-

Going-up-in-the-Air was wounded. Yet, seeing how many Sioux there were and how many of their own comrades were killed, the Flatheads ran back to their camp. It was a regular stampede. The Sioux started after them, but just then heard Chief Flying-By shouting: 'Stop! That will be all for this time! Some good men have been wounded already.'

So they turned back. The Sioux let the Flatheads go. If Flying-By had not given that order, all the Flatheads would have been wiped out that day.

Sitting Bull and a few others paid no attention to Flying-By. They ran after the Flatheads, and Sitting Bull was shot through the arm with an arrow.[1]

White Bull had jumped on the nearest horse to follow the Flatheads. When he came back to his party, he found that a Sans Arc Sioux had 'captured' his own war-horse. White Bull said, 'Friend, that is my horse, let me have it.' So Charging-Bear, somewhat crestfallen, handed over the lariat.

The Sioux gathered up their dead and wounded. Of the Minniconjou, Big Crow, Black Shield, Spotted Breast, Long Pine, Different Tail, Crow-Going-up-in-the-Air, Red Shield, Bull Head, had been wounded. Of the Oglala, Eagle Thunder, and of the Sans Arc, Big Hail and Bull Eagle had been hit. Thirty Flatheads had been killed.

They carried the dead Sioux, Standing Bull and Hunts-the-Enemy, across the Musselshell, roped them up in blankets and buried them in caves. They had no fear that the Flatheads would follow to desecrate these graves. The Flatheads had had enough of the Sioux.

The wounded who could ride were brought back on their

[1] An account of this battle from Sitting Bull's point of view will be found in my biography of that chief. Chapter XVII.

horses. The other wounded traveled on traveaux. Crow-Going-up-in-the-Air died on the way. Bull Eagle and Eagle Thunder died after reaching home.

On his return White Bull married White Cow. Soon after, he began courting the elder daughter of Standing Buffalo, a lively Sans Arc girl named Rattles-Track. One day he went hunting. When he returned, he found that White Cow's aunt had taken her home. It seemed he could never find two women who could get along with each other. They were always jealous.

CHAPTER XII

THE JEALOUS WIFE

Divorce in Lakota society was an incident rather than an occasion.
CHIEF STANDING BEAR, *Land of the Spotted Eagle.*

THE same winter (1871) White Bull stole Rattles-Track and made her his wife. She was a girl with a mind of her own and thoroughly able to take care of herself. According to Sioux custom, a man was expected to marry the younger sisters of his wife as they came of marriageable age, and it was not long until White Bull took into his home Eagle Woman, the younger sister of his wife. For a time they got along all right. Then White Bull met a young woman named Holy Lodge. He kept urging her to marry him, and at last she agreed. Perhaps Holy Lodge had heard of White Bull's checkered matrimonial career. At any rate, she demanded a pledge of his love. One day, when they were talking, she said: 'You are going away now. Give me your six-shooter to keep until you come back.' He gave it to her.

Holy Lodge was a popular young thing. She had many suitors, always seeking her out. One in particular courted her while White Bull was gone on a hunt. The girl carried White Bull's six-shooter on her belt, and when this young man saw it, he knew it was White Bull's. Soon everyone in camp had heard that Holy Lodge had White Bull's gun. Immediately some kind friend informed Rattles-Track that her husband was courting another girl.

Rattles-Track was not the woman to suffer jealousy inactive. Right away she went to the tipi of her rival's family, and, pointing out the six-shooter, said, 'This gun your daughter has belongs to my husband's uncle. He wants it.'

This news was a surprise to the parents and caused Holy Lodge great embarrassment. But rather than let them know the name of her real suitor, she said nothing and handed over the gun. Rattles-Track took the six-shooter home and hid it in the lodge. When White Bull returned, Holy Lodge told him of this and demanded reprisals. White Bull went to Rattles-Track and said, 'I am going on the warpath. I want my six-shooter.' Rattles-Track gave him the weapon.

From that day there was no peace for White Bull in his lodge. Rattles-Track made trouble all the time. She would lose her temper and hide White Bull's clothing. Sometimes she would pull his hair and scold and threaten. He never knew when she might whip out her knife and stab him. She was very jealous. But White Bull could not leave the girls alone. He would not let her bully him.

He went off to war. The day he returned he found the shamans performing an elk ceremony of some kind. Everybody was there looking on. White Bull found Holy Lodge and her sister together. White Bull said: 'My woman has been making trouble for me. I want you two to go home with me to be my wives.' Holy Lodge was ready. Her sister said: 'How many horses have you?' White Bull admitted that he had only two head at the time. The sister replied: 'You two go now, perhaps I will come along later.' She never did.

White Bull took Holy Lodge to his parents' tipi. Rattles-Track and her sister were there. This younger wife left him and went home.

But Rattles-Track was no quitter. She remained in his tent with Holy Lodge.

That winter of 1871 White Bull had a narrow escape from being frozen to death. The weather had been very cold. A man named Big Crow, walking from one camp to another, an all-day trip, had been found frozen to death, lying near his destination. Soon after, the camp moved from that place. White Bull was traveling with seven families. They needed meat, and he volunteered to go hunting.

That day was warm and bright, and White Bull set out wearing only a shirt, leggins, and a blue blanket. About sundown he saw buffalo passing. Tying up his horse in the brush, he tried to head the buffalo off, but they were moving so swiftly that he could not get a fair shot. He started back to his horse, but before he reached it, a sudden blizzard swept down out of the northwest. Within a few minutes the temperature dropped perhaps sixty degrees, and the snow was blinding. He blundered on and reached his horse.

He knew he was in great danger, but could not think where to go. As it happened, right at his side was a shallow wash-out. He dug into the drift there and squatted down in the hole he had made. Just in front he planted his ramrod vertically, so that, if buried in the snow, he could dig out, he would know which way to go. He covered himself with his blanket. He was very cold for a while, but at last the snow covered him over. He felt warmer and went to sleep.

When he awakened, his toes, chin, and forehead pained him severely. He knew they were frosted. With the guidance of his ramrod, he dug upwards and soon found himself standing clear of the snow. He climbed out of the wash-out and went to his horse, which was standing on higher ground. The storm had passed and the day was clear and bright. The morning sun shone warmly once more. White Bull looked around and saw a herd of buffalo not far off.

Before he could reach the herd, he sensed a change in the air. He looked back to the northwest and saw another storm coming. It was almost upon him. He had to think quickly.

Near-by, under the bank of the creek, he saw some box elders above the snow. He made a dash for them, and hurriedly began to dig a hole in the drifts as he had done before. Just as he got this hole finished, the blizzard swept over him. The hole was rapidly filled up by the drifting snow. His frosted feet were beginning to hurt him more and more. The air was so cold he could hardly get his breath. Something had to be done to keep him warm or he must die there. He wished he had a fire, but dared not leave his hole to gather fuel in the blinding fury of that blizzard. He sat there looking up, and then saw that by great good luck some of the branches of the box elders under which he cowered were dead and dry. He could reach them and break them off without leaving his shelter.

By this time his teeth were chattering and he was shaking so that he could hardly make a fire. But at last he succeeded, and, cowering over the blaze, he gradually warmed himself, adding fuel as the fire burned down, and eating a little snow to fill his stomach. He had had nothing to eat or drink since leaving camp the morning before. It was savagely cold.

Presently a coyote came and sat on the other side of the

fire in the hole the man had made. When White Bull saw this coyote, he looked at him and thought: 'I have had nothing to eat for two days. I will kill him.'

Then it occurred to White Bull that perhaps the coyote had come to him to tell him something or befriend him. White Bull spoke to the coyote; 'Friend, I came to this place and am having a hard time, but I wish only what is good.'

The coyote made no reply. The fire was dying down, and after a time White Bull stood up to get some more fuel. The coyote stepped to one side to let him pass. He went a few paces from his shelter and brought back wood. While he was out, he saw his horse shivering in the brush. White Bull called out to the horse, 'Stay where you are, friend, and we shall both pull through.'

White Bull went back to his fire. There the coyote remained, warming himself on the other side of it. They sat so near together that White Bull could almost have reached out and touched the wolf. At dawn out on the hills the coyotes began to yap. Then the coyote by the fire became restless, and whined a little, and trotted away.

When the sun rose the blizzard died away. After the wind had fallen and the air was warmer, White Bull got to his feet and gathered more fuel. He built up the fire and pulled some sage. Then he removed his moccasins and examined his feet. They were beginning to blister. He put sage leaves in his moccasins and put them on his feet again. His face also was frosted.

White Bull mounted his horse and started home. The camp was on Powder River. On the way he met a man who stopped, hand over mouth, astonished to see him. This man said: 'All of your folks are mourning. They think you are dead. They were out looking for you yesterday and today.'

As he approached the camp, he could hear the women singing. It was nearly sundown. He called out: 'I am home again.' This made his father happy. They told him they were about to give up. Three search parties had come in saying they could not find him.

All of White Bull's friends came into the lodge to kiss him and hug him. They were glad to see him safe again.

CHAPTER XIII

BULLET–PROOF

At Laramie I told the commissioners that I had seen the Sioux commit a massacre; they killed many white men. But the Sioux are still here, and still kill white men. *When you whites whip the Sioux come and tell us of it.* You are afraid of the Sioux. Two years ago I went with the soldiers; they talked very brave. They said they were going through the Sioux country to Powder River and Tongue River. We got to Pryor Creek, just below here in the Crow country. I wanted to go ahead, but the soldiers got scared and turned back. The soldiers were the whirlwind, but the whirlwind turned back. Last summer the soldiers went to Pryor Creek again; again the whirlwind was going through Sioux country, but again the whirlwind turned back. We Crows are not the whirlwind, but we go to the Sioux; we go to their country; we meet them and fight; we do not turn back. But then *we* are not the whirlwind! You say the railroad is coming, that it is like the whirlwind and cannot be turned back. I don't think it will come. The Sioux are on the way, and you are afraid of them; they will turn the whirlwind back.

'BLACKFOOT' (CROW CHIEF) *to United States Officials.*

LONG FORELOCK was one of White Bull's best friends and one of the best of the warriors. About this time (1871), Long Forelock, Owns-Swayback, Long Fox, and a lad named Left Hand, went hunting. They did not return.

Their relatives became alarmed and went looking for them. Near the place where Lame Deer was killed (Lame Deer, Montana), on a creek with a high bank at one side, they found a windbreak made of poles with a buffalo robe stretched around it. Long Forelock lay dead inside with his gun. The other three lay outside the windbreak with their guns by their sides.

Afterward it was learned that some Crow warriors, lying in wait on a high hill, saw these young men bringing buffalo beef to their camp. The Crows came down and surrounded them and began shooting. According to the Crows' story, they killed the three Sioux outside the windbreak one by one. The last man to stop shooting was the man concealed in the windbreak. Even after the shooting stopped, the Crows dared not go down to scalp their enemies. They thought Long Forelock might be lying in wait for them. That was why Long Forelock's relatives found the guns beside the dead bodies.

White Bull was not with the party which found his friend, but afterward when he was at Bear Butte, someone brought the skull of Long Forelock to the camp. That skull was all that remained of his comrade, killed by the Crows.

The winter after Long Forelock was killed, the Minniconjou camped near the Black Hills. One day at a dance, a man named Long Holy announced to the crowd that he had received power to make men bullet-proof, and that any young man who wished to share his power had only to say so. Long Holy stood up and called aloud: 'Those who wish to be my men may come with me. Those who join me will not be killed. We'll organize a big war-party. Let those who wish to show their courage come with me.' He ended his announcement by shouting, 'Whoever joins me must have a good gun and a six-shooter.' Thus Long Holy made his offer to the whole camp. Nobody took it up.

However, the man's words set young White Bull thinking. He was already convinced that men *could* be made bullet-proof. It was only three winters since he first heard of this 'way of making good warriors.' Only three winters back his friend Long Forelock had told him how the Cheyenne Chief Ice had gone to work and done it. Ice had made two Sioux boys bullet-proof: Long Forelock and High Crane. They had been tested out in a fight with the Crows over beyond the Musselshell. Both young men were hit, but the bullets did not go through. The more White Bull thought this over, the more it seemed to him that Long Holy's offer gave him an excellent chance to do something great. Long Holy, it was true, was not a professional shaman. But White Bull was eager to distinguish himself. He consulted his father, Makes-Room.

Makes-Room probably thought that, if anyone could make his reckless son invulnerable, it would relieve the family of a great cause for worry. After considering the matter, he replied: 'Son, it sounds all right. Long Holy is a good man, I suppose he is holy enough to do such things. If you wish to join him, go ahead.'

That night there was a gathering of young men in White Bull's tent, and after talking it over, four of them — White Bull, Bear-Loves, With-Horn, and Alone-on-One-Side — called Long Holy in and told him they were ready to join his Order. Long Holy was pleased. He instructed them to move the tipi into the middle of the camp circle. 'We shall sing there all night,' he said, 'and in the morning we shall be ready to try out my power and see how it works.'

The four young volunteers immediately moved the tipi, pitching it on the grass in the middle of the camp. Then they went inside the tent, and with their knives scraped the ground bare, and spread sprays of aromatic sage — a sacred plant — all round the walls to sit upon. Presently Long Holy came in, wearing a shirt and leggins. Around his head he wore a band of black fur, with a buffalo horn attached over each ear. His face was painted blue, with a white moon on his forehead and a star across the bridge of his nose. All night long he instructed them according to his vision, sometimes stamping and making sounds in imitation of the buffalo bull and the eagle.

Long Holy gave his men four face-paints, for their exclusive use. The first three could be worn at any time, the fourth only in battle. The first paint was yellow all over, touched here and there with flecks of black. The second was blue and yellow mixed, with a five-pointed star on the forehead. Long Holy gave each of them a small star cut out of leather for a pattern; by laying this on the forehead and tracing around its edge, they could make a perfect star in outline, and afterward fill it in with color. The third paint was red, with a white line across the forehead and down to the corners of the mouth. The fourth, or war-paint, was black all over, with a white sun-disk on the forehead and a star on the right cheek.

White Bull and his companions were told that they must observe certain taboos, also, or they might be killed. Each one must have a bed of his own in the family tent, and must allow no one to pass between that bed and the central fireplace. At meals he must be served first of all, and nobody else might use the wooden bowl he ate from. He must place a rock [1] between his bed and the fire, and, if he was absent from home when the family ate, a portion must be placed upon the rock before the others tasted food. Above all, Long Holy's young men must never wear anything red or blood-colored, and must keep away from unwell women. For if such a woman was in the lodge or ate from the kettle in which the young man's food was cooked, she would never stop flowing — unless the young man treated her with a medicine made of a root which Long Holy provided. Unless this were done, the power would not work; the young man might be killed.

Toward morning, when they were singing the last song, Long Holy leaned forward, placed his thumb and forefinger

[1] The rock was the patron god of war.

upon the bare ground, and, raising his hand, drew up a root a foot long. White Bull says there was no plant growing there when the young men scraped the earth bare with their knives, only grass. This root was the sacred medicine of Long Holy's vision; he could draw it out of the earth anywhere. He cut this root into five parts, one for each of them. He told them to chew some of it and rub it upon their bodies before a fight to make them bullet-proof. 'Rub yourselves with it now,' he advised them. 'It is time to try out my power.' They did so. White Bull says that root had a peculiar taste.

Then a buffalo robe was spread down in the middle of the lodge, and White Bull laid upon it his six-shooter, six percussion caps, six bullets, and a handful of gunpowder. That six-shooter was a new weapon then, it had hardly been used. White Bull says that afterward he killed more than thirty buffalo with that gun.

Long Holy then invited a number of leading men into the lodge to witness the loading of the six-shooter. Among those who sat in the tent as witnesses were Charging-Eagle, Feather-Earring, Thunder Hoop, Bull Eagle, Ghost Heart, Brave Heart, and Little. Little still lives at the Pine Ridge Agency.

Then White Bull loaded the six-shooter. No one else handled it. In each chamber he placed an inch of powder, and wrapping the ball in a scrap of thin buckskin, rammed it home. He charged the gun heavily. The powder was good powder; he had used some of it before, and used the rest of it later, with good results. Long Holy never laid a finger upon the gun, or the ammunition. Both White Bull and Long Holy were confident that his power would work. Otherwise they would never have taken part in what followed.

When the six-shooter had been loaded under the eyes of all those men, White Bull handed it to Long Holy, and they all went outside. The whole camp had turned out to watch Long Holy show his power. Long Holy announced, 'Now we are going to try this out, first with bullets, afterward with arrows.'

Long Holy called for a volunteer to come from the crowd and shoot at him and his young men. But nobody would do it. So he said, 'All right then, I will do the shooting myself.' He took his stand at one side of the camp circle, before the crowd, and the young men trotted past him in a circle, so that he could shoot at them. Four times they trotted around the camp, making a larger circle each time and coming closer to Long Holy. The fourth time he said he would shoot.

White Bull was in the lead, passing Long Holy within ten yards at a slow trot. When he was right in front of Long Holy, the man fired point-blank. The bullet hit White Bull in the ribs, and almost knocked him over, but ricocheted off his bare body 'as if it had hit a rock.' Says he: 'I could hear it *zing* as it flew through the air. It was no glancing blow; it hit me square on the side. But it did not break the skin. It made a bruise, but I did not bleed.'

Following him came Bear-Loves. He also was hit in the body, but the bullet did not go through, it did not hurt him much. The third man was With-Horn. Long Holy's bullet struck him in front, below the ribs, entering his body. With-Horn halted. He began to bleed, not only from his wound, but from the mouth. Long Holy went up to him and said, 'Do as I tell you next time,' and, taking a handful of earth from the prairie, he rubbed it on With-Horn's wound and stopped the bleeding. Soon after, With-Horn stopped spitting blood; he was all right again. Alone-on-One-Side also was hit. Then Long Holy said it was time to try out his power with arrows.

But the people were uneasy after With-Horn bled at the mouth. Someone called out: 'There must be an unwell woman in this crowd who is breaking Long Holy's power. It is not good to try the arrows at this time. Let's wait until we can do it where no women are about.' All the people were of that opinion, and Long Holy finally gave in and said he would omit the arrow test that day.

White Bull went home then, to wait for a big war-party which would give him a chance to show off his courage. He was satisfied with the proof Long Holy had given. None of the bullets had gone through, all four young men were alive and well. All four, and Long Holy, kept up the taboos of their Order. Later, others joined the Order. And soon after their big chance came.

The following summer the Minniconjou, Sans Arc, Oglala, and Hunkpapa Sioux encamped below the Big Bend of the Yellowstone to hold the annual Sun Dance. Two days after the dance, a party was organized to go to meet the white troops known to be approaching the mouth of Arrow (Pryor) Creek. Sitting Bull and Crazy Horse were the principal chiefs, and among the five hundred warriors in the party were White Bull's relatives, Feather-Earring and With-Horn (who had taken the name Runs-Against, now that Runs-Against was dead). Long Holy was planning to show off his power before all those warriors.

All night they rode, and toward morning halted not far from the camp of the troops,[1] which was opposite the mouth

[1] Four hundred soldiers (182 of them cavalry) under Major E. M. Baker, Second Cavalry, escort of a surveying party of the Northern Pacific Railroad Company. The engagement took place August 14, 1872.

of Arrow Creek. The Indian soldiers rounded up the young men, and tried to hold them together until dawn, the zero hour.

White Bull, however, was impatient. He had been much impressed by the great fame of the celebrated warrior, Crawler, and had heard that Crawler had made his reputation by always giving the Indian soldiers the slip and making an attack before the other warriors could strike the enemy. White Bull thought that a good plan, but could think of no way of escaping the vigilance of his comrades. Finally he got off his horse and said that he had to stop and relieve himself. The others rode on. White Bull stood there until they were out of sight, then mounted and rode around them through the darkness. As he advanced toward the enemy camp he met Crawler coming back with a bunch of captured horses! This encouraged him; he went on. But before he could accomplish anything at the enemy camp, the main war-party came up with him.

No sooner had the Indians come in sight than the troops began to shoot at them. White Bull estimates the number of white soldiers as four hundred, which exactly tallies with the figure given in the records of the War Department. The white troops were behind a cutbank, while the Indians lined the hilltop a quarter of a mile away. Between the two lines was open prairie. The fighting began at daybreak. Plenty Lice was the first man hit. He charged close up to the line of troops, was shot off his horse and killed before sunup. Soon after, High Hawk, a Brulé, was slightly wounded, hit in the ribs on the right side; oddly enough, the third man hit was another High Hawk, a Minniconjou, shot in the left shoulder. Then the sun rose.

Long Holy saw that this was ideal ground for a display of

his power. Just after sunrise he began to shout to the Sioux: 'Now I am going to make these men holy [bullet-proof]. We are going to make four circles toward the white soldiers, and each time we shall ride a little nearer to the enemy. When we make the fourth circle, we are going to charge, and all of you must charge with us.'

Long Holy called his young men together, and they all got ready. White Bull put on his battle face-paint, and rubbed his whole body, and the body of his horse, with spittle made of the root Long Holy had given him. His horse's body he painted iron gray, and all his joints were marked with white. He kept the sacred root in a little pouch tied to the quill of an eagle-feather worn in his hair. Bear-Loves and White Bull wore feathers exactly alike that day.

The seven young men mounted their fleet ponies, and away they all went at a run, circling toward the soldier lines, now fogged with smoke. White Bull led off, then came Bear-Loves, With-Horn, Little Bull, Leading-Him, and Takes-the-Bread. Last of all rode Long Holy. The soldiers were all shooting at them all this time. As they dashed along, they were singing the song Long Holy had taught them:

> There is nobody holy besides me.
> The Sun said so; the Rock said so;
> He gave me this medicine, and said so.

White Bull was expecting to be hit, he was waiting for a bullet to strike him or his horse. Suddenly, as he rode ahead, he heard Long Holy, and then Leading-Him, call out, 'I am hit!' He looked back, but they were still on their horses, galloping along, apparently unhurt. The second time they circled nearer the soldiers, within forty yards. White Bull could hear his comrades sing out, one after another, 'I am hit!' or 'I am shot!' He kept expecting to be hit himself. By the time they had finished the second round, four men had been hit. Leading-Him had been shot in the neck, below the chin; the bullet passed *clear through!* He bled freely.

As the young men were starting on their third circle, Sitting Bull galloped out upon the prairie between the lines. He was yelling at Long Holy and his young men: 'Wait! Stop! Turn Back! Too many young men are being wounded! That's enough!' He kept ordering them to turn back, to give up their circling. The young men hardly knew what to do. Leading-Him had been shot through the neck, Takes-the-Bread was hit in the ribs, With-Horn had been hit twice in the back, Long Holy himself had been hit in the right breast.

But Long Holy did not wish to stop; nobody had been killed, only one of the bullets had gone through. He was indignant at Sitting Bull's interference. Said he, 'I brought these men here to *fight*. But of course, if they *want* to quit, they can.'

Sitting Bull paid no attention to Long Holy. He kept insisting, shouting to the young men to stop. And so, reluctantly, they did. White Bull was the first to obey his uncle's orders.

Long Holy could see no reason for this high-handed conduct on the part of the chief. He pointed out that Leading-Him was wearing a red cord on his powder-horn, and said it was the young man's own fault that he was shot through. 'I told him not to wear anything red,' he declared. But Sitting Bull would not listen, he broke off the demonstration of Long Holy's power. They all rejoined their comrades on the hilltop.

Then for a time the Indians lay on the hilltop firing at the troops, and the troops kept firing at the Indians. Occasionally one or more of the young men would dash out into the open, ride at a run along the enemy line, and then speed back to safety on the hilltop. All this time Long Holy kept complaining because the chief had interfered with his demonstration, kept saying that Sitting Bull was getting 'mouthy.' That made the chief restive, touched his pride. The young men were also admiring Crazy Horse, who seemed very brave and lucky that day. Sitting Bull felt that he was being put in the shade. He thought it about time the head chief did something to remind them that he was the greatest man among them.

All at once White Bull, peeping over the hilltop, saw Uncle Sitting Bull lay down his gun and quiver, and carrying only his long narrow tobacco-pouch, with the pipestem protruding from its mouth, walk coolly out in front of the Indian line, as if he were taking a stroll through the camp at evening. He walked right out toward the soldiers, and sat down on the grass a hundred yards in front of the Indian line, right on the open prairie, in plain sight of the firing soldiers. There he got out his flint and steel, struck fire, lighted his pipe, and began to puff away in his usual leisurely fashion. Turning his head toward his own astonished men, he yelled to them, 'Any Indians who wish to smoke with me, come on!'

It was amazing. But his nephew, White Bull, was not the man to take a dare. He and another Sioux named Gets-the-Best-of-Them, went forward. With them went two Cheyennes. White Bull had his six-shooter and breech-loading rifle along. The other Sioux had a bow and arrows. They left their horses behind. When they reached Sitting Bull, they all sat down in a row.

Sitting Bull was calmly puffing away, and handed the pipe to his nephew, and so on down the line. They smoked, as usual, from right to left.

Says White Bull: 'We others wasted no time. Our hearts beat rapidly, and we smoked as fast as we could. All around us the bullets were kicking up the dust, and we could hear bullets whining overhead. But Sitting Bull was not afraid. He just sat there quietly, looking around as if he were at home in his tent, and smoked peacefully.'

While they sat there, Two Crow was making a circle between them and the soldiers at the gallop. Just as Two Crow passed between them and the troops, his horse was shot dead and fell headlong, kicking up the dust in their faces. White Bull, seeing the horse shot right in front of him, shut his eyes and dropped his head upon his knees in the face of all that shooting.

After the pipe was smoked out, Sitting Bull got out the little sharp stick he used for cleaning his pipe, cleared the bowl of ashes, and put the pipe and cleaner back into the pouch. Then he got up slowly, and sauntered back to the Indian line. White Bull and the other three ran back. Gets-the-Best-of-Them was so excited that he forgot his arrows, and White Bull had to run back after them.

Such absolutely reckless, cool daring beat anything those Indians had ever seen. It was the bravest thing Sitting Bull had ever done. There was no necessity for that stunt, no excitement to spur him on. It was sheer nerve — a grandstand play to teach those saucy young men a lesson and put them in their place again. It worked to perfection. None of them had ever seen anything like that. It was not a *coup*, of course, but it was braver than any *coup!* Long Holy had no more to say.

When Sitting Bull got back to his own line, he took up his weapons, mounted, and called out, 'That's enough! We must stop! That's enough!'

It was then about noon.

But Crazy Horse was unwilling to stop fighting. All the morning he had been the star performer of the Indian team, and he could hardly reconcile himself to being second — and a bad second — all at once. He had been too brilliantly outdone. He turned to White Bull and said, 'Let's make one more circle toward the soldier line.' That was all Crazy Horse could think up. 'You go first.'

White Bull was not the man to take a dare, and answered, 'Go first yourself, I'll follow.' And as Crazy Horse charged away on his fast war-horse, White Bull rode right at his heels. The soldiers fired at them as they passed. Just as they were turning back toward their own line, all the soldiers fired together and dropped the pony of Crazy Horse, stone dead. Crazy Horse was unhurt. He jumped up and ran back afoot. White Bull and his horse were untouched.

Plenty Lice was the only one killed. He was killed so near the soldier line that the Indians could not recover his body. They had to leave it behind when they went home. Some say that the soldiers tossed the naked body of Plenty Lice into a fire when the fight was over, and that the Indians found it there after the troops had gone.

When they got back to camp, Long Holy treated the wounded men, he healed them all — even Leading-Him, the man who had been wearing the red cord on his powder-horn. Long Holy's power was strong.

Sitting Bull, however, was always looking out for his reckless nephew. He advised White Bull to drop the whole

business. Said he: 'Nephew, you had better give this up.
Before long you will be going back to Good (Cheyenne)
River with your Minniconjou relatives. Down there, no-
body will know what this is all about; they will think it
foolish to keep it up. Besides, there are too many such
Orders.'

White Bull took his uncle's words. It had been understood that, if he captured horses, he would give Long Holy
one of them for his aid. But as it was, he had nothing to
pay. He no longer kept up the taboos of that medicine.
Not long after, the Minniconjou dragged south again, and
White Bull rode with them.

CHAPTER XIV

TAILS FOR MOCCASINS

An Indian mounted on an animal which he considers better than that of his enemies does not fear to penetrate into their very midst, and as a scout will be apt to do excellent service; but let him once feel that his mount is less fleet, less enduring, than are those of the enemy, and he is worthless — will take no risks....

W. P. CLARK, *The Indian Sign Language.*

IT WAS the season when the wild cherries ripen, the summer of 1872. A large camp of the Sioux was on the Big Horn River. Touch-the-Cloud and Charging Eagle led a war-party of some forty men to take horses from the Crow Indians. They followed up the Yellowstone, sending scouts ahead looking for enemies.

White Bull was one of the scouts. They climbed a hill, and White Bull began scanning the country through his binoculars. He had bought these glasses from an Agency Indian at Fort Bennett, the year before. Peeping over the hill, he saw Indians coming toward them, a big moving camp. There were many Indians — Crows, enemies. When this was reported to the leaders, Touch-the-Cloud got cold feet. He gave up hope, there were so many enemies. He decided to go home.

Most of the party followed his lead, but White Bull said: 'Well, what do you want? We came looking for enemies, and there they are.' Twelve others felt as he did — Wood-Pile, Hunka People, Dog-with-Horns, Talks-About-the-Girls (Lady-Killer), High Hawk, Brown (Yellow) Hat, Hole-in-the-Shin, Two Lance, Charging Bear, Low Dog, Fast Walker, and Bridger. These men advanced while the others fell back.

They all stopped in a ravine, and White Bull and another man went up on the hill to have another look. It was near sundown. They sat there watching the Crows make camp and planned how they would approach the camp and how they would leave it. They left nothing to chance. The camp was across the river.

After dark they swam the Yellowstone, but, when they got near to that great camp of enemies, four of the men turned back. The rest went on until they came to a big tipi. In it they could see the silhouettes of many enemies, cast by the firelight upon the sides of the taper tent. Then all but two turned back; only White Bull and Low Dog went into the camp. They left their horses behind and walked in. They found a number of fine horses picketed in the middle of the camp circle. White Bull selected a handsome pinto; Low Dog selected a bay.

They cut the lariats and tried to mount the horses, but the one Low Dog had stolen was so wild he could not mount it. They were afraid it would cause a commotion, so the two of them walked quietly out of the camp, leading the horses.

When White Bull and Low Dog turned up with these two fine animals, the other men in the group took courage. Though they had no heart for a second trip into the camp circle of the Crows, they thought they could steal some of the horses turned out to graze around the camp. Accordingly they rounded up a considerable number. White Bull caught a white horse, white all over. Then they set out for home as hard as they could ride, pushing the herd ahead of them.

They rode hard, afraid of pursuit, and White Bull's horse played out. He mounted the white horse he had captured, which promptly threw him. Again he got up, and again the horse threw him. But White Bull was no quitter. He mounted the third time and managed to stick on. Away they went at a gallop.

It was the custom that whoever first touched a captured horse, or caught it, became its owner. Most of the men in the party were nervous and fearful, for when one of their horses played out, they stopped; none of them would venture to mount a strange horse in the darkness. If a man were thrown and injured, they thought, he surely would be killed by the Crows, who were sure to follow. So this man called out, 'White Bull, rope a horse for me.'

White Bull roped the pinto he had captured in the camp, let his friend ride it, and they went on. Not long after, Wood-Pile's horse gave out; but he was a good man, he caught one for himself. The horse was so wild that they all had to help him mount. They choked the horse down and held his ears while Wood-Pile got on. Then they started running again.

Soon after, yet another man's horse played out. He called, asking White Bull to rope one for him, and this time White Bull roped a bald-face. All these horses he roped thus became his property. The other warriors were more interested in saving their lives than in acquiring horseflesh just then. Next, Hole-in-the-Shin's horse became exhausted. He called to White Bull, 'Friend, catch another horse.' By this time White Bull was tired of the repeated service and answered, 'Rope your own.'

Then it was found that Hole-in-the-Shin had no rope. He had to borrow White Bull's rope. White Bull always had the proper equipment for his raids and took care of his ropes, as his father had taught him. Every few minutes the same thing happened, all night long. But White Bull did not care: for by custom when a horse was roped with *his* rope, the animal became his property!

Dawn came, and they rode all that day as hard as they could and most of the following night, without food. Next morning early they saw some buffalo. It was raining. White Bull and another man killed all the meat they wanted and carried it back to their friends concealed in the timber. There they had a feast.

They pushed on until night and made camp. Early next morning, White Bull was up cooking breakfast when he saw a man on foot coming up the river. It was Elk Thunder, one of those who had turned back at the beginning with Touch-the-Cloud. When he came near, White Bull called to him. The man was startled, but recognized White Bull and came to the camp-fire. He seemed very nervous, and kept looking around as if afraid. White Bull offered him meat and said, 'Fear nothing, eat. You can talk when you have eaten.'

When the man had eaten, he told his story. He said his party were returning home with their horses and that the enemy had seen them. The Crows had charged, and there was a big fight in the timber. The Crows had captured nearly all the horses of the Sioux, had killed Long Bull, shot Brown Thunder in the side, another man in the breast, and shot the pony of Horse Shield in two places. The Sioux had scattered. Elk Thunder had remained hidden in the timber all night. The fight began at daybreak in the rain — at the same time White Bull was killing the buffalo. The Crows had been chasing White Bull's party and had run into the other one!

Elk Thunder led White Bull's party to the trail of his

comrades up in the hills, and they overtook some of them. They were scattered all over the country, plodding home afoot, in a very unhappy and frightened state. White Bull picked them up by twos and threes. Among them all there was only one horse left. Some of the men were not found at all, and came wandering into camp one by one days later. Their moccasins had got wet, the sinews had parted, and left them barefoot. They had had to wrap their feet in the strips of red flannel used for dress breech-cloths. The Indians refer to these cloths as 'tails,' because they are long and hang down behind. This warpath is therefore remembered as the Time-They-Used-Tails-for-Moccasins.

White Bull brought home seven good horses. One he gave to Wood-Pile, the pinto he gave to his uncle, Fast Horse; the others he kept. Having shown such courage when nearly everyone else was afraid, and having been so successful when nearly everyone else had failed, his name was high among his people.

Not long after, the Minniconjou, Oglala, and Brulé Sioux were in camp at the Big Bend of the Yellowstone River. Bull Eagle and Thunder Hoop led a party of fifty warriors up the Yellowstone toward Arrow Creek to attack the Crow Indian Agency. White Bull and his relatives, Wood-Pile and Feather-Earring, rode with them. It was late summer: the cherries were black. White Bull was twenty-three years old.

They reached the Crow Agency at night and rested until morning. At daybreak they saw ten head of horses grazing around the cabins and tipis of the Agency. The Sioux charged and swept away those horses. Fire-White-Man, Elk-Stands-on-Top, Charging Eagle, and Brown Wolf captured the horses.

The Crows came swarming out of their camp, yelling and shooting. Seven of them mounted, but they were reluctant to follow the Sioux. They rode back and forth, yelling and shooting.

White Bull, not having captured any horses, was anxious to do something, and tried to tempt the Crows to come out and fight. He and High Hawk and a man named Don't-Know-What-It-Is showed themselves on the hilltop. To tempt the Crows they danced and sang songs to show how brave they were, but nobody came to attack them.

The Sioux war-party started home. Then some of the young men decided to turn back and try to steal horses. White Bull, Yellow Owl, Crow Feather, Afraid-of-the-Enemy (Enemy-Fears-Him), Kicking Bear, and Feather-Earring made up this party. This Kicking Bear was the Oglala who later (1890) started the Ghost Dance in Sitting Bull's camp. They were all good men, but Feather-Earring was the best of the lot. Once before, at this Crow Agency, he had struck three Kootenay Indians who were fighting for the Crows.

White Bull was the one who proposed to go back and get horses. It was dark when they approached the Agency. But the Crows were on guard, and the horses were all in the corral. When the young men crept up, a dog barked and gave the alarm. The Crows shot at them and they had to give it up and go home.[1]

[1] 'Since the return of a number of citizens who accompanied the United States expedition under Colonel Baker down the Yellowstone River, reporting the late fight of that command with the Sioux, and the abandoning of the trip down the Powder River, the Crows think they have new cause for alarm; and no longer ago than yesterday (August 30, 1872) war-parties of Sioux were seen in this immediate vicinity; and the impudence with which they push these war excursions so very near us, and we entirely powerless to resist, or even to protect ourselves without the aid of the Crows, makes them look upon us with no little disdain.... (Agent for Crow Indians. *Annual Report, Commissioner of Indian Affairs*, 1872, p. 280.)

During these early years White Bull killed twenty-three bears. In those days, Sioux country contained black bears, bears in color like a wolf (black and yellow), and white bears (grizzlies). White Bull preferred to hunt bears horseback.

In those days bears of all kinds were very fierce. They generally ran in bunches of from two to five and very often would charge a man the moment they saw him.

One day when White Bull was out, he saw from a hilltop four bears, coming up the creek, and lay in wait for them with ready gun. When the foremost bear saw White Bull, it charged him at a run. His pony was frightened and ran away with him, all four bears hot on its trail. But at last the bears turned off and went into the breaks.

Then White Bull turned back and found them in a ravine. When he was close enough, he yelled aloud and the bears stood up to look. He shot the biggest one. The bear tumbled, but got up again, and White Bull rode forward. When the bears saw him, they turned and charged again. The frightened pony whirled and dashed away through the pines, almost rubbing White Bull from its back as it plunged under the branches of the trees.

But White Bull saw the wounded bear crawl under a fallen pine log, and there it stayed. The other bears drifted away. White Bull tied his horse at a distance and clambered up the sloping log. Below him he could see the wounded bear, with one forepaw over its eyes. The bear did not see White Bull. He shot the bear dead. It was good and fat, so he butchered it.

Another time White Bull was horseback and rode to the top of a hill. The bears must have caught his scent; five of them came up the hill after the man. He tied up his horse and took his stand behind two trees which grew close together. When the bears came near, he fired and shot the foremost. Then he ran for his horse. Soon after, he came back to see if he had killed the bear, but it was not dead. It was rolling and thrashing around in the brush.

When the four unwounded bears saw White Bull, they rushed him. White Bull called to his friend, 'Look out, they are after us.' The two men ran away on their scared mounts. For a time the bears chased them, then stopped in some cherry bushes.

White Bull sneaked up toward the bushes and again the bears ran him away. They retired up a ravine. The two men then rode back to find the wounded bear. White Bull's friend was mounted on a slow mule. When the crippled bear saw them, it took after them, and the man on the mule had a hard time getting away. The bear was right on his heels.

White Bull's gun was unloaded. He borrowed his friend's gun and killed the bear. The animal had been so fierce that the men were afraid to approach it for a while. Loading their guns, they cautiously advanced, and found it dead. White Bull took the hide and gave his friend half the meat.

The next day the two hunters went out again on the same two mounts. They stopped on the top of a bluff, and, looking down, White Bull saw a black bear eating cherries in the brush. He slipped back and told his friend what he had found. White Bull went to the top of the cliff very quietly. The bear did not see him. White Bull took good aim and shot the bear in the chest. The black bear then came to the foot of the bluff where there was a large per-pendicular rock. It stood up and leaned against this rock like an injured man, but could not get up, it was so steep. While White Bull was reloading, he heard another bear roaring in the brush. An instant later, a great white bear (grizzly) came charging out and ran up to the bluff where the wounded bear stood. The white bear seized the black bear around the body and hurled it aside. Then, standing on its hind legs and clawing, it tried to get up the bluff to White Bull.

By this time the hunter had reloaded. He fired. The white bear went down, and crawled to a cedar log which lay near-by. A second shot killed the grizzly. The body rolled into a water-hole below.

The two hunters found it very difficult to get down the bluff to where the bears lay, and knew that it would be impossible to carry the meat up again. However, they skinned both animals and took a little of the meat. The grizzly was large and fat and his pelt was in perfect condition.

When they got home, White Bull found his parents about to start for Fort Laramie to trade with the white men. Therefore the women made haste to dress the bearskins. His mother and sister tanned the hides. When they got back from Fort Laramie, they told White Bull that the trader gave more for the white bear's hide than for any other hide they had. The color of this bear was about the same as that of a gray fox.

CHAPTER XV

FIGHTING-IN-TRENCHES

The practice of the custom of trusting everything to a single effort undoubtedly has had its effect in their not harassing an enemy after their
first effort was made; but at any rate, it is a fact that Indians are woe-
fully lacking in enterprise in this way.

W. P. CLARK, *The Indian Sign Language.*

THE next spring (1873) the Sioux had a hard fight.

No matter how many times they drove the poachers
from their hunting-grounds, there was always another out-
fit coming in. As the range of the buffalo contracted and
the great herds shrank, all the surrounding nations were
forced to hunt in Sioux country, or go hungry. On every
side, Sitting Bull's Boys were hemmed in by desperate,
starving tribes, eager to get their teeth into fat cow,
watching their chance to raid the Sioux buffalo herds.
Policing that great range kept them busy.

Of all these poachers, none were more destructive than
the Mixed-Blood nations from Red River, in the British
Possessions. For more than half a century, these 'free people' had been making regular hunts, both spring and fall,
south of the present national boundary, killing thousands
of Sioux bison every season. In Canada, these tribes were
known as the Métis or Bois Brulés. They were the children
of the fur trade — offspring of French and English and
Orkney Islanders — and in their veins flowed the blood of
Cree and Chippewa, and indeed of half the Indian tribes
in Canada. They formed a distinct nation, of two grand
divisions, and their civilization was a curious compound
of Indian and European traits.

They were Catholic, spoke French, yet lived by the hunt.

Uneducated, devout, gay and pleasure-loving, with the dusky skin of the Indian and the flashing smile and mercurial disposition of the Frenchman, they preferred the hunt, the bivouac, the dance, the fiddle, the *chanson*, and a life of adventurous idleness to the drudgery of the farm. The culture of the Plains Indian had enchanted them, carried them away, as it had enchanted the Spanish *ciboleros* on the Staked Plains in Texas and the *vegas* of New Mexico. They had their own laws, their own customs. The Sioux knew them as the Slota, or Grease People.

Every season they came across the border, the men wearing blue Hudson's Bay capotes with big brass buttons, a gay sash, buckskin shirt, leggins and moccasins, with a case for the rifle with fringes a yard long from end to end. On they came, riding their fine horses in advance of the long lines of two-wheeled ox-carts, which squealed and creaked so loud they could be heard a mile in advance. For there was no iron used in these carts — only wood and rawhide; and buffalo grease was too good to eat to be used for quieting an axle! Such a caravan might comprise a thousand carts, eight hundred horses, five hundred oxen, four hundred armed hunters, eight hundred women and children, two hundred trained dogs, and any number of curs and mongrels. With them went the priest to say Mass at his improvised altar.

At night they formed a corral, pitched tents, stationed guards, fried their meat and potatoes, smoked their pipes, and after digestion had well begun, the fiddles would begin to squeak, and all joined in jigs, reels, and quadrilles, regardless of age or sex. They were a gentle, generous, polite people, and no friends of labor. But the havoc they made among the buffalo was terrible.

Exact statistics are available for several of the hunts of the Slota. One of their carts would carry about eight hundred pounds — the products of ten buffalo cows (pemmican, dried meat, tallow, marrow), the bulls and calves being left to rot on the prairie. These figures show that on the average the Red River Breeds made only seventy-five or a hundred pounds of meat from a single animal. In one such hunt, every man killed not less than seventy-seven cows, each cart devouring or carrying away forty cows. In twenty years it is estimated that these foreign poachers killed more than half a million Sioux buffalo. Moreover, these people were the children of Crees and Chippewas — eternal enemies of the Sioux. Sitting Bull rarely made truce with them, and then only for trade. And so, in that spring of '73, when the Slota appeared on the Rosebud, there was trouble.

One cold April evening, some young men came back to camp and reported that they had met some Slota horsemen. Shots had been exchanged, one of the Sioux had been hit, and his horse captured. Immediately Sitting Bull sent out ten scouts to locate the enemy: Old Bull, now living, was one of them. Then he turned out the guard. Nearly one hundred Sioux rode with him to strike the Slota. Fifteen miles they rode. At daybreak he found the Slota had corralled their carts above the mouth of Rosebud, the south bank.

The Slota were evidently expecting the Sioux. The carts were corralled around a big hole or depression, and this hole the Slota had been deepening, so that they could put their horses in safety. White Bull rode forward and around the corral, making reconnaissance, trying to charge the Slota. He could see the heads of about two hundred horses sticking out of the hole in the middle of the corral. That corral was very strong, with logs piled around it, and earthworks. They soon found that the Slota had good guns and plenty of powder. And when they fired a cannon at the Sioux, they all fell back to the hilltops. Nobody had been hit.

The rest of the battle was 'just shooting' from cover — a hard fight. No one could count *coup*. Because of this, the Sioux named this affair Fighting-in-Trenches. Most of the Sioux had only bows and lances. Guns were hard to get in those days: traders demanded a good horse or five robes for any kind of gun. Those Sioux who had guns kept shooting at the Slota from the hilltop. But whenever they raised their heads to shoot, the Slota would shoot too. Pretty soon the Sioux realized that the Slota were killing them. Sitting Bull called out, 'Lay low! Keep your heads down! Be careful!'

The Sioux could not tell how many enemies they killed, for they could not see them. But they did kill a great many horses: they could see the heads of the horses above the tops of the carts. Meanwhile, several Sioux were killed and wounded. Thunder Hawk and Kill Hawk were the first casualties.

White Bull was wearing his war-clothes; he was all dressed up. He wore beaded moccasins and leggins, a red shirt, and a bone breastplate. He had three eagle feathers in his hair and his face was painted yellow. On a thong over his right shoulder hung his medicine, and, like a kilt around his thighs, his black blanket was held in place by his cartridge belt. He lay on the hilltop peeping out between the clumps of sagebrush, firing at every enemy he saw. On his left lay His-Knife, wearing the sash and bonnet of his Society. His-Knife was a marksman. He had a fourteen-shot repeating rifle. Just then that gun jammed. His-Knife stood up to fix it. Before he could do so, he was hit in the forehead and instantly killed. He rolled down the hill some distance and lay under the fire of the enemy.

White Bull jumped up and ran to His-Knife, seized him by the right wrist and dragged him over the hill. He saved the body.

White Bull took him back, wrapped him in a blanket, and laid him across a horse's saddle. He laid him on his belly, and tied his neck to one side of the saddle and his legs to the other; that was the way they packed dead men from the battlefield. As soon as His-Knife had been dragged back, another Sioux named Two Crow took his place, and right away *he* was shot through the forehead, and instantly killed.

Jumping Bull and White Bull were lying side by side on the south bank, a little to the east of the river. Old Bull was there also, and Sitting Bull, armed with his Winchester and saber, was in the thick of things, giving orders.

After they had been fighting for some time, one of the Slota turned a pinto horse out of the corral. It ran away across the prairie, a great temptation to the Sioux. Cloud Man ran back to the ravine where the Sioux ponies were tied, jumped on his horse, and took after the pinto. All the Slota began to shoot at Cloud Man: the whole side of the corral was thick with the smoke of their rifles. They dropped Cloud Man's horse.

But Cloud Man was brave; he ran after the pinto afoot. Still the Slota kept shooting at him — all the Slota. They hit him — in the back — and also shot his penis off. He fell and lay on the prairie, only fifty yards from the Slota corral. Sitting Bull could see Cloud Man stirring: he knew the man was still alive. It was all open prairie, and the firing was terrible. But Sitting Bull ran down to Cloud Man, took

5. 1873. Rosebud River. Fighting-in-Trenches. White Bull saves the body of His-Knife from the Slota. (Chapter XV.)

6. June 17, 1876. The Battle of the Rosebud. He lames the Shoshoni Indian scout and shoots his horse. (Chapter XIX.)

ITEMS FROM WHITE BULL'S PICTORIAL AUTOBIOGRAPHY

hold of him, and dragged him back to the Sioux lines. That was a brave deed. It looked as if he could not live, but he was not hit. It was wonderful, with all these bullets kicking up the dust and whining around him. Cloud Man died a little later.

While Sitting Bull was dragging Cloud Man back, some of the Slota rushed out of their corral and tried to run off the Sioux horses. But White Bull saw them making for that ravine. He called out, 'Look out! They are coming! To your horses!' The Sioux ran to their mounts. That frightened the ponies. Some of them ran off and left their masters afoot. The men could not catch their horses.

Some of the Sioux started home, taking the wounded and dead. As they went away, the Slota advanced to the hilltop and began to shoot. As it happened, some old Sioux and a few boys were sitting under a pine tree on a hilltop, smoking. The Slota came upon them, shot them, killed them all: Grindstone, Two-Men, Holy Eagle, Stands-Him-Off, and others whose names are forgotten. The Slota had long-range guns.

When Sitting Bull had carried Cloud Man to safety, he came running back to the front. It was about noon. He saw how things were going. He yelled, 'It is impossible to kill them all. You see for yourselves how it is. They are lying in trenches, we cannot see them.'

Nevertheless, all that day they kept trying to recover the dead bodies of their friends. But it was impossible. The fire of the Slota was terrible. At last Sitting Bull gave it up. He called out an order: 'We have fought enough. We can do no more. Let's go home.'

This time the young men obeyed him. The Slota did not attempt to follow.

Next day, after the Slota had gone, the Sioux went back
and recovered the bodies of their dead. They found a great
many Slota horses lying dead in the big hole where the corral had been. The Sioux believe that the Slota were bound
for the Black Hills to look for gold. It was unusual for them
to go so far south into Sioux country. As a rule they hung
around Mouse River and the Missouri near the Ree village
(Fort Berthold).

One tragic incident has come down to us from those who
defended the corral that day. It appears that, after the
fight, the Slota women cooked supper for their men, before
the carts pulled out. One of these women was carrying her
baby on her back in an Indian cradle. She went happily
about her work of cooking supper, bending over her kettle,
unaware of the Sioux arrow which was sticking through the
heart of the child on her back.

The Sioux, however, knew nothing of this. They resumed
their interrupted hunting.

They struck their camp on the Rosebud, and moved
after buffalo. That day, White Bull was one of the soldiers
guarding the moving camp. As he was riding along, he
saw a commotion at the head of the column, and galloped
forward to see what was wrong. A bull elk had crossed the
trail and the people were chasing him. White Bull had a
fast horse under him and joined the chase. The bull was
swift and soon outdistanced all his other pursuers, but
White Bull's running horse came up with the bull. He
fired and dropped it on the run.

Ordinarily, Sioux hunters stalked the elk on foot or
made surrounds on foot. Once, that cold season, while
camping on the Yellowstone (sometimes known as Elk
River because of the great numbers of wapiti along its

course), a scout reported a herd of these animals in the Bend. Next morning the men all got on their horses. The river was frozen, but they threw earth on the ice to make a road for their horses, and crossed safely. In the Bend they found nearly a thousand elk in one herd. They surrounded them, running them like buffalo. More than two hundred were killed. White Bull dropped only one; his fingers were so stiff with cold, he could do no more.

Vast as the numbers of elk and buffalo were upon the Plains, the white-bellied deer or pronghorn antelope far outnumbered them. Because the buffalo was large and dark-colored and easily seen, travelers have made much of the bison in their accounts of wild life on the prairies. But the pronghorn, because of its speed and protective coloration, abounded everywhere. Indian hunters tell of traveling thirty miles at a stretch through a single herd of antelope, which extended as far as they could see on both sides. They were so swift that men had to stalk them on foot. But once in a while somebody succeeded in shooting one from the saddle.

One day, when the camp was on the march, White Bull was riding ahead on his fast sorrel. He flushed some antelope. They sped away, light as smoke, swift as cloud-shadows, over the flat. Quirting his pony, he took after them. After a hard race, he came within bowshot of the hindmost and let his arrow fly. The arrow went through the animal's slender body so far that only the feathered end remained in it. As the dying antelope plunged on, the projecting arrow wagged up and down, up and down, almost falling out.

Bighorn Sheep were also plenty in the Bad Lands, in the Black Hills, and around Bear Butte. White Bull hunted them often; their hides were used for making fine war-shirts. When stalking these wary animals, White Bull wore a gray cloth robe and a gray kerchief tied over his head to keep from being seen on the skyline. He would tie his horse at the bottom of the hill and go up afoot. When he had made his kill, he would drag it down to a place where he could go with his pack-horse.

Sometimes, when hunting in the hills, he would see the tracks of mountain lions. But he was a plainsman; he was afraid of the lions, and never hunted them. Besides, there is no hunt like the man-hunt.

CHAPTER XVI

WHITE BULL THINKS OF HIS MOTHER

Prisoners, unless women and children, were rarely taken, and hence scenes of fiendish delight in inflicting exquisite torture were unusual.

W. P. CLARK, *The Indian Sign Language.*

IN JULY, 1873, the Sioux were in camp on the Rosebud River, near the spot where Lame Deer was buried (Lame Deer, Montana). Minniconjou, Oglala, and Sans Arcs were all together. White Bull proposed to organize a war-party. Wood-Pile and White-Man-Shoots-Him joined, and from Sitting Bull's camp came High Bull and Gray Eagle (Sitting Bull's brother-in-law).

Following down the Rosebud River, the five of them crossed the rushing Yellowstone and kept on north to Little (Milk) River, intending to take horses from the Slota or Red River Half-Breeds. They found the Slota camp and planned to capture the horses that night, as they were a small party and could get a good start during the hours of darkness. But that evening the Slota put all their horses in the center of their camp. This was so unusual that White Bull thought the Slota must have seen his party. He decided to clear out.

They rode south for two days. They saw no game, killed no meat; they were hungry all the time. Next day, near the Spoonhorn (Mountain Sheep) Butte on the Big Dry, they saw two people, a man and a woman, afoot on the prairie. Here at last was a chance to do something.

All five young men whipped up their horses and started after these strangers. White Bull was in the lead, but three of his comrades were better mounted; one by one they passed him. The woman was nearer than the man. One after another, the three young men tapped her and raced on to strike the man: White Bull was the fourth to reach the woman. As he galloped up to her, he saw she held a knife in her hand. She held it raised, ready to stab him. He struck her wrist sharply with his bow, knocking the knife from her hand. That made her cry.

Just beyond her was the man, armed with a bow and arrows. None of the Sioux dared go near this man. They could not strike him; they feared his arrows. White Bull raised his gun to shoot the stranger. When the stranger saw this, he was frightened. He turned and ran. White Bull dashed after him, and with his bow struck the man's weapons from his hand. Both enemies were now disarmed. The other young Sioux counted *coup* on the unarmed man.

All the young men had counted *coup:* there was nothing left to do but kill these enemies. In those days Plains Indians had no compunction about killing mothers of enemies, for their wars went on forever. High Bull raised his gun to shoot the woman.

When that lone woman saw the rifle leveled at her, she called out in Sioux, 'Take pity.' She was crying.

When White Bull heard the voice of this pleading woman, he thought of his mother. His heart softened. He called to High Bull, 'Wait, don't shoot.'

White Bull rode up to the woman and questioned her. She explained that she belonged to the Hohe or Assiniboin nation. Long before, the Hohe had been a part of the Sioux nation; she spoke a dialect which White Bull could readily understand.

The woman explained that her daughter had married one of the Slota. She said that she and her husband, White

Boy, were walking up there on a visit. She showed the young men a bundle of presents she was carrying to her daughter. Said she: 'If you *must* kill someone, there is another man following us back there. He is a *bad* one. Kill him. Let us go!' All this time the woman was pleading, first with one of the young Sioux, then with another, until Gray Eagle said to her, 'White Bull here is our leader, he is Sitting Bull's nephew.'

Then she turned to White Bull and went up to him and stroked him with both hands, calling him 'Hunka.' White Bull took pity on her and said to his comrades, 'Leave them alone, let them go.'

All this time the Hohe man had stood there motionless, saying nothing, leaving everything to the woman. But now he relaxed and came forward. The woman had food, and they all sat down on the grass and picnicked together. The young men were hungry. When they had eaten, the woman took from her bundle the presents intended for her daughter and gave them to the young Sioux. They made friends. White Bull felt sorry for these foolish Hohe, walking across the prairie in broad daylight that way. He says the Hohe were always like that: they never seemed to know how to take care of themselves, they were always getting killed and captured.

After a while White Bull stood up and said, 'I advise you to stay in the timber until dark, and then go on your way.' To his comrades he said: 'Let's go. Maybe we can find that man this woman tells of.' The Sioux mounted their horses and started off on the lookout for that 'bad man.' They did not find him. Perhaps he saw them coming.

As the five of them rode on, they grew hungry, but could find nothing to eat. The country seemed to be empty of game, and, though they scattered over the prairie and scouted through the timber, they could kill nothing. There was nothing to eat anywhere. Day after day it was the same, until the five young men were so faint and dizzy they could scarcely sit their horses. Had they been white men they might have killed a horse for food, but the Sioux reverence for this animal made such a course impossible. They might have eaten a horse already dead, but would never have killed one for food.

Dizzily they rode along at a walk, and on the fifth day as they went over a hill their eyes were gladdened by the dark forms of grazing buffalo.

When the young men saw those buffalo, one of them called out: 'Whoever is a man, let him go get one of those bison.'

White Bull said: 'I am a man. I will get one.' Wood-Pile said the same. The two set out.

They were so faint with hunger that they dared not run their horses, so they left them and plodded on afoot. They crept along a wash or gully, trying to get a fair shot, and finally reached a position within easy bow-shot of a fat cow. The sight of all that fat meat made their mouths water. But they could not kill the cow because of a bull which persisted in standing between them and the cow. And in any case they dared not shoot the cow for fear the bull would charge them, helpless as they were to run away. Advancing up the gully, they found a hole in the bank about four feet deep, and narrow, like a shelf. There they waited for a chance to shoot. Finally another, fiercer bull came along. He drove the first bull away.

It was all Wood-Pile could do to draw his arrow to the head, but by both shooting together, they managed to

drop the cow. *There was meat!* Yet even then, they dared
not approach it, for the bull which had so fiercely driven
off the first bull kept hanging around the dead cow, after
the other animals had run away. The two young men must
have been very light-headed at that moment, for they
decided — of all things — to scare that bull away!

The moment they showed themselves, the bull charged.
In desperate haste, the two men feebly staggered back and
dived into the hole in the bank, dropping White Bull's gun
on the way. They cowered there in the hole while the bull
tore at the bank with his sharp horns and kicked and
pawed to get at them. After some time the bull left them
and returned to his former position near the cow. They
could just see his hump over the bank. Creeping out of the
hole, they picked up the gun and decided to keep it in
reserve and shoot an arrow at the bull's hump. So it was
done. Wood-Pile shot and hit it. The moment the bull
felt the arrow in his hump, he came charging back at them,
and they staggered toward the safety of the hole once
more.

White Bull was in the lead, and Wood-Pile was right at
his heels, yelling, 'Hurry, friend, he is close!' The bull was
right after them, but both of them managed to scramble
into the hole before he could gore them. They had the
gun with them this time, but were so exhausted by their
running that neither had the power to raise the heavy barrel
and shoot. Again the buffalo tore and pawed at the caving
bank. But at last it went away, this time to a distance of a
quarter of a mile.

Then White Bull and his comrade crawled out of the
hole and wearily plodded across the grass, dragging their
weapons, to the dead cow.

They managed to open the carcass and take out the liver, the kidneys, and the paunch. They ate a few bites only of these raw dainties and then started to rejoin their party, carrying the meat along.

When they came within calling distance of their friends, they dropped down, worn out, and White Bull called, 'Here's the meat; come and get it.'

But their comrades had lain down to rest, exhausted. One of them called faintly back: 'We are lying down, we cannot get up again. You will have to bring the meat here.' After a time, White Bull and his companion were able to rise again and carry the meat the rest of the way. When they arrived, everyone ate a few morsels, then all fell asleep. They remained there all night. Next morning they all went down to the dead cow and ate some of the lean meat. It tasted *good!* They had been riding without food for five days.

Loading their saddles with fresh meat, they set out, and reached home without further adventure.

CHAPTER XVII

CROW HORSE

Indians! Good shots, good riders, and the best fighters the sun ever shone on.

GENERAL FREDERICK W. BENTEEN.

THE Sioux were in camp on the Yellowstone, 1874, when a large body of Crows came and made camp on the bank opposite. The young men of both tribes fired at each other across the water.

White Bull, now twenty-five, jumped on his pony and rode behind a large cottonwood tree where he could fight from cover. On the side of the river held by the Sioux there were only two groves of trees. Whenever one of the Sioux tried to go from one patch of timber to the other, all the Crows would shoot at him. Five Sioux were wounded here, including Male Eagle and Brings-Plenty, an Oglala. This was not the Brings-Plenty who captured Fanny Kelly in 1864.

After this battle across the water, the Crows moved their camp down-river. A small party of the Sioux followed down on the opposite bank. They lay in wait on a bluff, and when the Crows came down to the river to water their ponies, the Sioux fired and made the Crows run. These young Sioux then returned to their own camp, intending to swim the river and capture horses. Jumping Bull was going with this party, and White Bull was anxious to go. But Uncle Sitting Bull did not approve. He thought it too dangerous. Sitting Bull advised White Bull not to go with the others. White Bull made no reply.

Now, in those days, young men who wished to go on the

warpath asked nobody's permission. Sitting Bull knew
this, and, seeing White Bull so eager to go, said to him:
'Nephew, I must go away for a while. I need a good horse.
Lend me your running horse.'

White Bull found it practically impossible to refuse any
such request made by his uncle, Sitting Bull. He therefore let him take the horse. Sitting Bull mounted and
rode over the hill. All that day, White Bull waited for his
return, but he did not get back, and next morning he was
still absent. Then White Bull realized that his uncle had
probably tricked him to keep him from going to war, but
he said nothing to anyone. He thought turn-about was
fair play. He knew that Sitting Bull's daughter, Has-
Many-Horses, owned a fast pony named 'Back.' He went
over to his cousin and asked her to lend him that horse.
She agreed.

Then White Bull, Gray Eagle, Little, Bear-Loves,
With-Horn, and five others, swam the river and rode down
on the Crow side to take horses. White Bull had no war-
charm along.

The ten young men cautiously approached the Crow
camp and among them ran off nine head of Crow ponies.
The Crows were numerous and on the alert. They took
after the Sioux and chased them hard. It was a long chase,
and the horse White Bull was riding played out. He had
to get down and stand off the Crows on foot. Seeing him
afoot with his gun, the Crows slowed down and rode back
and forth, shooting at him and trying to get to close quarters. But White Bull stood them off, threatening them
with his gun and shooting. It was almost sundown when
he dropped one of the Crows. When that happened, the
Crows held off. White Bull jumped on the horse he had

captured, and driving 'Back,' galloped to his brother One
Bull and Wood-Pile, who were anxiously waiting and
calling to him to come on.

They overtook their party. The Crows did not follow
farther. They all got home that night.

When Sitting Bull turned up next day, White Bull said:
'I have captured a fast Crow horse, seven years old. I
would like to give it to you, Uncle. Yonder it is.'

Then Sitting Bull laughed, and replied, 'Nephew, you
captured that horse. Keep it for yourself.'

All the horses captured by the Sioux that day were fast
animals. White Bull's prize he named 'Crow Horse.' This
war with the Crows is known to the Sioux as Fighting-Over-
the-Water-with-Crow-Indians.

Whenever a tribal hunt was on, the Sioux camp was
policed by the members of one of the warrior societies.
These policemen, or 'soldiers,' as they were called, had the
duty of preventing individual hunters from going after
game. If anyone disobeyed these orders and hunted, he
might frighten away the herds and leave the camp hungry.
When the soldiers caught such a man they dealt with him
severely, killing his horses, cutting up his tent, and slashing
his buffalo robes to pieces.

One day, when White Bull was twenty-six, the Fox
Soldiers, of which he was a member, were ordered by the
chiefs to police the camp, then on Big Cottonwood Creek.
They announced that no one was to shoot or hunt until
the tribe had made its surround.

Soon after, the Fox Soldiers learned that certain men
had fresh deer meat in their lodges. They went in a body
and searched the tipis of these men. In one of these tipis
they found meat. With their knives they slashed the tent

to pieces and broke the poles. Riding on around the camp circle, they came to another suspected tipi. There they found the owner, a Fox Soldier himself, riding back and forth with his rifle in his hands. He was a Hunkpapa named Sitting-White-Buffalo. They attempted to enter his tent, but the man would not permit it. He shoved away the soldier at the door with the shoulders of his horse. Then all the Fox Soldiers halted and hardly knew what to do. The man was a well-known warrior, a dangerous fighter. By custom, only one who had a better war record than he had could legally punish him. So this warrior dared the soldiers to meddle with him, saying, 'I am a Crow standing' (i.e., 'I am an enemy; look out'). White Bull was sitting his horse in the rear of the line of Fox Soldiers and took no part until the rebel pushed away the soldier at the door of his lodge.

Then White Bull started at him, calling out, 'You are a Fox Soldier and now you are going back on your Society.' Without waiting for a reply, White Bull raised his gun and shot the man's horse under him. Down it went. The man jumped to his feet and started to run. White Bull took one shot at him, but missed. The man ran off among the tipis. White Bull said to his companions, 'Tear down his lodge,' and compelled them to do so.

Then the soldiers mounted their horses and dashed away toward their Society lodge within the camp circle. White Bull yelled after them, 'You were all scared,' and fired his rifle into the air over their heads in derision. Then all the Fox Soldiers gathered in their lodge and had a good laugh over this affair.

There was always danger to be enjoyed. Sometimes it came from men, sometimes from animals.

One day, that year, White Bull was out herding horses with two other men. He had only his knife in his belt and wore his blanket folded and belted around him like a kilt, extending from the waist to a little below the knees. That was an easy way to carry a blanket.

Not far off the hunters were running buffalo, and a cow, separated from the herd, came running in White Bull's direction.

White Bull thought he would like to kill this cow, which was a fine-looking four-year-old, fat and in good condition. One of the men with White Bull had a bow and two arrows, one of them without a point. White Bull borrowed the good arrow and the bow, and, riding up to the cow, took aim and let his arrow fly. The point struck the buffalo on a rib and did it no harm.

The cow, however, feeling the prick of the sharp point, jumped into a narrow ravine which had been washed out in the hillside. There it remained, with the arrow still sticking up, for the point was caught in the buffalo's wool.

When White Bull saw the cow standing motionless under the cutbank, he dismounted and crept up to the edge of the bank, which was just level with the buffalo's hump. There he began reaching out his bow and fishing for that arrow. If he could get it, he hoped to have better luck with his second shot. Though on foot and unarmed, White Bull felt perfectly safe, as the bank seemed too steep for the cow to climb.

But the moment the cow felt his touch upon the arrow, she whirled and charged up that bank as if it had been level ground. Before White Bull could realize what had happened, the cow was right behind him. He tried to run, but he was hampered by the blanket belted about his legs. The cow was swift. In another moment he knew he would be tossed on her sharp black horns. White Bull stopped and whirled around, and, as the cow came up, grasped it by the horns, one in each hand. The cow did not give way, but kept butting and pushing, trying to hook him. Fortunately for him, White Bull had powerful shoulders and was very strong. He tried to twist the cow's head to one side so that she could not hook him. He began to yell for help: 'Come on, friends! Hurry! Get out your knives and hamstring this cow.'

But his friends were afraid, though on horseback. They dared not approach the cow. White Bull stood there wondering what to do, for something must be done before he became exhausted. He could not kill the cow, he could not hold her long, and he dared not let go. He thought his only hope was to get rid of the hampering blanket and take to his heels. Accordingly, he slowly forced the cow's head to one side, pressing against it with his chest to hold it there until he could get one hand free and jerk open the buckle of his belt. This took only an instant. The belt was loosened, the blanket fell to the ground.

Then White Bull seized the horns with both hands again, and, twisting the head of the cow toward his two companions, called to them once more: 'Ride up close, friends, come near, so that this cow can see you. Then she will chase you and I can get away. Come on, now. Help me.'

But the men were afraid. They were unwilling to approach the cow. However, the men did yell at the cow, hoping to attract her attention. White Bull, twisting her head to face them, suddenly let go of the horns and raced away in the other direction, out of her sight. But the cow whirled and took after him. She paid no attention to his yelling companions. Within a few yards was a cutbank, steep, and as high as a man's shoulder. White Bull ran as hard as he could to this cutbank, dived up on it just as the cow came charging on his heels. One of her horns touched his moccasin as he went up the bank. She tore furiously at the caving earth with her sharp horns.

White Bull did not spare the feelings of his cowardly companions who had left him to save himself in that dreadful difficulty. Said he: 'I might have been killed!'

White Bull was angry. He was determined that the cow should pay for her attack on him with her life. He was going to kill her — and kill her on foot. He made his comrade give him the second arrow, which had no point. The other man happened to have an arrow-point in his pouch. White Bull fixed this iron point in the shaft of the arrow, and, taking some of the sinews which held the feathers on, lashed the point securely enough for use. White Bull, still afoot, selected a sloping tree-trunk close by as the point from which he would shoot the cow. Then he went after the buffalo. The moment she saw him, she charged. He raced to the tree and scrambled up its trunk. The charging buffalo stopped underneath. White Bull took careful aim at her and sank his arrow to the feathers in her vitals. Thus he killed her. He had his revenge.

White Bull had faced all the danger and done all the work of this hunt, but his companions insisted on helping him butcher, and according to custom the meat had to be divided into three shares. Worse, the man who had supplied the bow and arrows demanded the hide. Considering his cowardly behavior while his friend was wrestling with the cow, White Bull thought that a good deal more than he deserved. But he was generous; he let him take it.

One day while his people were camped on Powder River, White Bull left his wife and family to visit the Agency at Fort Bennett. There he met an attractive girl named Helper Woman. He stayed with her for a while as her husband. When he had to leave the Agency, he asked his new wife to go west with him.

She said, 'My mother is very sick, she asks me to stay with her.'

White Bull said, 'I will come back for you.'

But somehow he never got around to that.

CHAPTER XVIII

COLONEL REYNOLDS ATTACKS

Neither the wild tribes, nor the Government Indian Scouts ever adopted
any of the white soldiers' tactics. They thought their own much better.
CAPTAIN LUTHER H. NORTH, of the Pawnee Scouts.

EARLY in 1876 the War Department was ordered to attack
the Western Sioux and force them to leave their hunting-
grounds (guaranteed them by the treaty) and to come in to
settle at the Agencies.

On March 1, 1876, General George 'Three Stars' Crook
set out from Fort Fetterman, Wyoming, heading for Powder
River. With him went ten troops of cavalry, two companies
of infantry, four hundred pack-mules, eighty-six wagons,
and four ambulances. It was one of the strongest single
outfits ever seen in Sioux country.

Early on the foggy, bitterly cold morning of March 17,
1876, Scout Frank Grouard, faithless to Sitting Bull (who
had saved his life and adopted him in 1869), led six troops
of Crook's cavalry, under Colonel J. J. Reynolds, to the
village of Two Moon's Cheyennes. A few Oglala were
camped with the Cheyennes in the timber on Powder River,
some miles above the mouth of the Little Powder, in
Montana.

The warriors, tumbling half-naked from their beds into
the frosty air, and outnumbered by fifty per cent, successfully fought off the troops while their families scurried
to the snowy hills. Colonel Reynolds, who had foolishly
sized up Grouard as untrustworthy, appears to have feared
a trap or ambush of some kind and did not press his advantage. He bungled the attack. Yet, with superior

numbers, superior arms, and the great advantage of complete surprise, he could hardly have failed to capture a small camp of one hundred and five tipis. He took it, with a loss of four killed, six wounded. The Indian loss was one man killed and one old woman wounded — and afterward captured. But (to use Grouard's words) 'as nobody in the command wanted her, she was left there.'

Besides the old woman, some seven hundred ponies were captured. So far everything had gone off according to schedule — except that Reynolds had let the Indians get away! Yet he feared a trap still. He did some very foolish things.

Because of the severe weather his men had not been permitted to sleep the night before, for fear they might freeze. They had less than one day's rations. Yet Reynolds immediately burned the tents he had taken, all the warm buffalo robes, and tons of prepared meat, and then marched his sleepy, tired, and hungry men back upon the frozen prairies to spend another sleepless night. The frost was terrible: the mercury froze solid in the thermometers. Sixty-five men were frost-bitten on the march home.

Yet those men were admirably outfitted: heavy underwear, a second suit of perforated buckskin, a blouse and cardigan jacket, leggins and moccasins lined with wool, heavy lined overcoats with fur collars and wristlets, sealskin caps and gloves. Nevertheless the Sioux and Cheyennes, half-naked and outnumbered as they were, not one in three with a gun, and all afoot, soon had these soldiers scuttling for the south. Reynolds pulled out and left his dead in their camp, and — it is believed — one wounded man, whom — some writers say — the Indians cut to pieces.

Reynolds wanted to kill the seven hundred ponies he had taken, but could not 'because of lack of ammunition.' An odd statement, that, when one considers that he reported the camp to be 'a perfect magazine of ammunition, war material.' Apparently this 'magazine' did not contain enough cartridges to shoot seven hundred ponies, or even one smoothbore to be used with the powder and lead found so 'abundantly.' At any rate, Reynolds tried to take the ponies off with him. Two Moon soon had them back, and with them the beef herd brought along by General Crook. The soldiers ate horseflesh, when they ate anything, from then on.

It was claimed that the tents were full of Agency goods, and that this proved that 'these Indians were in copartnership with those at the Red Cloud and Spotted Tail Agencies,' and 'that the proceeds of raids on the settlements had been taken into those Agencies and supplies brought out in return.' Not even the most blindly prejudiced officer would have had the nerve to suggest that the tents contained goods captured in raids on the settlements. For there were no raids on settlements, unless one can call the outlaw mining camps in the Black Hills 'settlements.' As a matter of fact, the Indians in that camp had a perfect right to rations and Agency supplies until February 1, 1876, and in their camp were many friendly, peaceable Indians who intended to go back to the Agencies in the spring. But when people begin to shoot at your wife and children and burn down your house and take your property, no man who is a man but will fight back.

Even after Reynolds and Crook joined forces, the Indians harassed them. But at last the hungry, frost-bitten soldiers got back to barracks at Fort Fetterman, only 'to be redistributed to their various winter stations to protect them from the extreme cold.'

The winter campaign was abandoned, and Colonel Reynolds had charges filed against him, along with several other officers who faced courts-martial. All the reports are adverse to his work: General Sherman put the complaint in a nutshell — 'The result was only the destruction of the tents or tipis of the Indians, with their contents....' It was apparent that something more ambitious and better executed would be required to deal with the hunting bands.

This affair has been commonly described in the histories as a wonderful victory for the Indians, and lavish praises have been showered upon the genius of Crazy Horse (who was not present) for his alleged generalship in this affair. No generalship was required. Reynolds was a bungler, and the two forces never really came to grips. When the Indians ran off the captured ponies, only half a dozen civilian scouts offered any resistance whatever, and they were so outnumbered that they had no chance. The soldiers were exhausted, and Reynolds had no initiative. Neither Sioux old-timers nor Cheyennes who were present regard this skirmish as of any importance. George Bird Grinnell barely mentions it in his history of Cheyenne warfare.

However, White Bull tells an interesting story of this fight which may account for the persistent rumor that the Indians cut to pieces the wounded soldier left behind. White Bull was not in the camp at the time, but his friend Little Shield told him about it. After the soldiers had pulled out, some of the Indians came back to the burned camp to look for something to eat. Most of them had had no breakfast. When Little Shield arrived, he found three Cheyennes roasting fresh meat over a hot fire.

Little Shield stood by the fire for a while, warming himself. Close by on a big platter were several pieces of raw meat awaiting their turn at the blaze. Little Shield was hungry; he thought the meat looked very appetizing that cold morning. He could not speak Cheyenne, so after a while he just went over and helped himself to a piece of meat and began to cook it for his breakfast. The Cheyennes watched him take it, but made no objection. They began to talk among themselves.

When Little Shield's meat was done to a turn, he began to eat it. He had swallowed half a dozen juicy morsels when one of the Cheyennes came over and talked to him in the sign language. Said he, 'We found a dead fat soldier lying over yonder. We cut him up. That meat you are eating is part of him. That is soldier meat.'

The Cheyenne spoke seriously. Little Shield did not know the Cheyennes very well; he did not know but what their customs permitted cannibalism. Yet, being a Sioux, he was horrified; the Sioux never ate human flesh.

But it was too late. Little Shield could not get the meat up again.

Probably the Cheyennes were playing a joke on Little Shield because he had helped himself to their meat. But some of the Sioux believe to this day that the Cheyennes ate the dead soldier. Little Shield says it tasted pretty good, at that.

After they had chased the soldiers away, the warriors brought back the ponies and the cattle they had taken, salvaged what they could of their half-burned camp, and set out to look for succor. That terrific weather was hard on the half-clothed women and children: some were frost-bitten, several froze to death. Two Moon led his Cheyennes over to the mouth of Otter Creek on Tongue River, looking for friends. Finding none, he went back toward Pumpkin Creek, and came upon an Oglala camp in the breaks there. But Crazy Horse had nothing to spare: he could not help Two Moon. The Cheyennes pushed on, along with the Oglala, cold and hungry. And at last, in the Blue Mountains on Beaver Creek, some sixty miles down the Powder, they found the camp of Sitting Bull.

These Cheyennes and Oglala belonged to Red Cloud Agency. Many of the people in their camp had come out to hunt, because there was not enough to eat at the Agency. In January, 1876, the Agent at Red Cloud Agency had reported that his supply of beef and flour would be exhausted before March 1, and Congress hastily passed an emergency appropriation of $150,000 in April. The supplies failed to reach the Agency until mid-summer. These Indians had to hunt or starve. That was where the Agency goods found in their tents came from: many of them were Agency Indians. But now the Grandfather, after driving them from the Agency by starving them, was trying to kill them because they were not at the Agency.

Said Crazy Horse: 'This is it. The Grandfather's young men have been trained to the warpath. For the last few years (I have heard) he has been trying to get them to stop fighting and give up their guns and horses and follow the plow. But these white soldiers would rather shoot than work. The Grandfather cannot control his young men, and you see the result.' Crazy Horse spoke seldom: when he did speak, he hit the nail on the head. He and Two Moon plodded into the camp of Sitting Bull.

White Bull saw these cold and hungry refugees come dragging into his uncle's camp. They had lost their saddles, their winter's meat, all their ammunition. But they were not entirely destitute: they had their horses, and some of them had tents. It would appear that the soldiers failed to burn all the lodges, or else these folks had extra supplies stored at some other place. But most of them needed help, and needed it badly.

Sitting Bull heard their story, took them in, fed them, gave them horses and saddles, powder and ball, and told his own people to double up and let the visitors have some of their tents. He made them welcome. Right away he sent runners to summon all the chiefs of the hunting bands to a big council on Tongue River, and soon after moved his camp to that stream. This was the beginning of the war in which General Custer lost his life.

White Bull had no part in Two Moon's victory, but in the following month he went to war again. The chiefs were sending out young men to rustle horses for the war. From the camp of the Minniconjou and Sans Arc Sioux, then on the stream Where-the-Woman-Broke-Her-Leg, Long Horn led a party of thirty men toward Bear Butte. On the way, they joined forces with another war-party of forty Hunk-papa. They needed meat, and made camp south of Bear Butte to hunt. White Bull and a comrade went after meat: White Bull killed three deer, his comrade two. The main party remained in camp, but twenty men set out to steal horses from the whites.

Wood-Pile and White Bull found this party too cautious and slow for their taste; they went on ahead. That evening they ate a haunch of venison, and rode all night into the Black Hills — until they saw a log cabin with seven horses near-by. They charged, and swept away with all seven head. Five white men came out of the cabin and fired at them. Nobody was hit.

White Bull got four of the seven horses. But as the pony he was riding belonged to Wood-Pile, he presented one of the captured horses to his friend. On the way home the two of them passed the place where Rapid City stands now. There White Bull picked up two more horses. When he got home he gave one to Sitting Bull, another to his father. After that, he went hunting for eagles. He wanted feathers.

The Sioux usually hunted these birds in the traditional, ceremonial manner, lying in a pit near the top of a hill, concealed from sight by a covering of brush. On this covering they would place raw meat as bait, and when the eagles alighted to eat, would seize them by the feet, pull them down into the pit, and strangle them.

This method did not appeal to young White Bull, for on one occasion a Sioux eagle-hunter, lying in the pit, had been surprised and rubbed out by a Crow war-party. Moreover, White Bull liked action, and he was by no means the kind of man to be unduly careful about the ancient taboos of eagle-hunting. He shot his eagles.

One day when hunting, he came upon the carcass of a deer. Many black crows were circling around it, and among them a lone eagle. White Bull crept up and shot the great bird as it perched on the carcass. Another day he saw an eagle perched on the point of a butte. He crawled within gunshot, but just as he was taking aim, the eagle launched itself into the air, circling away. White Bull kept his finger on the trigger of his rifle, and, as the eagle soared over, fired, and dropped him from the sky. That he considers one of his best shots.

CHAPTER XIX

THE 'THREE STARS' BATTLE ON THE ROSEBUD

They [the Plains Indians employed as Government Scouts] are un-
equaled as riders, know the country thoroughly, are hardly ever sick,
never desert, and are careful of their horses. Moreover, I have never seen
one of them under the influence of liquor, though they have had every
opportunity of getting it.

THE SECRETARY OF WAR

AFTER the attack on Two Moon's village on March 17,
Sitting Bull summoned the Sioux and Cheyennes 'to have
one big fight with the soldiers.'

During May and June, Sitting Bull's great camp was
hunting on the Rosebud and the Little Big Horn, and all
this time Sitting Bull kept scouts out. But for a long time
they had nothing to report. By the middle of June, the
game and the grazing on the Rosebud had become exhausted and the camps were moving back to the Little
Big Horn looking for buffalo. On the evening of June 16,
the tipis were pitched on Reno (Ash) Creek, between the
Rosebud and the Little Big Horn. That night, Cheyenne
scouts came in and reported the valley of the Rosebud
black with soldiers. General George 'Three Stars' Crook
was coming from Fort Fetterman, Wyoming, with more
than a thousand white soldiers and two hundred and sixty
Indian Scouts — Crows, Shoshoni, Rees — a force of more
than thirteen hundred men.

Makes-Room was attending a meeting in the Cheyenne
camp when the scouts came in. He hurried back to his own
camp circle and spread the news. All the Sioux began to
prepare for battle. They expected a hard fight.

White Bull put on a pair of dark blue woolen leggins decorated with broad stripes of blue-and-white beads, and beaded moccasins to match. Before and behind he hung a long red flannel breech-cloth reaching to his ankles, tucked under his belt over his regular loin-cloth. He put on a shirt, and over his right shoulder he hung the thong which supported the small rawhide hoop, to which was attached four small leather pouches of medicine (earth of different kinds), a buffalo tail, and an eagle feather. This was his war-charm. It hung under his left arm. Around his waist, like a kilt, he placed his folded black blanket and belted it there with his cartridge-belt containing a hundred cartridges. He borrowed a fine war-bonnet from his brother-in-law, Bad Lake.

This bonnet had a long tail of eagle feathers reaching to the ground. The feathers began at the crown of the head and went straight down the back. There were no feathers around the head on this bonnet. All the way down the tail this bonnet was colored red and white alternately — seven white feathers, then four red, and so on. These red feathers commemorated wounds received in battle. A man who wore such red feathers dared not tell a lie or he might be wounded.

This bonnet had no protective power: White Bull wore it for its beauty. If he were to be killed, he wished to die in these fine war-clothes. Otherwise those who saw him lying on the battlefield might say: 'This was a poor man. He must not have been a good warrior. See how shabby he lies there.' Besides, such fine war-clothes made a man more courageous.

White Bull took his seventeen-shot repeating rifle, which he had purchased from an Agency Indian at Fort

Bennett. Then he went out and saddled a fast horse. He tied an eagle feather in its forelock and tail and fastened an imitation scalp made of woman's hair to his bridle-bit. Only horses which had been used to ride down an enemy could wear such a decoration. Then White Bull rode over to Sitting Bull's tent where the warriors were gathered.

Almost a thousand warriors had assembled — Cheyenne, Oglala, Minniconjou, Sans Arc, Brulé, Hunkpapa. It was late at night when they set out. They rode until nearly daybreak, then stopped, unsaddled, and let their horses rest. At daybreak they saddled up and rode on until they came near a big hill. There they halted again and sent scouts forward to the top of this hill to look for the troops. When these scouts had traveled halfway to the hilltop, Indian Government scouts appeared there, and firing was heard.

The whole war-party whipped up their horses and charged for the hill. There they found a Sioux wounded, and a horse killed. They rode over the hill and saw five Government scouts dashing downhill to the troops. They charged these five men, shooting all the time, and wounded one of them. Still they pressed on, following the five scouts, close to the soldiers.

The soldiers advanced, firing at the Indians. A Cheyenne had his horse shot under him. The Sioux who rode with him were all surrounded and killed. They got caught between two bodies of enemies. It was a hard fight.

White Bull was not much given to singing war-songs, but as he advanced into that fight he was inspired to sing a song composed on the spot:

> Friends, try your best.
> I do not wish my father to be made ashamed.
> Because he is a chief.

There was a brave Cheyenne wearing a war-bonnet and red leggins who led the attack. White Bull kept trying to get in front of this brave man, but could not; the Cheyenne had the better horse. But as the Government scouts and the soldiers came charging back, White Bull stood his ground and the Cheyenne retreated past him. White Bull was out in front at last. The enemies kept coming, and in the lead dashed a brave Shoshoni. He was riding a fast bald-faced sorrel with white stockings. His horse's tail was tied up in red flannel and a red flannel strip was tied about its neck. This Shoshoni had a cartridge-belt and a repeating rifle. He came straight for White Bull.

On came the Shoshoni, and White Bull sped to meet him. When he came near, the Shoshoni fired twice — but missed. White Bull pumped two bullets into the right fore-shoulder of the sorrel horse and dropped it. He ran the Shoshoni down and lamed him in the right leg, then wheeled away to join his comrades in retreat.

Afterward White Bull learned from the Crows that this Shoshoni was one of the bravest of their warriors. This Shoshoni was still living a few years ago: he may be alive today. This was considered one of the bravest of White Bull's many deeds, and, when President Coolidge visited the Black Hills and White Bull was chosen to make the address of welcome for the Indians, the Chief was pointed out as The-Man-Who-Lamed-the-Shoshoni.

It may be interesting to know White Bull's opinion of the various enemies he fought with: Says he: 'The Rees are good fighters. The Flatheads fight well on foot with guns, but if you once get them to running, they sure do run. The Crows and the white soldiers are about the same at long-range shooting, but in hand-to-hand combat the

Crows are more dangerous. But of all the enemies I have fought, the Shoshoni are the bravest and best warriors.'

It was back and forth that day. All day long the Indians of both sides charged back and forth horseback and not a few were killed on both sides. The troops lost nine men killed and twenty-one wounded. Of White Bull's immediate friends, Little Crow, Black Bird, Sitting Bear, and Little Wolf perished.

There were many thrilling rescues. White Bull's brother, One Bull, saved Yells-at-Daybreak (His-Voice-is-Loudest-at-Daybreak, sometimes translated Rooster). White Bull himself saved Hawk Soldier after he was shot from his horse. He carried him back to his uncle. In another part of the fight a horse was shot and the Indian rider was pinned down. His leg was caught under the dead horse. White Bull ran forward and protected him until he could get his foot free and escape.

There was a Cheyenne in this fight named Sunrise. He was painted yellow all over and wore a stuffed water-dog tied in his hair for a war-charm. He was shot through the belly from behind and lay helpless. White Bull dismounted and ran forward under fire. He seized the Cheyenne by the wrists and dragged him back to safety. The Cheyennes still honor White Bull for saving this man. Sunrise died after they got him back to camp. Because of his war-charm some of the Sioux remember him as Water-Dog.

This was one of the hardest fights White Bull ever saw. It lasted all day, but when it was over 'Three Stars' took his troops and hit the trail back to his base. The Sioux and Cheyennes rode home, leaving scouts behind to watch 'Three Stars' movements.

Two days later the Sioux returned to the battlefield.

They found the body of a Government scout there. Some
say the Indians dug up the bodies of the white soldiers
buried there, but White Bull knows nothing of this.

There is one strange thing about the Three Stars battle.
A certain Cheyenne rode into the fight, singing:

> I do not wish to be an old man.
> This day is mine to die.

That Cheyenne was killed in the fight. White Bull is puzzled to know how the Cheyenne knew he was to die that
day. He says he never saw an Indian throw his life away
deliberately in battle or commit suicide in a fight.[1]

[1] In discussing such matters with the Chief, I often stimulated his interest
by matching his stories from my own experience, and in this connection told
the Chief of an instance in the Great War in which an officer had said that he
was sure his friend, another officer, would be killed in battle, as afterward
happened. It may interest psychologists to read the Chief's reply: 'Perhaps
God put that thought into his mind, or perhaps' (with a smile) 'that officer
wanted his friend's woman!' It happened that the doomed officer was not
married. When informed of this, the Chief's comment was: 'Well, perhaps he
was jealous of him for some other reason.'

CHAPTER XX

LONG HAIR CUSTER IS KILLED

When the Sioux Indian was armed with a bow and arrow he was more formidable, fighting as he does most of the time on horseback, than when he got the old-fashioned muzzle-loading rifle. But when he came into possession of the breech-loader and metallic cartridge, which allows him to load and fire from his horse with perfect ease, he became at once ten thousand times more formidable.

GENERAL GEORGE CROOK, *Report of the Secretary of War*, 1876–77.

THE morning of June 25, 1876, that fatal day on which General George Armstrong Custer and five troops of the Seventh United States Cavalry rode to their doom, dawned brightly, giving no hint of the bloody scenes that were to make it memorable. During the ten years since the Fetterman fight at Fort Phil Kearny, White Bull had been constantly on the warpath, fighting the whites and neighboring tribes, killing enemies, counting *coups*, stealing horses by the score. That morning he was twenty-six years old and already a famous warrior. It was not yet sunup when he stepped out of his wife's tipi in the Sans Arc Sioux camp circle, loosened the picket-ropes of the family horses and drove his ponies to the river for water.

The Sioux and Cheyennes had pitched their camps, three miles of tipis, circle on circle, in the wide flats along the east bank of the Little Big Horn River. There they rested after the fight with General George Crook on the Rosebud only a week before. Their scouts reported that Crook was retreating, and, though they knew that other troops were in their country, they did not expect them that day. Besides, they were not afraid, there were too many Indians in the camp.

The Little Big Horn flowed to the north, its shallow, winding course marked by clumps of tall cottonwood timber above which White Bull could see the abrupt bluffs, scarred by ravines, rising steeply from the eastern bank. When the horses would drink no more, he drove them north of the camp to grass, and when they had settled down to graze, left them and went home for breakfast. Later he returned, trying to keep them in a bunch about a hundred yards west of the river. As usual, he carried his seventeen-shot Winchester and wore two filled cartridge-belts.

It was a hot, lazy day, almost windless, and the trails were dusty. White Bull remained herding his horses without a thought of any danger, though all that while General Custer's command was rapidly approaching. Custer's scouts had warned him that he would find more Sioux on the Little Big Horn than he could handle, but he refused to be frightened, divided his command into three bodies, and pushed on. Captain Frederick W. Benteen had orders to strike the village from the west, Major M. A. Reno was to attack on the south, while Custer rode over the bluffs to jump the Sioux from the east bank of the stream. The General expected the Indians to run and was anxious to prevent their escape.

It was not yet time for the midday watering when White Bull, watching his horses north of the camp, heard a man yelling the alarm. Immediately he jumped on his best running horse, a fast bay, and ran his ponies back to camp. Before he reached it, everyone in camp had seen the tower of dust coming from the south, and below it the blue shirts of soldiers, the flash of rifle-barrels in the bright sunshine. The column of soldiers spread into a line, smoke burst from it, and White Bull heard the noise of the carbines.

All through that great camp was the confusion of complete surprise. Old men were shouting commands and advice, young men running to catch up their horses, women and children streaming away to the north afoot and on horseback, trying to escape the soldiers. They abandoned their tents, snatched up their babies and called their children. White Bull saw young girls clutching shawls over their frightened heads, fat matrons puffing and perspiring, old women, shriveled as mummies, hobbling along with their sticks, trying to save themselves.

White Bull saw his own family started to safety, then sped up-river hard as he could ride to the camp of his uncle, Sitting Bull, which the soldiers were already nearing. There, he knew, his father's tipi stood on the north side of the circle. By the time he arrived, the woman and children had fled, and about a thousand warriors were gathering to resist the troops, whose bullets were already crashing through the tipis too high to hurt anyone. When White Bull reached the south end of the great camp, he saw a lively fight going on in the open, where the Ree and Crow Government Indian scouts were trying to run off the Sioux ponies. Everything was smothered in a great cloud of dust and smoke as the Indians on both sides dashed back and forth, fighting for their horses. Already some of the Cheyennes and Sioux had been shot down by the Rees, and the white soldiers, firing from the saddle, kept advancing, pushing the Sioux back. But before long the Sioux had gathered in such numbers that the Rees retreated, leaving most of the ponies to their enemies. Immediately after, the soldiers dismounted and formed a line in the open facing the north. White Bull saw them set up a flag (guidon).

White Bull yelled aloud, 'Whoever is a brave man will go get that flag.' But everyone was busy. Nobody volunteered, and before he himself could do anything the soldiers moved the flag, falling back into the timber along the river. By this time great numbers of Indians had gathered. Some of them made charges toward the troops while others stood and fired. After some hot fighting on foot in the timber, Major Reno's troopers climbed into their saddles and fled south up the river, looking for a place to cross. The moment they turned tail, the swarming Sioux were on their heels, striking them with war-clubs and the butts of their guns, shooting arrows into them, riding them down. The soldiers did not wait to resist. It was like a buffalo hunt. Away they went, plunging through the river and up the steep, sprawling ridges of the high bluff to the top. Most of them got over, ran up the bluff and dug in. But three soldiers kept up the west bank on the level. White Bull took after these. There was one soldier on a gray horse. White Bull singled him out for his victim and fired, but failed to hit him. Reno had left behind him three officers and twenty-nine men killed.

Just then the foremost Indians halted and White Bull heard some one behind him yelling that troops were coming from the east toward the north end of the camp three miles down-river. White Bull was near the water and turned downstream with the rest to meet this new danger. Some of the Indians rode through all the camps and crossed the stream above them to block Custer's advance. White Bull and many others crossed almost at once, streaming up the ravine to strike Custer on the flank. As he advanced, he saw Custer's five troops trotting along the bluffs parallel to the river. White Bull saw there would be a big fight. He stopped, unsaddled his horse, and stripped off his leggins. He thought he could fight better so.

The Indians rode in many small parties, streaming northeast up the ravine toward the troops passing along the ridge. With White Bull rode Iron Lightning, Owns-Horn, Shoots-Bear-as-He-Runs, and two Cheyennes. They rode up the ravine with a great horde of warriors. Most of Custer's five troops of cavalry had passed the head of the ravine by the time White Bull was near enough to shoot at the soldiers. From where he was, the soldiers seemed to form four groups of mounted men, heading northwest along the ridge. He was shooting at the group in the rear (Lieutenant James Calhoun's command).

All the Indians were shooting, and White Bull saw two soldiers fall from their horses. The soldiers fired back from the saddle. Their fire was so effective that some of the Indians, including White Bull, fell back to the south. Soon after, the white men halted. Some of them got off their horses to fight. By this time the Indians were all around the soldiers. Many were between the camp and the troopers, ready to defend the ford. Others took their stand wherever they could obtain cover, each small party acting independently.

When White Bull was driven out of the ravine by the fire of Lieutenant Calhoun's men, he rode south and worked his way over to the east of that officer's command, and there joined a party of warriors with Crazy Horse. By this time a large number of Indians were gathering around Calhoun's troops. They were particularly numerous south of him. The troopers at the tail of the column were falling back along the ridge, leaving their dead and wounded behind them, trying to join forces with Keogh's troop. Keogh's men were fighting on foot.

Seeing these soldiers on the run, White Bull, in bravado, dashed across their line between the two troops, hugging the neck of his fleet pony. They fired at him, but missed him. He circled back to his comrades. Encouraged by his success in this desperate stunt, he called out, 'This time I will not turn back,' and charged at a run on the fleeing troopers of the last company. When the Sioux heard him yelling and saw him dashing forward, many of them followed. This charge seemed to break the morale of the survivors of Calhoun's troop. They all ran to join Keogh, every man for himself, afoot and on horseback. All around, the Sioux were firing, dropping the fleeing soldiers.

One of the Sioux shot a mounted trooper. White Bull saw the man waver in his saddle, and, quirting his pony, raced forward to strike him and count the first *coup*. Before he could reach the trooper, the dying man fell from his saddle. White Bull reined in his pony, jumped down, and struck the body with his quirt, yelling, 'Onhey! I have overcome this one.' He took the man's revolver and cartridge-belt. Did-Not-Go-Home struck this enemy immediately after; he counted the second *coup*. Then White Bull leaped on his barebacked bay and dashed on with the charging, yelling warriors through the dust and smoke drifting down the bluffs.

By that time the last of Calhoun's men had joined Keogh's troopers, and all together they were falling back northwestward along the ridge to their comrades of the third group. A bugle blared. Those soldiers who still had horses were mounting.

White Bull found himself side by side with Chief Crazy Horse. Knowing him for one of the bravest of the Sioux, White Bull dared Crazy Horse to lead a charge. Crazy Horse refused. White Bull led the charge himself.

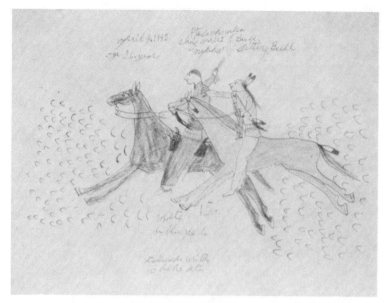

7. June 25, 1876. Custer's Last Stand. White Bull drags a soldier from his horse. The trooper fires in the air. A first *coup*. Chief Crazy Horse counted the second *coup* on this soldier. (Chapter XX.)

8. October 15, 1876. Yellowstone River. Fight with Colonel E. S. Otis. White Bull circles towards the soldiers and is hit in the left arm. (Chapter XXII.)

ITEMS FROM WHITE BULL'S PICTORIAL AUTOBIOGRAPHY

He saw a mounted trooper left behind; his horse had played out. White Bull charged this man; Crazy Horse followed him. As White Bull dashed up from the rear, the trooper tried to turn in his saddle and bring his carbine to bear on White Bull. But before he could shoot, White Bull was alongside, seized him by the shoulders of his blue coat, and jerked furiously, trying to unhorse the man. The soldier fired in the air, and with a scream fell from his horse. Crazy Horse struck this man second. White Bull had outdone the famous chief.

Some troopers were left afoot. One of these, finding the Indians all around him, stood turning from side to side, threatening them with his carbine. In that way he kept his enemies at a distance. However, White Bull was not daunted. He rode straight for the soldier. At close quarters the trooper fired. White Bull dodged: the ball missed him. A moment later he flung the shoulders of his horse against the trooper and rode him down. Bear Lice counted the second *coup*.

The remnants of Calhoun's and Keogh's troops had now joined the troopers around Custer to the north and west, near where the monument is now. The fourth mass of soldiers (the commands of Captain G. W. Yates, Captain Tom Custer, and Lieutenant A. E. Smith) was then below these, down the hill toward the river. The air was full of dust and smoke. Here and there a wounded man had been unhorsed and left behind.

One of these men, bleeding from a wound in the left thigh, with a revolver in one hand and a carbine in the other, stood all alone, shooting at the Indians. They could not get at him. White Bull dashed up behind the man, who did not see him come. White Bull rode him down. Brave Crow counted the second *coup* on this enemy.

By this time all the troopers on the hill had let their horses go. They lay down and kept shooting. White Bull was to the east of them, Crazy Horse at his side. Then White Bull charged alone through the soldiers at a gallop. It was all open ground. He lay close to his horse's neck and passed the troopers within a dozen feet, but was not hit.

The horses turned loose by the soldiers — bays, sorrels, and grays — were running in all directions. Many of the Indians stopped shooting and chased these loose horses. White Bull tried to head some off, but the Indians swarmed in ahead of him. He caught only one sorrel. The firing was very hot, so hot that, immediately after, White Bull's horse was shot down. The animal was shot through the fore-shoulder and chest, through the ribs, and through the head just behind the ears. White Bull was left afoot. Other Indians had dismounted. It was hand-to-hand fighting by that time. White Bull rushed in.

A tall, well-built soldier on foot tried to bluff White Bull, aiming his carbine at him. But when White Bull rushed the man, he threw his gun at him without shooting. They caught hold of each other and wrestled together there in the twilight of the dust and smoke. The soldier was brave and strong. He tried to wrest White Bull's gun from him, and almost succeeded. But White Bull lashed the enemy across the face with his quirt. The soldier let go, then grabbed White Bull's gun with both hands, until White Bull struck him again. But the soldier was desperate: he struck White Bull with his fists on the jaw and shoulders, seized him by his long hair with both hands, drew his face close, and tried to bite his nose off. White Bull thought his time had come. He yelled for help: 'Hey, hey, come over and help me!' He thought the soldier would kill him.

Bear Lice and Crow Boy heard his call and came running to his aid. They tried to hit the soldier, but in the rough-and-tumble most of their blows fell on White Bull. He was dizzy from the blows, but yelled as loud as he could to scare his enemy. At last he freed himself, struck the soldier several times on the head with his pistol, knocked him over, took his gun and cartridge-belt. Hawk-Stays-Up struck second. That was a close shave, a hard fight, but White Bull says: 'It was a glorious battle, I enjoyed it. I was picking up head-feathers right and left that day.'

Then for a time all the soldiers stood together on the hill near where the monument is now, ringed in by the Sioux, dying bravely one by one, as the Indians poured a hail of lead and arrows into their dwindling strength. They lay or knelt on the bare ridge, firing across the bodies of dead horses or taking cover behind the shallow shelter of a fallen comrade, selling their lives dearly. Only a few remained alive.

A Cheyenne named Bearded-Man charged these soldiers. He rushed right in among them and was killed there. His body lay in the midst of the soldiers. When the fight was over, the Sioux found him there. They did not recognize his body. They thought he was an Indian Government scout. Little Crow, brother of Chief Hump, scalped Bearded-Man. Afterward, when Little Crow realized his mistake, he gave the scalp to the dead man's parents.

By this time many of the Indians had armed themselves with carbines and revolvers taken from the dead troopers, and filled their belts with cartridges found in the saddle-bags of captured horses. The volume of their fire constantly increased, while that of the soldiers diminished. White Bull lay in a ravine pumping bullets into the crowd around Custer, aiming always at the heart. He was one of those who shot down the group in which Custer made his last stand.

All this time White Bull was between the river and the soldiers on the hill. The few remaining troopers seemed to despair of holding their position on the hilltop. Ten of them jumped up and came down the ravine toward White Bull, shooting all the time. Two soldiers were in the lead, one of them wounded and bleeding from the mouth. White Bull and a Cheyenne waited for them. When they came near, he shot one; the Cheyenne shot the other. Both ran forward. White Bull struck first on one soldier. But the Cheyenne beat him to the other one. He got only the second *coup*. The eight remaining soldiers kept on coming, forcing White Bull out of the ravine onto the ridge.

White Bull snatched up the dead soldier's gun and started up the hill. Suddenly he stumbled and fell. His leg was numb, it had no feeling in it. He searched himself for wounds, but could find none. Then he saw that his ankle was swelling. The skin was not broken, only bruised. He had been hit by a spent ball.

He found a shallow ditch, crawled into it, and lay there until all the soldiers were killed. At the time he stopped fighting, only ten soldiers were on their feet. They were the last ones alive. The fight began before noon and lasted only about an hour, he says.

White Bull found very few cartridges in the belts he captured. Though he was in the thick of the fighting from start to finish, he did not see a single soldier commit suicide. 'The soldiers seemed tired,' he says, 'but they fought to the end.' However, Did-Not-Go-Home saw one soldier shoot himself. He was running away, horseback. The Indians were chasing him, when all at once he put his revolver to his head, pulled the trigger, and fell from his saddle, dead. (This was probably Lieutenant H. M. Harrington.) The Indians were puzzled by the man's action.

Soon after, With-Horns found White Bull, put him on his horse, and led him back across the river. The tipis had not been moved up there. The people had rigged up tent-flies and were camping as best they could on the open flat.

Makes-Room made his son White Bull lie down under a shade there, and sent for Sitting Bull. Sitting Bull put 'wounded medicine' on White Bull's ankle and wrapped the swelling in buffalo wool. Sitting Bull said: 'Nephew, you had better be careful. One of these times you might be killed.' Meanwhile, the herald was calling out that the camp must be moved to where the people were. The women went after their tipis and moved them.

Meanwhile some of the men were singing mourning songs for the dead. Chief Makes-Room sang one:

> The people called him Elk-Stands-on-Top.
> He was a brave man.
> Now he is gone.
> Oftentimes they called him Elk-Stands-on-Top.
> They took him for a brave man.
> Now he is gone.

Chief Makes-Room had taken no part in the battle. It was the duty of a chief to look out for the women and the children in such a defensive fight. As a young man he had distinguished himself in battle nine times. Now he was fifty-one years old. Long before this, the other chiefs had told Makes-Room to give up the warpath and devote himself to caring for his people.

After a while the Indians had lunch. Then White Bull asked for his horse. They brought it and helped him upon its back. He crossed the river to get his leggins and the sad-

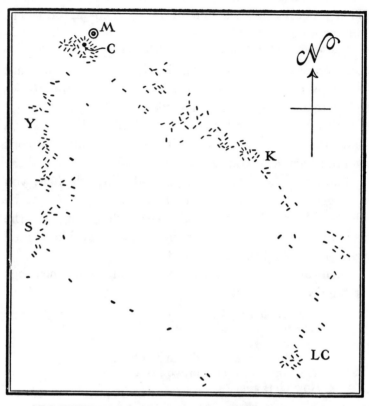

MAP SHOWING POSITIONS OF DEAD BODIES OF TROOPERS
FOUND ON THE CUSTER BATTLEFIELD

M. Monument
C. Body of General Custer
K. Command of Captain M. W. Keogh
Y. Commands of Captain G. W. Yates and Captain T. W. Custer
S. Command of Lieutenant A. E. Smith
LC. Command of Lieutenant James Calhoun
   Note: The river lay to the south and west

dle he had left there, and afterwards went over the battle-field to see the dead. He says he did not see anyone mutilat-ing the dead. He thinks that the parents of Indians killed in the fight must have gone up there later and mutilated some of the soldiers. On the hilltop he met his relative, Bad Soup (Bad Juice). Bad Soup had been around Fort Abra-ham Lincoln and knew Long Hair (General Custer) by sight. The two of them found Custer lying on his back, naked. Bad Soup pointed him out and said: 'Long Hair thought he was the greatest man in the world. Now he lies there.' They did not scalp Custer, because his hair was cut short.

White Bull took two pairs of trousers from the soldiers. On his way home he washed them in the river. He gave them to his father.

The Custer fight was over. In that fight, White Bull had counted seven *coups*, six of them 'firsts,' had killed two men in hand-to-hand combat, captured two guns and twelve horses, had had his horse shot under him, and had been wounded in the ankle. Few, if any, of the Sioux or Chey-ennes in that fight could show such a record of reckless bravery and good fortune.

White Bull gives the following list of Indians killed in the fight with Custer's immediate command. Of the Sans Arc Sioux, Long Dog, Elk Bear, Cloud Man, Kill-Him; of the Hunkpapa Sioux, Rectum (Guts), Red Face, Hawk Man; of the Oglala Sioux, Many Lice, Bad-Light-Hair, Young Skunk; of the Cheyennes, Left Hand (son of Chief Ice), Owns-Red-Horse, Flying-By, Black Cloud, Swift Cloud, and Bearded Man (Mustache).

Two men were killed in the fight with Reno on the bluffs that afternoon: Dog's-Backbone (Minniconjou); he was shot down right in front of White Bull. Long Road, a Sans

Arc, was shot while trying to count *coup* on the soldiers in the trench.

In the fight with Reno in the bottoms that morning two Minniconjou, Three Bear and Dog-with-Horns, were killed; also two Hunkpapa, Swift Bear and one White Bull; a Two-Kettle Sioux named Chased-by-Owls; an Oglala named White Eagle; Elk-Stands-on-Top (Standing Elk), a Sans Arc Sioux, and a Cheyenne, name unknown.

Some of these dead were brought to camp and laid out in a big tipi. Some were buried elsewhere. Those wounded who died on the way to the White (Big Horn) Mountains next day were buried where they died. A few of them had other names.

After White Bull reached camp with his saddle and leggins, he rode to the bluff and took part in the fight with Reno's men. He remained there all night.

After fighting all night and part of the morning against the soldiers entrenched with Major Reno on the bluff, White Bull came back to his tipi and went to sleep. About noon his father came and woke him up, saying, 'Son, something is going to happen over yonder.'

White Bull took his weapons and his horse and rode over the hill. There he found several warriors assembled. They told him that a scout had just come in from below to report that white troops were coming up the river. Immediately White Bull, Many Lice, and another Sioux set out to scout toward these troops. After riding ten miles down the Little Big Horn, they saw a white soldier. On seeing them, he galloped back, and soon after White Bull saw the troops of General Alfred H. Terry and General John Gibbon coming up the west bank of the river.

The three scouts lay low for a while and watched the troops, taking care not to show themselves. They saw that the troops had horses with them. Later they saw these horses grazing at long rifle range from the troops. White Bull took the lead and the three men rounded up the horses and started them back up-river. On their way home they met Indians moving camp, who said they were moving because soldiers were coming and that the soldiers were camping at the place where the Sun Dance had been held. These Indians asked White Bull how many soldiers were below on the river. He told them, 'Not as many as we have just killed.' Two of these Indians asked White Bull to give them horses from his captured herd. White Bull said, 'Go get some for yourselves.'

White Bull, Many Lice, and their comrade rode on back to camp with the captured horses. Nobody had fired a shot at them.

When the three got back to the Custer battlefield, they found that the camp had pulled out to the southwest. It was almost sundown, so they divided their horses. They followed the trail of the camp. Many Lice was in a hurry; he went on ahead. White Bull found a bundle of food that had been dropped, and made his supper of it. Here and there he would see a lodge-pole, or some other object left behind.

When he approached the camp in the darkness, he heard his father singing, for Many Lice had already reached camp and had told White Bull's father of his son's success. So Makes-Room was singing:

> White Bull, whenever there is something going on,
> You are always out in front.
> This makes me love you.

White Bull brought home eleven horses. None of them had shoes on.

CHAPTER XXI

WHITE DEER IS RESCUED

Indians are bred up to trailing, scouting, and horse-stealing, until, like game-dogs, their natural and instinctive powers are wonderfully increased.

W. P. CLARK, *The Indian Sign Language.*

IT WAS the end of July, 1876.

White Bull's people were in camp on Beaver Creek between the Yellowstone and Thick Timber (Little Missouri) River. White Bull was anxious to lead a party to the Black Hills in search of enemy horses. He wished only a small party, one or two men, for the Indians had found that the troops seldom pursued such small bodies of men.

White Bull first asked his brother, One Bull, to join him, but One Bull had other plans. White Bull then invited Iron Claw (Horseshoe) to go. Iron Claw had no gun and was unwilling. In order to persuade him, White Bull had to lend the man his own gun and ammunition. They set out toward the Black Hills.

When the two of them reached the Captive Butte on the headwaters of Owl (Moreau) River, a party of Indians tried to run off their horses. It was a Sioux chief and a party of ten or a dozen warriors! They had thought White Bull and Iron Claw were enemy Indians! When the mistake was discovered, the two groups decided to camp together there.

White Bull went to shake hands with the leader of these Sioux. He saw a slender, quiet man with a sharp, aquiline nose and a light complexion, standing under six feet. His face was unpainted. He was wearing white cloth leggins and a white muslin robe. White Bull recognized Chief Crazy

Horse (also known as Breaks-the-Head). He was glad to see him.

With Crazy Horse were Black Fox, His-Horse-Looking, Short Bull, Low Dog, Dog-Goes, also four Cheyennes and a Cheyenne woman. Most of the men were Oglala. Crazy Horse said they were on their way home from hunting enemies in the Black Hills. White Bull did not ask for the story of that warpath. He saw no scalps or captured ponies. That night, however, they danced the Victory Dance, and White Bull therefore believes that Crazy Horse had been successful. Crazy Horse was usually successful. He was always getting his horse shot under him, counting *coups*, and stealing ponies.

That night White Bull and Crazy Horse, the two leaders, slept side by side. Before they dropped off, they talked of the Custer fight.

Next morning, Crazy Horse and his party set off for the home camp. Iron Claw and White Bull pushed on toward the Hills.

One night, about two hours after sundown, White Bull and Iron Claw came to a camp of white men. There was a wagon; two horses, a bay and a black, stood at the tail of the wagon, eating hay from the wagon-box. Their owners were snoring in their bedrolls close by.

White Bull left Iron Claw at the edge of the timber and rode quietly up to the wagon. The unshod hoofs of his pony made little sound on the grass. The horses had on halters with short halter-ropes, but, for a wonder, were not tied. White Bull drove them quietly away without awakening their owners. He gave one of the horses to Iron Claw, and they set out for home. White Bull describes this exploit as 'A-Good-Job-Well-Done-While-They-Slept.'

Toward the end of August, 1876, White Bull decided to go on a hunt. The camp was then west of Slim Buttes. For some time the Indians had been hunting on Grand River, and were now moving west — Oglala, Minniconjou, Hunkpapa, and Sans Arc.

Sitting Bull, however, had halted on Grand River because his little son had been kicked in the head by a mule and killed. White Bull rode down to Sitting Bull's camp to get his brother, One Bull, and, learning of this tragedy, remained for a while to mourn with the family.

White Bull and One Bull set out for the Black Hills. When they reached the Hills, they rode along east of them until they reached the spot where Rapid City stands now. There they met two Sioux, Lame Dog and His-Iron-Horse, and two Cheyennes, one of whom was a brother of Touch-the-Cloud. These Indians had three women with them — good-looking women. White Bull joined forces with this party, and they rode on together. Soon after, they saw houses ahead and horses grazing alongside.

One Bull, White Bull, and Touch-the-Cloud's brother whipped up their ponies and started for the grazing horses. It was near the middle of the day. The white men saw them, came running out of the houses, and began to shoot. There were so many of them that the Cheyenne turned back. But White Bull and his brother kept on and succeeded in running off fifteen head.

The white men had plenty of horses left, however: they mounted and came after the Indians, shooting all the time. They rode hard and gained on the Indians. Lame Dog and the Cheyennes were riding for their lives. They ran their ponies as hard as they could, leaving White Bull and One Bull in the rear.

WHITE BULL
As a young warrior

ONE BULL
As a young warrior

White Bull called to One Bull: 'Go ahead with the horses. I'll stand them off. Somebody will have to fight here, for those other Indians are scared to death.'

One Bull answered: 'All right, Brother, but look here: if these other Indians get killed, you and I can marry their women.'

White Bull looked at One Bull and laughed; One Bull already had two wives. White Bull thought perhaps his brother was joking.

One Bull pushed on with the captured herd. Their pursuers kept shooting, and White Bull began to look for cover. He saw a large circular object made of wood set up on three poles. It was painted with alternate rings of black and white, it was round like a shield. White Bull got behind this and fired at his enemies. They stopped and kept on shooting and many of their bullets hit that round object above White Bull's head. It seemed to draw fire. Then White Bull realized that it was a target, set up by the whites for rifle practice. He galloped away.

All afternoon the white men chased the Indians. White Bull could not stand them off, they kept on coming. They pushed him so hard that he kept yelling to the women ahead what they must do to save themselves if the men were killed. They had a hard run to get away. Just at sundown White Bull dropped one of his enemies. He saw him tumble from the saddle. Then the whites halted, and after a while the two brothers halted to let the horses rest. But the Cheyennes and Sioux with the good-looking women never stopped. They kept going. They were scared.

The two brothers found their camp on Duck-Lives (Prospect Valley) Creek. It flows into the Little Missouri below the Short-Pine Hills. When the two victors rode into camp,

White Bull gave his share of the horses (eight head) to his parents and relatives, as they came rejoicing to meet him.

That night they told him of the battle with the soldiers at Slim Buttes (September 9, 1876). The battle had taken place while he was away on the warpath.

These raids in the summer of 1876 were dangerous enough to prove interesting. But White Bull says that during the winter before he took part in a battle in the snow which was far more thrilling, and memorable besides for a feat he performed — a feat which has made him renowned ever since. During the early part of that winter (1875–76) his people had been camping on the Little Missouri, a favorite winter camp-ground because of the sheltering timber there.

From the Little Missouri the camps moved over to the Yellowstone. One night, while the tipis stood on a small creek east of Tongue River, the Crows came and stole many horses. Red Horse immediately organized a party of fifty warriors to follow the enemy trail. White Bull and his relative, Feather-Earring, rode out with the others.

They followed that Crow trail for three days. Then snow fell and covered the tracks in places. Nevertheless, the Sioux kept on until they ran into a party of white men. By this time the Sioux had almost despaired of recapturing their ponies, and some of them wished to attack these white men. They said, 'We ought to have something to show for this warpath when we get home.' Others objected, for they saw that the white men had good fast horses and rifles. It was left to Red Horse to decide. He said: 'Leave them alone. We cannot kill them, and they might kill some of us.'

It began to snow heavily, covering the trail. The whole party turned back. On the way home White Bull and his brother shot a buffalo. The meat of that buffalo was all they brought home with them. They found the camp at the mouth of Tongue River.

Some of the people made fun of the young men when they came back empty-handed. This made the young men eager to go to war again to silence the scoffers, and very soon after, though the snow was deep, Spotted Thunder and Hunts-the-Enemy set out with almost a hundred warriors. They stopped at the Big Bend of the Yellowstone over-night. During the night their scouts returned and reported that they had seen some white men and the smoke of a campfire rising from the timber not far up-river. Here was the chance the young men wanted.

Early next morning they all mounted their war-horses and advanced cautiously through the deep snow, led by their scouts. As they pushed on, they saw a white column of smoke rising from the trees into the quiet, frosty air. As they came nearer, they saw a man — he ran into a thicket of willows. On the hillside near-by they saw horses pawing for the grass on the wind-swept slopes where the snow was not deep.

Most of the Sioux started for the man they had seen, White Bull and some others advanced on the campfire. Woody Hill (Feather-Earring's brother) and White Bull ran off the horses grazing near the camp. As their ponies plunged through the drifts, three white men appeared at the edge of the timber, running toward them and shooting. White Bull was left behind. They were shooting at him all the time, but missed him. He rounded up several ponies and ran them off.

While this was happening, the white men drove their re-maining animals into the timber, where the Sioux kept try-ing to get at them. Of course the Indians could not charge on horseback through the deep snow. They dismounted and advanced through the timber from tree to tree, driving the white men back until they had captured the campfire. Around this fire they found proof that the white men were buffalo hunters and wolfers. They had many hides of these animals there, also strychnine.

The Sioux kept advancing and the white men kept firing from cover at them. Suddenly White Bull heard someone calling: 'One of us is killed. White Deer is dead, and King Man has been shot in the knee.'

Someone helped King Man back out of danger. He sat with his back against a tree while they bandaged his wound. White Bull went to his friend and said, 'Where is this dead man, White Deer?'

King Man answered, 'He is lying over there under that tree.' The tree under which White Deer lay was in front, under fire of the enemies. White Bull belted his blanket around him like a kilt, and, carrying his rifle, ran dodging back and forth to the body of his friend. He was not hit. He found that White Deer had been shot in the side. The bullet had come out below his left hip. He lay on his face in the snow, apparently dead, but still bleeding freely.

Ordinarily, when White Bull rescued a comrade, he took him by the wrists and dragged him to safety. But that day the snow was knee-deep. White Bull knew he would have to carry his friend on his back. With the help of another Indian, White Bull got White Deer's body on his back, holding him by his arms over his shoulders. Then he started back. The snow was deep and hampered him. The white men in the timber kept on shooting, and part of the way there was no cover. Twice they shot at him. But he went as fast as he could, and finally carried White Deer out of the field of fire. Says White Bull: 'That rescue was one of the hardest things to do, and is one of the best things to tell. That was the kind of deed which put a man among the famous.'

The Sioux gathered around White Deer, examining his wound. Suddenly White Deer 'came alive.' The Sioux removed his blue blanket coat, stopped the bleeding, and bandaged him. They made a travois to carry him home.

The fight went on until Blue Horse and Sits-in-the-Timber were wounded. Blue Horse had his arm broken by a bullet.

Then Bad Lake was angry. He shot and killed the white man who had wounded his friend. Immediately they all charged in and captured this white man's body. Peace-Pipe-Bearer took his gun and counted the first *coup*. Goes-in-the-Center struck second, Young Skunk third. Iron Claw (Horseshoe) was fourth. They took the white man's silver money and his cartridges; those cartridges were as long as a man's finger. They found the white man dressed in shabby clothing, his hair was cut short. Therefore they did not strip or scalp him. After this, they all went home.

That was the end of White Bull's adventure in the snow, that winter of 1875–76. But when he reached home, he found his wife Rattles-Track ready to make things lively for him there.

All this time, the jealousy of Rattles-Track grew worse and worse. When White Bull lay down to sleep with Holy Lodge, Rattles-Track refused to lie alone on her couch across the fire. They slept three in a bed. Rattles-Track clung to White Bull's arm and leg on one side, and Holy Lodge clung to him on the other. Neither woman would allow him to face the other. He had to lie flat on his back all night. This jealousy was not diminished when Holy Lodge presented White Bull with a fine boy in his twenty-third year. This was White Bull's first-born, and he was delighted with his son. Rattles-Track was so angry that she took White Bull's war-charm and threw it away, thus leaving him without protection when he went to war. Her temper grew worse and worse until he became afraid of her. He did not know what she might do.

One day the warriors held a Grass Dance to initiate some new members. White Bull attended the meeting. A man named Long Lodge had been seriously ill. He believed that by joining the Grass Dance Society he might be cured. He took his place in the center. The members sat in a circle around him.

The Grass Dancers wore on their heads a roach made of porcupine hair and sometimes decorated with one or two eagle feathers. Such a roach was very handsome, standing as much as six inches above the head, and would swing gracefully with every movement of the dancer. It extended from the middle of the forehead to the nape of the neck behind and was fastened to the hair beneath it by hidden thongs. The hair on either side of the roach was clipped short or shaved away. Therefore, when a man joined this Society, the members clipped his hair. White Bull and Swift Eagle were appointed to act as barbers for the new member. Men chosen as barbers were by custom required to do some great thing at the meeting.

White Bull took the shears and cut the hair on the right side, Swift Eagle on the left. When they had barbered Long Lodge, White Bull walked around the circle of members of the Society until he came to one who had a fine crest or headdress made of porcupine hair. He asked this man for the headdress to be given to Long Lodge, the new member. Again he approached a man having a fine pipe-hatchet made of iron, a hatchet with a pipe-bowl above the blade, the hollow handle serving as a pipe-stem. In this way White Bull collected one garment or weapon after another until Long Lodge was fully equipped with the costume of the Society.

When this was over, it was time for White Bull to make his announcement, telling what he would give away for being honored as the barber of this Society. Some men would give horses, some weapons, but the greatest thing a man could do at such a time was to give away his wives.

White Bull therefore announced, 'I leave my wives for the young men.' By these words he renounced his rights as a husband and turned his women loose for anyone who might successfully win them. This announcement brought White Bull great applause. Not every man's heart was strong enough to give away his women.

White Bull, however, was well content. Says he: 'Those women were jealous and making trouble for me all the time. I was glad to be rid of them!' When he got home the women were gone.

At this time White Bull had three sons, one by Rattles-Track, two by Holy Lodge. He was devoted to his children and kept them when the women left. The youngest was a year old at the time (1876). He thought that his mother and sister could care for it. But that did not work out well. Having no baby-food and no cow's milk, Sioux mothers nursed their children much longer than is customary among the whites, sometimes for four or five years. (Indeed, White Bull's earliest recollection is of crying for his mother's milk — when four years old.) Though the father hugged the boy and sang to it and did his best to feed it, he could not quiet it. He could not hunt and fight and care for an infant too. Within three months Holy Lodge was back in his tipi caring for the child.

They got along happily after that. While Holy Lodge was in his home, he had another wife for a time, Light-in-the-Face. She remained three months in his twenty-sixth year. Again he married Elk Tooth. She remained only during his fortieth year. Holy Lodge died when the Chief was forty-five.

CHAPTER XXII

SURRENDER

Even with their lodges and families, they can move at the rate of fifty miles per day. They are perfectly familiar with the country; have their spies and hunting parties out all the time at distances of from twenty to fifty miles each way from their villages; know the number and movements of all the troops that may be operating against them, just about what they can probably do, and hence can choose their own times and places of conflict, or avoid it altogether.

GENERAL GEORGE CROOK
Report of the Secretary of War, 1876–77

AFTER the battle of Slim Buttes, the Sioux camps moved north to the Yellowstone for the fall hunt. Now that Long Hair Custer had been rubbed out, the Grandfather at Washington was filling up the Indian country with pony soldiers, walking soldiers, wagons and cannon, and wherever the troops went they disturbed the game and ruined the hunting for miles around. Therefore, the Indians tried to keep out of their way, and warned them off whenever possible. Since the soldiers had their orders to proceed, a fight generally followed.

Early in October, 1876, an Indian brought into camp a stranger, a very dark, handsome, heavy-set man with an open countenance, who wore a mustache, and long hair under his big hat. Because of his cowboy chaps, the Sioux dubbed him 'Big Leggins.' It was Johnny Brughière. Brughière was an Indian, but also a white man; he was fleeing from a charge of murder.

Dauntless, he rode into Sitting Bull's big camp with his Winchester across the saddle before him. The Sioux came running from all sides and surrounded this stranger. They were always suspicious of men in white men's clothes; they thought he must be a spy sent by the soldiers. They began to mill around him, and Jaw kept calling out, 'Kill him, kill him!' Then Sitting Bull learned what was going forward and sent word: 'Leave him alone. I want to see him.' They led Big Leggins to Sitting Bull's painted tipi.

Big Leggins spoke Sioux, the language of his mother's people. He handed the reins of his horse and his rifle to the Chief, and said, 'Brother, I have come to stay with you.'

Sitting Bull led Big Leggins into his roomy tipi and made him sit down. By this time a great crowd of Indians had come running to see the daring stranger. They pulled up the pegs of the tipi all around and raised the lodge cloth, crowding round to peer in at him. Big Leggins did not tell Sitting Bull why he had come to the camp, but he was frank and fearless. His Indian blood showed in his face. He spoke Sioux. Surrounded by that mass of dark, hostile faces, hemmed in by a ring of rifles, sharp spears, and arrows as he was, he did not flinch or show any anxiety. This pleased Sitting Bull.

Sitting Bull said to his comrades: 'Well, if you are going to kill this man, kill him. If you are not, give him a drink of water, something to eat, and a smoke.'

Seeing that Sitting Bull had taken the part of Big Leggins, the Indians relaxed, smiles appeared, and they hastened to do as Sitting Bull had suggested. Sitting Bull was glad to have a bold man in his camp who could read and write English. Perhaps this was the reason he spared the stranger.

Sitting Bull began to joke Big Leggins, now that he was one of them. The Chief knew they might have to fight the soldiers. He said to Big Leggins: 'Now you are one of us. I

JOHNNY 'BIG LEGGINS' BRUGHIÈRE

have a good running horse. Perhaps *you* can do something brave!' Thus Sitting Bull joked his new brother. Perhaps he did not think Big Leggins had a strong heart. Then all the warriors laughed, and the crowd dispersed. White Bull made friends with the man Sitting Bull had adopted.[1]

On the night of October 10, the Sioux stampeded and captured forty-seven mules from the camp of Captain C. W. Miner and four companies of infantry, and next morning, when the crippled train tried to advance, the Indians quickly forced it to turn back. As soon as that happened, the Sioux let the wagons go: all they asked was to be let alone. But the civilian teamsters were so terrified that they refused to go with the train a second time; they had to be replaced by enlisted men. Then the train started out again.

Four days later, White Bull learned that soldiers were coming again. He stripped to the gee-string and put on his fine war-clothes. He thrust each sinewy leg into a dark blue woolen leggin, decorated with handsome stripes of blue-and-white beadwork, and fastened the straps to his belt on either side. Under his belt, before and behind, he tucked a bright strip of scarlet flannel hanging to his ankles. Then he pulled over his head a white buckskin shirt and around it buckled his cartridge-belt, heavy with cartridges of red metal. Over his right shoulder he slung his war-charm, so that the eagle feather and buffalo tail attached to it swung under his left arm. In his back hair he fastened two upright eagle feathers, lustrous white with black tips, and, carrying his Winchester, stepped outside the tipi. There stood his war-horse, a spirited pinto, red and white, reared from a

---

[1] For Johnny Brughière's own account of this interview, as given by his nephew John E. Brughière, see *Winners of the West*, October 30, 1932, page 8.

foal by his mother. He tied up its tail in flannel red as blood, and attached two eagle feathers there. Then he bridled the horse with a bridle decorated at the brow-band with eagle feathers and at the bit with a flaunting tassel of woman's hair, evidence that this horse had been used to run down an enemy. Folding his blanket, he laid it on the animal's bare back. Then he mounted his eager war-horse and rode out with eight companions.

Somewhat later, they heard shooting over the hill and, quirting their ponies, rode to the sound of the guns. From the hilltop they saw wagons, with many soldiers on foot all around them. The Sioux were riding around, trying to get at the wagons, but the soldiers would not let them. All the Sioux were on horseback.

The wagons never stopped; they kept right on going. All the time the footsoldiers were charging back at the Indians, and then running to catch up with the wagons, and the Sioux were all around, circling and shooting and yelling. White Bull saw his friends firing into these soldiers. He did not know why, but he did not pause to ask questions. He charged right into the middle of the fight. Afterward someone told him: 'We saw these wagons and rode down to ask them for something to eat, we were hungry. But the soldiers started shooting, and that's the way the fight began.'

For a while White Bull was in the thick of it. He rode up within seventy-five yards of the wagons, looking for a chance to charge in and count *coup*. The soldiers were firing all the time, and there were a lot of them, nearly two hundred. Then the first thing White Bull knew, he was shot. He was hit in the left upper arm. The bullet went clear through and broke the bone. He wears the scar still. The shock of the wound knocked White Bull out. But he stuck on his horse, and right away two of his friends came and led him back to camp. The only other Indian wounded in this skirmish was Broken Leg; he was shot in the sole of the foot. Bad Hair's son was killed. The fight did not last long.

But it was a hot fight while it lasted. There was much shooting. The Indians made a most determined attack. They set the short grass of the prairie afire. The wagons had to advance through the flames. They moved in four lines close together, surrounded by the infantry escort. Every once in a while the Indians would see a soldier fall, then his comrades would carry him and put him into one of the wagons. Four soldiers were wounded that day.

Johnny Brughière rode out with the Indians to fight the troops on a horse given him by Sitting Bull. It was a fast bay named 'Hohe Horse.' Johnny remembered Sitting Bull's taunt. He said to the Sioux around him, 'Watch me; I'll show you how to fight.' Away he went on the swift bay, straight for the center of the white men's line. He rode right up within a few yards of them, then turned and galloped boldly along their marching line to the head of it before he turned back to join the Sioux. He was unhurt. After that, the Sioux liked him better than ever: they knew him for a brave man. Ever since, the Sioux have honored the memory of Big Leggins, and he in turn remembered Sitting Bull as 'a kind, good-hearted man, and generous.' [1]

Sitting Bull did not approve of all this fighting. He wished to hunt in peace. Accordingly next day he told Johnny Brughière he wished to write a letter to the white soldier chief. Brughière took a piece of white cloth and said he was ready to act as Sitting Bull's clerk.

[1] Statement of his nephew, John E. Brughière, for copy of which thanks are due to Brigadier-General William C. Brown, U.S.A., Retired.

Sitting Bull dictated as follows:

Friend:

I am coming up here to hunt. Ever since I was grown I have been unwilling to fight with soldiers or white men. But wherever I camp, you come and begin shooting at me. Now again you are shooting at me, but still I have come only for hunting. Therefore, when you see my letter, move away. I am coming there to hunt.

I am Sitting Bull.[1]

The note was left in sight of the soldiers in a cleft stick:

YELLOWSTONE

I want to know what you are doing on this road. You scare all the buffalo away. I want to hunt in this place. I want you to turn back from here. If you don't, I will fight you again. I want you to leave what you have got here and turn back from here. I am your friend.

SITTING BULL

I mean all the rations you have got and some powder. Wish you would write as soon as you can.

When Colonel E. S. Otis received this note, a conference was held. Three chiefs talked for Sitting Bull. Otis made them a present of one hundred and fifty pounds of hard bread and two sides of bacon. He said he had no authority to treat with them, but suggested that the Indians could go to the mouth of Tongue River to make peace. The Sioux did not molest the train further.

On October 20 and 21, Sitting Bull held councils on the prairie with Colonel Nelson A. 'Bear Coat' Miles, verbatim accounts of which will be found in my biography of Sitting

---

[1] Here follows the Sioux text of Sitting Bull's dictation:

'Kola: Le wana wasin kta ca wa u welo. Imacage ehantan Isantanka ki wica wa kiza wacin sno yelo. Tka tu kte wati canna el ya u na mayaku te helo. A ke ma ya ku te tka ini han sni wa u welo. Wana wasin kta ca wowapi ki le wan la ke ki reyap iyayayo he wana wasin ktaca wa u welo.

'Tatanka Iyotake Miyeyelo.'

Bull. Immediately after the second council, the troops attacked the Sioux without warning. This treachery so enraged young White Bull that he yelled, 'Come on, let's go and rub them out,' and immediately charged on the troops alone. No sooner had he started than Sitting Bull rode out, caught his bridle-rein, and stopped him, saying: 'It is only six days since your arm was broken. You are not fit to fight. Fight no more.' Sitting Bull led him back and sent him to the camp with Jumping Bull, away from the battle, with a message to Makes-Room to keep an eye on his reckless son, and keep him out of mischief.

Sitting Bull's mounted warriors stood off the troops for a time and then fell back to their camp. War Department records would have us believe that Bear Coat's infantry (three hundred and ninety rifles) 'pursued' the mounted Indians ('estimated at upwards of a thousand warriors') forty-three miles! This 'pursuit' was so effective that the soldiers lost the trail altogether and missed the crossing on the Yellowstone.

After this fight the camps divided. Sitting Bull and the Hunkpapa went on with their hunting. However, some of the Minniconjou were tired of being chivvied about the country by the troops. When Bear Coat Miles asked them to sit in council they crossed the Yellowstone and held a talk (October 27, 1876). Big Leggins acted as interpreter. Miles questioned him and promptly engaged him as a Government scout. Miles afterward described Brughière as 'The man to whom I am largely indebted for the success of my campaign against Sitting Bull and Crazy Horse.' Brughière eventually stood trial for murder at Fargo, North Dakota, in the United States District Court, December 27–31, 1879, and was acquitted.

After the talk with Bear Coat, some four hundred lodges of Minniconjou decided to make peace. The official reports describe this agreement as a 'surrender.' The Minniconjou did not understand it so at the time.

Colonel Miles was plausible. He said, 'Now we shall get on a steamboat and go to the Agencies down-river, and the families of those who go on the boat can go overland.'

Some of the head men went on the boat. Most of the people went overland. White Bull's uncle, White-Hollow-Horn, was one of those who went on the boat.

When those going overland reached Slim Buttes, they heard that the troops were taking away all the horses and guns from the Indians at the Agencies. This had been done at the Red Cloud Agency, October 22, just five days before they had their talk with Colonel Miles. They learned all this from some Sioux who had become frightened and were running away from the Agency. They did not know what to do.

While they were camped at Slim Buttes, two young Sioux came, horseback, from the Agency, carrying a white flag. White Bull met the two and took them to his tipi. They explained that they had been sent to the bands on the prairie to ask them to come in. One of these young men was a Sans Arc named Crow Feathers. The other was Rock-in-the-Mouth, a Two-Kettle Sioux. They reported that the troops had taken away the spears and even the knives of the people; very few had got anything back, and these few only one horse per man.

Now, the Sioux warrior loved his horse quite as much as any cowboy; he lived and died horseback. The last words of more than one prairie warrior were addressed to his horse. More than one warrior, in his last moments, facing death, threw his arms around the neck of his pony, and, with tears streaming down his face, cried, 'I love you; good-bye, my friend!' A Sioux warrior afoot felt like a sailor ashore, a cowboy on the pavement, a grounded aviator. His horse and his weapons were all that he possessed; all else was his woman's. Without his horse he was helpless to feed or defend himself. And so, all that night, the people were crying and wailing because they were going to lose their ponies, and the men sang sad songs about comrades who had been killed by the enemy.

The two young men who had brought the news dared not urge these people to go in to the Agency. Said they: 'Any warriors who go in will probably be killed. It is up to you to decide what you will do. Those head men who went on the steamboat are as good as prisoners now. But maybe, when their families go in, they will be turned loose.' All the people gathered to hear what the young men said. Finally Little Bear spoke up, 'Well, Uncles and Brothers, it is for you to say what we shall do.'

All agreed. Then Little Bear stood up and said, pointing to White Bull, 'Brother, whatever you decide to do, we'll do it.'

White Bull was Sitting Bull's nephew, his opinion had weight. He was, moreover, a famous warrior, with thirty brave deeds to his credit, though only twenty-six years old. They listened to hear what he would say.

'Uncles and Brothers! Not long ago I was taking part in a fight with the troops, and my uncle, Sitting Bull, came and stopped me and led me off the field. He said I was not to fight in a war again. That was why I made peace — it was his orders. And so Bear Coat got some of our men to go on the steamboat, and now he is holding them prisoners. Those men are our relatives, we cannot let them down. We must go in to the Agency. From this day on, the Grandfather will take over the nation that used to be ours; he will take our guns, and knives, and horses — everything. That is the price he demands for peace — *everything!* Therefore, I am going to give you a chance to go in with me. Those who do not wish to go may remain.'

Some of the Sioux refused to go with White Bull; they said they would rather try the Oglala Agency. Next day the camp split up and pulled out on different trails.

When White Bull's party reached the Agency at Fort Bennett, they made camp close to the warehouse and the interpreter at the post asked the Sioux warriors to come out on the parade ground and line up in a row with their weapons. Some of the Indians, afraid to be left defenseless, had concealed their best guns on the way in, but not White Bull. He was afraid that, if he had a weapon, he might lose his temper later and use the weapon and kill someone. Then the white troops would punish his relatives and things would be worse than before.

The fifty warriors with White Bull followed him out to the parade ground where the troops were drilling, and formed in line, carrying their weapons. All had guns. Then the soldiers marched up facing them, and halted. The Captain came forward with ten Sioux Indians and his interpreter. This Captain informed White Bull's party that these ten Indians were to have their guns given back. He then asked White Bull for his gun.

White Bull replied: 'I cannot give up my gun. I have a family to support. They will starve unless I hunt for them, and I cannot hunt without my gun.'

A second time the Captain demanded White Bull's gun,

and again White Bull refused. He was doing a brave thing.

Then the Captain barked out a command, and the soldiers brought their rifles to a position pointing toward the Indians. White Bull glanced down the line of Minniconjou warriors beside him. There stood Little Bear, Eats-with-Bear, Woody Hill, Fast Horse, Has-Two-Wives, Yellow Owl, Two Elk, Bear-Loves, Shot-by-White-Man, Red Bull, White Horse, and the rest, and every one of them looked strange. Their faces were 'different.'

A third time the Captain asked for White Bull's gun. White Bull felt alone then, yet he could not bear to surrender his weapon. He refused to do so.

Once more the soldiers pointed their guns at the Indians. The Captain asked the others for their weapons. All but White Bull handed their weapons over to the ten Indians with the Captain. He was the only one left with a gun. When he looked at his comrades' faces, he saw that something had happened to their courage.

Then the Captain said to White Bull: 'We are taking all the guns and the names of the Indians here. Some day, when the wars are over and the Sioux have cooled off, these guns will be given back or will be paid for, or shot-guns will be issued to the Indians for hunting.'

White Bull trusted this officer and believed he was telling the truth. He was the only Indian armed now. He did not wish to start trouble for his people. He gave in and handed his rifle to Four Bears, one of the Two-Kettle Sioux with the Captain. The Captain was pleased. He smiled, and shook hands with White Bull.

When this was over, the Indians went back to their camp. And when White Bull went to water his ponies, he found that the Indian Government scouts had come along and had driven them away. Immediately after, rations were issued to his party — beef, sugar, baking powder, coffee, bacon, and flour. These foods White Bull had tasted before, on visits to the Agency.

White Bull's people remained camped close to the warehouse all winter. Having no horses and no weapons, they could neither travel nor hunt. That was a hard winter, a dismal time. All winter, at intervals, the women would cry and the men sing sad songs.

Soon after, the Indians were forced to cede the Black Hills. They were told they could have no rations until this was done. 'And that,' as White Bull puts it, 'was the end.'

PART III
THE WHITE MAN'S ROAD
1876–1933

CHAPTER XXIII

AGENCY INDIAN

The scout was the man... whose outstanding quality was scrupulous
honesty.   CHIEF STANDING BEAR, *Land of the Spotted Eagle.*

IN 1881, White Bull's thirty-second winter, the head men
of the Minniconjou Sioux called a council to appoint new
chiefs. At the time, only three of the six head chiefs, or
Scalp Shirt Men, were living. The head men decided to
name five more chiefs and hold a Sun Dance. Chieftaincy
among the Minniconjou was hereditary in theory, but in
practice only an able man could step into his father's
moccasins. When the council had assembled, two men were
detailed to bring the newly appointed chiefs into the center
of the Grand Council.

White Bull knew nothing of the purpose of this council,
but, seeing the crowd assembled, he rode up to see what was
going on. When the two officials saw him sitting his pony
looking over the heads of the people, they pushed through
the crowd, took him by the hand, and led him into the
center of the circle. Thus he was appointed in place of his
father, Makes-Room, and thereafter had the privilege of
wearing a buckskin shirt decorated with fringes of human
hair. Big Crow was named second, Touch-the-Cloud third,
White Swan fourth, Touch-the-Bear fifth.

At this meeting they sang a song:

> It is hard to be a chief,
> But I do my best to be a chief.

Then Makes-Room, the oldest of the retiring chiefs,
made a speech advising their successors:

God sees you. Guard the Black Hills and also this Reservation. Do not let white men fool you. Use your head and take care of your people. Be wise, be patient. Try to get along with the people of this Island [the United States]. God made these people as well as ourselves. We do not wish to fight them. Hold fast what we have told you. Never forget these words.

Love your people, there are many helpless — old folks and orphans. Take care of them. Be good friends to good men: good men are your friends. Use all your mind to look out for the future of our young folks. Be fair with the Grandfather, and try to make a good bargain and a fair agreement for both parties. Never let the Sacred Pipe go out, and when you pray to Wakan Tanka with this peace-pipe, He will hear you. Do not step out of the Indian road; that is the road Wakan Tanka made for us. See that your children learn those things which the Grandfather wishes them to know. Try to secure a good agent and a good Commissioner of Indian Affairs. As we live now, everything comes through them; keep them satisfied. Be thoughtful, think every day. These are my words.

Thus White Bull automatically became a member of the Chiefs Society and took up the burden of leading and providing for the Minniconjou. This had been no light burden when the Indians ran wild on the Plains, but at the Agency it seemed even heavier.

Nevertheless, White Bull pushed along the white man's road with the same vigor which had distinguished him on the warpath. He made his home in a log cabin, gradually acquiring a wagon and more than a hundred horses. In time he joined the Congregational Church, and from the missionary learned to write in his own language, so that he could record the story of his life and of his people.

As Chief he frequently entertained visitors of other tribes, acted as peacemaker when quarrels arose among his people, soothed and made presents to neighbors frantic because of some bereavement, and on one occasion rode day and night to Pierre for a white doctor, thus saving a woman in labor. Repeatedly he acted as a private or officer of the Agency Indian Police, and served as Judge of the Court of Indian Offenses on his Reservation. He also exerted his influence against rot-gut whiskey, introduced illegally among his young men, for though White Bull has tasted good liquor on occasion, he thinks it bad for Indians, and was never drunk in his life.

A great part of his energy has been devoted to keeping possession of Indian lands and resisting the encroachments of white settlers. More than once he has refused the bribes and flattery of commissioners sent to purchase Sioux lands, and has steadily supported the claims of the Sioux to damages for the Black Hills, taken from them by force in violation of their treaty rights.

When the Ghost Dance came to Cheyenne River, he took no part in it. He saw that the dance was *wakan*, and it was revealed to him that those who took part in it would be killed, as afterward happened at Wounded Knee.

Yet all these things, necessary and useful as they were, meant less to him than the old ways of the hunter and warrior. So long as game remained in Sioux country, he was always ready for a hunt.

The Indians at the Agencies were not allowed to have guns. However, they made bows and arrows secretly, and would slip off and hunt small game along the river. This varied their rations a little. Sometimes a few Indians were able to get a permit to go on a hunt. In 1882, White Bull got such a permit. He was allowed to go with three others to hunt with ten white men; the Sioux acted as guards and hunters. They left in August and went to Bear Butte. They were gone three months. The interpreter had a good new gun which he gave to White Bull.

As White Bull was an Indian Policeman at that time, he was allowed to keep this weapon.

Somewhat later, some Indians visited Slim Buttes and saw buffalo there. When this good news was brought to the Agency, a large party of hunters obtained a permit to go after them. They sent five scouts ahead over the snow, after they had made camp near the Buttes. To be chosen to act as a buffalo scout was a high honor. The scouts were White Bull, Puts-on-His-Shoes, Bay, Turtle, and Red Horse.

The scouts reached Slim Buttes at night. It was very cold. Next morning they climbed to the western peak of the Buttes, and through his binoculars, White Bull saw buffalo. Immediately they started back to the camp. On the way they shot a deer and had a feast. When the scouts neared camp, they fired a gun to announce their coming. When they came in they found the people waiting in a semicircle with the leader of the hunt, Eats-with-Bear, seated in the center holding a pipe. Eats-with-Bear asked the scouts to sit down beside him where the snow had been scraped off. He filled the pipe and White Bull smoked it, thus pledging himself to tell the truth. All the scouts smoked this pipe.

Eats-with-Bear laid his palm flat on the ground and questioned the scouts.

It was the custom for game scouts to use their thumbs in pointing toward buffalo. To point with the thumb indicates that the pointer speaks truth.

Eats-with-Bear said, 'Have you seen anything?'

White Bull answered, 'Yes.'

Eats-with-Bear asked, 'Can I reach what you saw?'

White Bull replied, 'I saw a herd of buffalo.'

All the people were thankful. They called out: '*Hie!*
Hie!'

Eats-with-Bear then demanded, 'Is there enough to
feed my people?'

White Bull answered, 'There are as many buffalo as
there are people.'

Then all the Sioux called out: '*Hie! Hie!*'

Eats-with-Bear demanded: 'Is there enough to cover my
people?'

White Bull replied, 'More than enough.'

Having questioned the scouts four times according to the
ritual, Eats-with-Bear asked White Bull to tell just what
he had seen.

White Bull replied: 'I saw buffalo west and north of the
Buttes. They covered the earth.'

Then the people were happy. They went back to camp
and tried out their best running horses. Everyone was
happy; even the horses seemed to know what was going to
happen. Next morning, they moved the camp to a place
where there was a big spring — plenty of water. The
morning after, they went on the hunt.

When the soldiers gave the word to charge the herd, all
the men dashed away on their best horses. White Bull was
among the foremost four. He killed three buffalo and
stopped. They butchered and packed the meat back to
camp. Next morning they made a second hunt. The herd
was so big that the party divided and charged from two
sides. White Bull remained between the two parties. He
killed seven cows. It took some time to butcher these, and
that night the people made camp on a creek not far off.

On this stream there were only a few box elders, no
timber. Therefore, White Bull and three companions rode

on all night. White Bull saw something ahead. It looked like buffalo. He halted. When the other three came up, White Bull told them he intended to run these buffalo, though it was dark. He shot twice, but hit nothing in the darkness. Then a cow came out of the herd close to him. He fired, but did not drop her. He was loading his gun for a second shot when he heard the buffalo coughing blood. Then he knew she was dying. The hunters skinned the cow's hump in the darkness to see how fat she was. White Bull says she was the fattest cow he ever killed.

They butchered the cow, but White Bull took only the hind quarter and the flesh from one side of the ribs. The rest he covered with snow. Then he returned to the main party about midnight, got another saddle-horse and a pack-horse, and in the morning returned to the buffalo he had killed. The snow had kept the beef from freezing.

That day the hunters saw two more buffalo and killed one, covering the meat with snow as before. Again they saw four, and White Bull killed one and again buried the meat. Next day he collected all this meat and went back to camp. The whole camp made a hunt that day.

On that hunt White Bull carried a fourteen-shot rifle. It was very cold. He and another were in the lead when the hunters rushed the herd. He dropped four cows dead with one shot each; the other seven died within a few minutes. He used only eleven cartridges and dropped eleven cows. Some of the hunters got one or two, some none at all that day.

The unsuccessful hunters helped him butcher for a share in the meat. The hide, of course, belonged to the man who killed the animal, though the butchers would borrow the hides to pack the meat in. It took two or three horses to carry all the meat of one buffalo, and that day his five pack-horses were kept busy. On one horse would be put the meat, cut off the ribs from the neck to the hind quarters. This would be packed in the hide with the heart, liver, and intestines. The head was packed on a second horse, and everything else on a third. So many helped butcher that by the time he got his kill home, he had parted with fully half of it. But it was a good hunt all the same.

He has killed countless buffalo, sometimes with a gun, often with a bow and arrow. The greatest number of buffalo he ever killed in a single hunt with a bow was eight. Those eight buffalo constituted a record in more ways than one. There was a little snow on the ground that day. He had a fast horse and was riding bareback. The hunters rushed the herd and began shooting. White Bull was well in the lead. Each time he drew his arrow back to the head and took careful aim. Each time the arrow went true, sunk to the feathers in the flesh of his quarry. He loosed eight arrows and brought down eight buffalo. Then his hands were so cold and stiff, he could not shoot at all. He had to get down and rub his hands with snow. This happened east of Arrow Creek near the butte Where-the-Fifteen-Sioux-Were-Killed, when he was twenty-four years old.

Four times during his lifetime, White Bull shot his arrow entirely through the body of a buffalo. The first time he did this, he was nineteen years old. The people had set out on a hunt, leading the pack-horses, planning to camp at a creek beyond the herds. They made a surround. White Bull singled out a cow and let fly an arrow. It did not go deep enough to kill the cow. The cow whirled, plunged into the young man's pony and rolled it over.

White Bull and the horse both had a fall. When the pony
gained its feet, White Bull was on its back. He galloped
to within ten yards of the wounded cow. The cow and the
pony both stopped, but before the cow could attack again,
White Bull drew his arrow to the head and shot. The
arrow passed clear through the cow and stood in the snow
beyond. This happened opposite the mouth of Powder
River. White Bull was riding a bald-faced horse.

Two years later, at the mouth of Tongue River, a hunting
party found buffalo, just at sunrise. White Bull shot two
cows. The arrow passed entirely through the first one.
White Bull says that to look at the arrow one would
hardly suppose it had been used at all. There was only
a little blood — around the feathers.

In the spring of his twenty-fourth year, White Bull went
out in the morning to catch his ponies. The ground was
frozen. On the way back he rode up to a three-year-old
cow and shot at her. He picked up his arrow ten yards on
the other side of the cow. It had passed clear through.

Next autumn he killed three cows on a hunt. His arrow
passed completely through the first one. In those days few
rifles would send a bullet through a buffalo. The 'muzzle
velocity' of a Sioux arrow was very great.[1]

In September, 1883, Sitting Bull and the Sioux from
Standing Rock joined other Sioux bands in the last great
buffalo hunt. They found the herds northwest of Slim
Buttes. They made three surrounds. White Bull killed
five buffalo the first time, six the second, four the third.
Some of the young men roped a buffalo cow, a bull calf,
and four heifer calves, and brought them back alive. Two

[1] See *Arrow Wounds*, by Thomas Wilson, *American Anthropologist* (n.s.),
vol. 3, 1901, p. 513.

white men were on this party, Alex and Dupree. They were not Government employees. Dupree was a well-known frontiersman after whom the town of Dupree, South Dakota, was later named. He took the six live buffalo and raised them.

One day during this hunt White Bull was out scouting and saw three white men camped west of Slim Buttes. They had a tent and a four-horse team. White Bull knew they were buffalo hunters because of the hides stacked in their camp. He went back unseen and reported these poachers to the hunting party.

The Indians decided that these men must be caught and kept from killing their game. They decided to go into the camp of the white men in a friendly manner and capture them before they knew what had happened. Three young men were appointed to seize and disarm each of the whites. White Bull was one of those appointed for this duty.

According to plan, the Indians entered the camp of the white men, smiling and talking, and crowded around them. When everything was ready, their leader called out. At this signal, White Bull and other Indians appointed grasped the white men and took their guns away. No one was hurt.

The white men said they had come from the Black Hills. The Indians brought them home and old man Dupree interpreted. It was agreed to let the prisoners go, provided they would return home and stop killing buffalo on the Reservation. The white hunters readily agreed. These white men had only beef to eat; therefore the Indians gave them sugar, flour, and coffee. However, the Indians kept their guns.

One of the white men told the Indians that the Grandfather at Washington had said that any man could kill buffalo, and that when a man had got a hundred hides the Grandfather would give him one hundred and sixty acres of land. He said the Grandfather wished to starve the Indians into settling on the Reservation.

This white man said: 'After we have cleaned up the buffalo, we are going to clean up the deer. We were sent out here by Uncle Sam.'

These white men carried heavy Sharps rifles. Soon after, White Bull traded a horse for one of these guns and the tools used in reloading cartridge-shells. The Sharps rifle was of 40-90 caliber, and used cartridges about four inches long. Later, White Bull accidentally cracked the stock of this rifle and mended it with rawhide. It is now in my possession. The Chief says he kept this gun in a buckskin case. He used oil from the marrow of leg-bones of deer or buffalo on all his guns.

White Bull finds it difficult to accept the stories of white hide-hunters. He says a herd of buffalo will not stand to be shot at after one has been dropped. When one is dropped, they all run, in his experience, and though on level ground a man might shoot several as they ran away, in rough country that would be difficult. Says he: 'I have heard lots of white men tell lies, and Indians too. Even at the Agency, some men tell lies. I do not believe that a white man afoot could shoot thirty head of buffalo without moving, as is claimed. If such methods had been practical, we Indians would have used them.'

That last buffalo hunt brought trouble to the Sioux. Though they had done no harm to the three white poachers on their Reservation, white officers came from the Black Hills and arrested Bull Eagle. They took him back with them and put him in prison.

Soon after, the Chief took to wife White-Buffalo-Shawl. She lived five years in his lodge and bore him one child. In 1906, White Bull married a Ute woman. In 1907, Smoky Woman married White Bull: later they parted. In 1908, White Bull married Her Shawl, his present wife, a handsome, competent woman who makes excellent coffee. They get along well. Her Shawl says, 'I never was jealous.'

Life on the Reservation seemed humdrum, after the excitement of war and hunting. White Bull believed that he was being kept in one place as a punishment. For it *was* a punishment to an old rover like him. At times he was roused to anger at the way he was treated. He was a man and a chief, yet sometimes they treated him like a child.

Once White Bull was punished. At the time, cattlemen wished to lease the Cheyenne River Reservation, offering what White Bull considered a very low price per acre. The Indians held council, and most of them were willing to agree. But White Bull would not give in. He held out for a better price, and the Agent threw him into the guard-house.

The guardhouse was in the same building as the head-quarters of the Indian Police. There were three prisoners in one cell, but White Bull was kept in a cell by himself. He was in solitary confinement for three months, for the Agent gave orders that no one could see him.

At intervals during that time the Agent called White Bull to his office. Each time, two Judges of the Court of Indian Offenses, three Policemen, and three old men belonging to the tribe sat with the Agent. Each time the Agent demanded White Bull's signature on the lease. But White Bull had given his word not to sign. Each time he refused. He was not a man to be bullied when he felt himself to be in the right.

At the end of three months, the Agent called him in for the fourth time. He said: 'Now I am going to turn you loose. All your people from Cherry Creek are coming up to the Agency. You can stay here with them if you wish to.' Then the Agent had the gall to add: 'Now, White Bull, I want to be your friend. I will do anything I can for you.'

White Bull was outraged. He told the Agent what he thought of him. He said: 'You are a Government Agent, sent here to help the Indians, but instead of doing that you are cheating them. You are doing things the Indians do not like. I cannot be friends with a man like that.'

White Bull said: 'You are trying to scare me, but you are only scaring yourself. You will be the one afraid of what has been done. What you have done is no good to the Indians. This Reservation belongs to the Indians and I will use all my power to make the best of it. I will not stay here. I am going home to see my father.'

The Agent said: 'How are you going home?' (The Cheyenne River Agency is some sixty-five miles, as the crow flies, from Cherry Creek, White Bull's home. White Bull was fifty-two years old.)

White Bull answered, 'On foot.'

As White Bull came out of the Agency office, an Indian met him and asked him to go to his lodge for the night. It was already near sundown. This friend was a good man and wanted to hear what had been said in the office. He said he had only two horses, but would lend them to White Bull and let him send them back from Cherry Creek by someone who might be coming to the Agency.

But White Bull would not remain. He mounted one horse and led the other. He rode all night and got home about sunrise. Next day he sent the horses back.

CHAPTER XXIV

WHITE BULL CAPTURES THE UTES

Only the brave and fearless can be just.   Lakota proverb.

IN HIS fifty-seventh year, White Bull was singled out from all the chiefs in America and given a difficult mission to perform by the United States Government. Many old chiefs have been honored, but few indeed have been commissioned to carry such a responsibility and have carried it so well. The exploit was one of which the Chief is justly proud.

In July, 1906, several hundred White River Utes, under their leaders Appah, Soccioff, and Red Cap, left the Uintah and Ouray Agency in Utah and set out across Wyoming for the Sioux country in South Dakota. For generations they had hunted on the Plains, they had never liked their Reservation in Utah, and after negotiations with one of their chiefs (without the knowledge or consent of the tribesmen), their lands had been allotted in severalty and the Reservation suddenly thrown open to white settlement by legislative enactment.

Though the Utes were not hostile toward the whites, the Governor of Wyoming was in no mood to welcome a band of Indians who could no longer support themselves by hunting. The citizens of Wyoming were few and far between, and did not wish to be burdened, and possibly terrorized, by a horde of homeless nomads. Yet the Federal Government, having just conferred citizenship upon the Utes, could hardly send United States troops to force them to return to Utah, because citizens of the United States had the right to travel peaceably wherever they chose. Nor

was the State of Wyoming anxious to call out the militia
and thus cause bloodshed.

Accordingly, the Indian Bureau sent Inspector James
McLaughlin, who found the Utes early in October on
Black Thunder Creek. Inspector McLaughlin, formerly
Agent at Standing Rock at the time of Sitting Bull's
death, was a very able man. But he found the Utes stubborn, sullen, and unmanageable. After some days' negotia-
tion he was only successful in persuading forty-six Utes (one
eighth of the party) to return to Utah. The other Utes
declared they would fight to the last man rather than
return, and on McLaughlin's recommendation, eight
troops of the Tenth Cavalry and eight troops of the Sixth
Cavalry were ordered out to overawe them. It was a
ticklish situation for all concerned.[1]

One evening White Bull was sitting beside his cabin
when a breed came bringing a letter. He said it was from
the Grandfather at Washington, and said it read as follows:

White Bull:
    When you get this message, go now to Wyoming and take
a good interpreter along. The United States troops and the
Ute Indians are about to fight. Go see the Captain.

Next morning the Chief rode in to Cherry Creek and was
given a Government team of horses and a spring wagon.
He took Henry Fielder as his interpreter. It was raining,
and they took two sleeps to reach the bank of the Missouri

---

[1] The official report on these absentee Utes will be found in *Reports of the
Department of the Interior*, 1907, volume II, pages 121–29. For Inspector Mc-
Laughlin's account of this matter, see James McLaughlin, *My Friend the
Indian* (Boston, 1910), Chapter XX. Of course none of these officials makes
any mention of White Bull's services. The War Department records are a
trifle more generous. See *Annual Report*, Brigadier-General Edward S. Godfrey, Commanding the Department of the Missouri, dated August 12, 1907.

River opposite Pierre. They crossed in a boat. From Pierre they took the train to the Black Hills. One day about dark they reached a station east of the Hills and stopped for dinner.

There a white man met the Chief with a buggy and a trotting team and gave him a rifle. The white man said, 'We have seen the Utes.' White Bull drove the team all that day and the day following. In the afternoon he reached the country where the Utes were supposed to be, and about nine o'clock came to a camp of soldiers. These troops were short of rations, but gave the Chief some coffee. Next day someone shot an antelope. White Bull ate part of this animal and next morning reported to the commanding officer at Fort Meade. The following morning an officer and the Chief started off, driving the doctor's four-mule team (an ambulance). The driver demanded seven dollars a day on such a dangerous mission; they sent the driver home.

That day the two of them reached the camp of the army in the field. There they remained four days.

The Captain said, 'White Bull, will you go to the Utes?' White Bull replied, 'I don't care.'

The Captain misunderstood him and thought he must be afraid, but White Bull explained that he was perfectly willing to face all the Utes in the world. He asked the Captain, 'What am I to say to these Utes?'

The Captain answered: 'These Utes are about to start trouble. I cannot tell you what to say to them. You are an Indian and a Chief. Use your head.'

Afterward the Captain asked what White Bull was going to do. White Bull replied: 'I will take these Utes to Fort Meade. I will talk to them, and if they take my words, I will take care of them.'

The Captain asked, 'Do you think these Utes will take your words?'

White Bull answered confidently, 'Yes, they will take my words, for I have been thinking what to say on my way up here.'

The Captain said he would give White Bull two good saddle-horses and a wagon full of rations, ready to start next morning. When the horses were brought out, one was nervous and the other quiet. White Bull chose the gentle horse.

The Utes were said to be on Powder River in Montana, just across the Wyoming line. Captain Carter P. Johnson (Tenth Cavalry), White Bull, and the interpreter rode away ahead of the wagon toward the angry Utes. As they approached the Ute camp, they saw the heads of Indian scouts — black dots — on the hilltop. An instant later these disappeared. Then they saw all the warriors of the Utes approaching. They dismounted.

A man with an eagle feather tied in his hat came from among the Utes and said, 'Is this White Bull?'

White Bull answered, 'Yes.'

Immediately all the Utes gathered round and shook hands with him. One of these Utes could speak Sioux. White Bull told him to unload the wagon and share the rations. While this was being done, the six head men of the Utes, Captain Johnson, and White Bull sat in a circle and smoked the peace-pipe. It was time for White Bull to speak. Before he spoke he filled the pipe and made a prayer:

> Wakan Tanka, look at me;
> I do not ask for anything bad
> When I wish good things,
> I carry my peace-pipe.

Then he advised the Utes: 'One half of my body is a chief and one half is a man. While I am here, I am going to use only the half of me that is chief.'

He talked over their trouble until he knew what it was. A chief of the Utes had made an agreement with the Indian Bureau and the people did not know of it, so he was told. When the survey was completed and the allotments were made, there was dissatisfaction. The Utes said they did not want their allotments in Utah; they wished to go and live with the Sioux in Dakota. They told White Bull that Inspector McLaughlin had talked with them. McLaughlin, they said, had told them: 'In Washington they know all the chiefs. Of all these chiefs, White Bull is the only wise man. He is Sitting Bull's nephew and a famous warrior.' When the Utes heard that, they told McLaughlin they wished to see White Bull.

'Now,' said they, 'in spite of being held back, we have come to meet you.'

White Bull made his speech then, urging the Utes not to make trouble.

When he had finished, one of the Utes stood up and said: 'Chief White Bull, you have made a speech full of good sense. We take your words. We put ourselves in your hands. Hold us tight. Tomorrow we want you to come here, and we will go where you wish us to go. Your words have covered us up. We cannot go under or over or around your speech.'

White Bull and the officer went back to the army camp.

The Captain said, 'White Bull, I want you to tell us what you said to the Utes.'

White Bull repeated his words. All the officers were well pleased. The Captain said: 'White Bull, tomorrow you can have twenty-five soldiers and rations. Where do you wish to go?'

White Bull replied, 'I wish to go to Fort Meade in the Black Hills.'

White Bull knew the commanding officer at Fort Meade. He asked to have the troops follow the Utes three miles behind. There were nearly three hundred Utes in the party.

Captain Johnson said: 'White Bull, you surely are a leader. You are like an eagle that catches a rabbit in one claw and another rabbit in another. You take the soldiers in one hand and the Utes in the other.'

Next morning (November 6) it was very cold. When White Bull reached the Ute camp, his party warmed themselves. Then a herald made an announcement to the Utes. He named four camp-leaders to direct the march. He told the Utes to break camp. They did so, but it was so cold that they traveled only three miles that day. The storm stopped them and held them for two days, but at last they reached Fort Meade and made camp in the timber.

Thus White Bull solved the problem.

White Bull remained a few days with the Utes. They were determined to go with him to his Reservation. White Bull promised that he would try to arrange this for them. Then his interpreter took sick, and the Chief decided to return home.

Before he left, White Bull advised the Captain and the soldiers to be careful not to scold or abuse any of the Utes, but to treat them kindly and in that way avoid any cause of trouble. He also advised the Utes to do whatever the Captain and the soldiers asked them to do. Said he: 'Think of God at all times. I am going home now, but I will be back. When I return, I will lead you to my home, to live where I can look after you.'

While White Bull was with the Captain that day, he was given a glass of whiskey. Once before, as a young man, he had tasted whiskey in Sitting Bull's tipi. It was given him by some traders to warm him up one cold day. He had not tasted that 'medicine' since, but he had seen the trouble it caused on the Reservation. So now he advised the Captain not to let the Utes have any whiskey. Both the Captain and the Utes agreed to follow his advice.

All that winter the white men kept trying to persuade the Utes to return to Utah, but they were determined to go to White Bull's Reservation on Cheyenne River. Even when a delegation of their chiefs went to Washington to present their grievances personally to the President, they insisted on going to stay where White Bull could look after them. Accordingly, in the spring, June, 1907, White Bull came back for them and led these Utes to his home, where the Government had leased Sioux lands for them for a period of five years. They settled peaceably there, and the trouble was at an end.

While White Bull was looking after these Utes on Cheyenne River, he married a Ute woman. As neither of them could speak the other's language, they communicated by signs. This marriage lasted about a year, until the Utes returned to their Reservation at White Rocks, Utah.

When White Bull got back to Cherry Creek, the Sioux sang a song in honor of his exploit. The words of the song were:

> The soldiers fear the Utes;
> Come on, White Bull.

That winter, White Bull thought his time had come. He was so ill that he went out of his head. His soul left his body. He saw a man coming from the west all in white. The man said, 'I came after you.'

White Bull rose and followed him. They halted and looked across Cherry Creek. There he saw four other men coming, four from the north. The man in white said, 'Look, these men say they wish to befriend you.' Soon they arrived.

Immediately the skull and horns of a buffalo emerged from the ground. The skull moved, the earth cracked and trembled as the skeleton struggled to come forth. The hump and ribs emerged, the forefeet came out, and at last the whole skeleton heaved up and stood on the prairie. White Bull watched. Flesh covered the bones, hide covered the flesh, hair grew. The buffalo was alive.

The buffalo said, 'Behold me; I wish to be your friend, before we all go into the ground together.'

The buffalo said, 'You have a good name, because you took it from our brother, the buffalo.'

The buffalo said, 'I am strong and hearty, therefore they have appointed me to help you.'

The buffalo said, 'Observe what I eat: I eat these. They make me strong. These four roots I eat. Do likewise.'

They all moved about over the prairie and found four plants growing. Then suddenly they vanished, and White Bull found himself in his bed again.

This happened in April, 1907. As soon as the spring was far enough advanced, the Chief sent his wife out to look for these four plants, which he described. She found them. He ate them, and was cured.

CHAPTER XXV

THE HAPPIEST DAY

The man who gives much will live a long life, while the selfish man will live a short one.

Lakota proverb.

WHITE BULL'S old age has been accompanied by honor, love, obedience, troops of friends, not only at Cherry Creek among his own band (who hold themselves superior to other bands on the Cheyenne River Reservation), but all over that Reservation, among the Sioux everywhere, and indeed all over the Plains. Moreover, white men have singled him out on many occasions.

But his greatest public honor came to him in 1926, when, on the fiftieth anniversary of the battle in which General George Armstrong Custer fell, he was invited to attend the Semi-Centennial Ceremonies held on the Custer Battle-field. Some of the Indians invited to this ceremony hesi-tated to accept. Said one, 'I am afraid that, when the soldiers get us together there, they will get to thinking about their dead comrades and rub us out.' But White Bull was not afraid. He was told that great crowds would be there, both Indians and whites, from all over the country. And when he arrived, he was not disappointed. Reports of the gathering estimate the number of visitors at forty thousand.

Delegations of the Sioux came, led by James Red Cloud from Pine Ridge, Red Tomahawk ('Slayer of Sitting Bull') from Standing Rock, Chief Standing Bear, the celebrated author, and others. Chief Little Wolf brought the Cheyenne delegation from Lame Deer. The Crows swarmed in from their Agency near-by, led by the three surviving Crow scouts of Custer's command, Curly, White-Man-Runs-Him, and Hairy Moccasin. There were Arapaho, Shoshoni, Rees: almost every tribe on the Northern Plains was represented.

The white men came in special cars and automobiles or on horseback. Eminent historians, such as George Bird Grinnell, A. E. Brininstool, W. M. Camp, and Grace Raymond Hebard, were present. Governors of surrounding States and representatives of commercial clubs and leading corporations of neighboring cities, reporters, and well-known writers, such as Mary Roberts Rinehart, the famous movie star Bill Hart (there christened 'Crazy Horse' by the Sioux) — all were on hand, together with thousands of tourists and spectators. Best of all, in White Bull's estimation, were the many old veterans of Indian wars, including Captain Luther H. North, leader of the Pawnee Scouts, and Brigadier-General E. S. Godfrey, U.S.A., Retired, who had exchanged shots with White Bull in the fighting with the troops under Major Marcus A. Reno on that fatal day fifty years earlier. With these, White Bull was pleased to see the khaki-clad troopers of the new Seventh United States Cavalry, inheritors of that regiment's great renown. The Seventh was commanded by Colonel Fitzhugh Lee.

But from all those Indians White Bull was chosen to be most highly honored. He was not only photographed, interviewed, entertained, and given presents, but was chosen as the Representative of the Red Race in the Peace Ceremonies on Custer Ridge. On the morning of June 25, the Peace Ceremonies took place.

Simulating Custer's advance, the Seventh Cavalry, led

by General Godfrey, one of the four surviving officers of the fighting, rode up over the ridge from the south toward the shaft which marks the spot where Custer fell.

With the General rode seven troopers, veterans of the battle. The Seventh Cavalry was divided into five troops, and to their guidons were attached streamers bearing the names of Custer's five troop commanders. Slowly they advanced toward the National Cemetery to the strains of a funeral dirge played by a band of the Seventh concealed in a near-by ravine. From the north in a far-flung column, hundreds of mounted Indians in full war-costume, led by eighty Sioux and Cheyenne survivors of the battle, advanced behind White Bull to meet the troops.

Near the monument the two parties met. White Bull raised his open palm vertically in the sign of peace. General Godfrey replied by sheathing his sword as he rode forward to greet the Chief. They clasped hands, and, as a pledge of friendship, White Bull presented to the General a fine blanket, while General Godfrey gave White Bull a large American flag.

Afterward, while General Godfrey and the seven veterans laid wreaths upon the monument, a detachment of the Seventh fired three volleys over the graves on the hillside and sounded taps for the men buried there.

Then Indians and troopers paired off, and in column of twos rode slowly away down past the National Cemetery to camp. They rode as brothers-in-arms, following Old Glory from the spot where half a century before the men of their races had met as deadly enemies.

Major Alson B. Ostrander, formerly of the Eighteenth Infantry, U.S.A., had heard how Bad Soup had pointed out the body of Custer to Chief White Bull on the day of the battle. The Major asked White Bull to point out the spot where he saw Custer lying on his back that day. White Bull immediately complied. The Major said, 'That is the spot.'

From the description of the battle given by the Indians, Major Ostrander concluded that White Bull was certainly among those who shot down Custer and the men immediately around him. He asked White Bull, 'Are you the man who killed Custer?'

White Bull could not be sure, as he never saw Custer to know him until after the battle, and no one could tell him just where Custer was wounded. He answered, 'Maybe.'

Of course the Chief would like to believe himself the slayer of so famous an enemy. But he cannot be sure. White Bull has thought a great deal about this.

Next day there were other ceremonies. The body of an unknown soldier recently discovered on the battlefield was buried with military honors. Red Tomahawk and various white men made speeches, and a marker was raised on the bluffs where Reno stood off the Indians. But none of these things could add to the satisfaction of the Chief. He and General Godfrey had been honored above all men that day.

White Bull went back to Cherry Creek carrying the flag the General had given him. He still keeps it, a treasured memento of that glorious day.[1]

[1] For accounts of these ceremonies, see *Winners of the West*, August 30, 1926, or a separate reprint, *The Custer Semi-Centennial Ceremonies, June 25–26, 1926.* (*The Custer Semi-Centennial*, Major A. B. Ostrander; *Hasty Notes on the Semi-Centennial*, R. S. Ellison; *The Official Report*, General E. S. Godfrey; *The Burial of the Hatchet*, M. E. Hawkins.) The Casper Printing and Stationery Company, Casper, Wyoming, 1926. Also press notices throughout the States.

CHIEF WHITE BULL, 1932

He carries the flag presented to him by General E. S. Godfrey at the
semicentennial of the Custer Fight, June 25–26, 1926. He also wears
a saber given him by the author

It has been said that he who fills his youth with creditable actions and in his age can talk of them has lived a happy life. Certainly this seems true of Chief White Bull. When he had finished telling me the story of his life, I had planned to ask him if he thought life worth living, and if he would live his own life again, if he could. But when the day came, I did not ask that question. Long before that, it was obvious that the Chief has found life well worth while and would jump at the chance to live again. And this in spite of the defeat and squalid poverty which have befallen his people.

However, I asked him what was the worst day of his life. He said: 'That was the day my eldest son died. He was just thirteen, and died of a hemorrhage. I could do nothing. I thought I should go crazy. That was the most dreadful day of my life.'

Seeing how the old man was moved by this memory, I did not press him for details, but turned the talk to pleasanter things.

I asked, 'What was the happiest day of your life?'

Then a smile broke over his strong features. He smacked his lips and answered: 'It was the day I was honored on the Custer Battlefield. Thousands of people were there, great generals, great chiefs. I was honored above all the Indians. I was a great man that day. Ever since, I have thought *that* the happiest day of my life.'

Then the old man smiled graciously at me and added: 'But perhaps I was wrong. I was greatly honored that day, but now today you have taken down the story of my life. You will make it into a book, my friend. At the Custer Battlefield, I was honored for one day. But when our book is published, my name will be remembered and my story read so long as men can read it. You have done this, and I think you have made this the happiest day of my life.'

It is my hope that Chief White Bull may find one happier day even than these — the day when he holds in his hands the first copy of this volume.

THE END

APPENDIX

APPENDIX

A MINNICONJOU CALENDAR
or
WINTER COUNT
1781–1932

WHEN White Bull was twenty-nine years old, he began to compile and record the history of his people and their wars. He had heard that a wise old man named Steamboat (Fireboat) had counted years by memory, and had a hide on which he had painted, in a sunwise spiral, beginning at the center, a series of mnemonic pictures for the years. After Steamboat died, his brother-in-law, Hairy Hand, owned this calendar, which Steamboat had taught him to interpret. White Bull purchased this calendar from Hairy Hand, and afterward called in a number of other old historians (men with good memories) to discuss it with him. In this way he became thoroughly familiar with the history of the Minniconjou Sioux as far back as 1781, at which time the calendar began.

Having learned to write in his own language, White Bull saw no need to rely upon painted hides for his chronology, and transcribed the events of each year in a book purchased for that purpose. On one page he wrote out the story of the events in the history of his people, year by year, and on the page opposite noted events of a more personal nature, concerning himself, his friends, and family. Here follows White Bull's calendar, giving the names of the Winters.

1781 *Swimming for Buffalo.* After the ice broke up in the Missouri, the Indians swam out and retrieved carcasses of buffalo drifting down.

1782 *They First Saw Steel Knives.* An Englishman came to the camp and saw the people using knives of stone and bone. He went away and returned with steel knives.

1783 *Ant's Brother Died.* This man Ant and his brother were celebrated men.

1784 *Pemmican-Bag's Brother was Murdered.* Apparently this was remarkable because of the man's prominence, or by reason of the rarity of such a crime.

1785 *Pine-Shooter was Captured.*

1786 *People Speaking the Same Language Quarreled.* This was a feud within the tribe.

1787 *Helping on Each Side.* Each party to the feud begun the previous winter gained helpers. The cause of this feud is unknown, but when the fight was over, one party left the tribe and disappeared. White Bull thinks they went to Canada, for when Sitting Bull was brought back from Canada in 1881, he said to White Bull: 'We went hunting away up north. We found a band of Indians speaking Sioux. I asked an old man where they came from, and he told me that his grandfather had come up there because of a quarrel.' (White Cap's Sioux?)

1788 *Wears-Mask Died.*

1789 *Devil Goes Crazy.* There was a man who claimed he was a shaman. He kept talking about it all the time until he went crazy. (Apparently the word here translated *Devil* is *not* the proper name of this unfortunate.)

1790 *Mandan Houses were Burned.* The Minniconjou attacked the Mandans and burned their houses.

1791 *Three Going After Wood were Killed.* Three women, wood-gatherers, were cut down by the Crows within a quarter of a mile from camp. The Crows had such good horses that they were not caught.

1792 *Made-Himself-Like-the-Man-in-the-Moon Died.*

1793 *A Scout Looking was Killed.* The Crows killed a Minniconjou scout east of the Missouri River. At this time, the Minniconjou made their headquarters on the Missouri, though they had gone as far as the Black Hills in 1765.

1794 *The Oglala Get Cedar.* A shaman put an end to an epidemic among the Oglala by burning cedar in the lodges.

1795 *They Made no Winter Camp Until Spring.* That winter

the people kept moving constantly, instead of camping in one place as usual.

1796   *The Hoop Stops Against Penis.* While playing a game of hoop-and-sticks, a man named Penis lost his temper and attacked two other players. One of them killed him. In that game some object like a log was used to stop the course of the rolling hoop. The dead man was so disliked that his comrades continued the game, using his body for this purpose.

1797   *Owns-Club was Killed by the Crows.*

1798   *Smallpox Epidemic.* This was along the Missouri.

1799   *Second Smallpox Epidemic.*

1800   *They were Frozen to Death.* The Minniconjou were moving camp over the high prairie from one stream to another. A blizzard caught them. In those days they had few horses. One by one the older people succumbed to the cold. When one of them gave up, the survivors would carry him.

1801   *A Man Wearing a Red Blanket was Killed in Battle.* He is remembered for his bravery.

1802   *They Came Home Four Times Victorious.*

1803   *Lone Man Came Home Dead from a Fight.* Lone Man was leader of a war-party. Three of his men were killed. Lone Man survived. Such a leader, who lost some of his men, was called a coward and 'not worth a bunch of buffalo hair.' White Bull explains: 'Being a leader is a hard job. Yet all the young men wish to be leaders so much that they *will* keep trying. A leader should be in the thick of the fight. He should shoot, capture horses, and strike the enemy. If he is killed, his comrades will say he is a brave man. If his men come home without him, the people will say they should revenge him, or vindicate themselves by some brave deeds.'

1804   *A Clown was Killed.* A Clown (Heyoka) is supposed to do everything backwards. If he is given a command, he will do the opposite. This Clown acted very foolish. In a fight with enemies he shot his arrows straight up in the air. He led the attack against the enemy, but, when almost halfway between the two forces, he turned his back on the enemy and shot arrows at his own people. The first time he shot above his people, the second time above them, the third time at the enemy, and the fourth time at his own people. He was killed by the enemy.

1805 *Many Crows (Birds) Died.* There was a place where the crows roosted in trees. The Sioux used to go there to pick up feathers. One day they found the ground covered with dead birds. No one knew what had killed them.

1806 *An Hidatsa Woman Came.* When she turned up in the Sioux camp she explained that she had had trouble with her folks. She did not say whether she was married or not. After a while some Sioux men took her home, making presents to her parents. Her family were glad to see her.

1807 *They are Taking a Book Around the Country.* Some white men employed an Indian to carry a book to other white men settled in Sioux country (trading posts). An Oglala named Red Dog carried the book far to the northwest to the head of Little (Milk) River, and then returned. No one knows what this book contained.

1808 *Mandans, Rees, and Hidatsa Moved Together.* The Minniconjou camped with the Mandans.

1809 *Still with Them.* That is, the Minniconjou remained with the Mandans.

1810 *Little-Face was Killed in Battle.*

1811 *They Went out and Killed Four Enemies with Long Hair.*

1812 *They Have Him Stand with the Water-Bag.* One winter a good-looking married woman left the Sioux camp and went after water. At the river a stranger asked her for a drink of water. She was startled, but kept her head, and gave him a drink from a horn cup. The man said, 'Come home with me and be my woman.' The girl feared that this enemy would kill her if she went with him. She replied: 'I think you are a handsome man, so I will go with you. But first I must return to the camp to get my moccasins, and awl, and sewing things. Please hold my water-bag until I return.' He agreed.

He let her go to the camp. She immediately told the men about this enemy. When she went back to meet him, the Sioux were hidden all around. They surrounded this enemy and killed him. When his body was frozen stiff, the men, for a joke, propped it up with sticks and hung the water-bag on the dead man's arm. Hence the name of this year.

1813 *Wears-War-Bonnet Died.* He was a famous Minniconjou.

1814 *Little-Buffalo-Cow, a Minniconjou Hunter, Killed a White Buffalo.*

1815 *Many Pregnant Women Died.* An epidemic killed eleven women.

1816 *Two Horses with Big Manes Captured.*

1817 *Charred-Face Strikes Two Enemies.* Charred-Face was a young boy, an orphan fourteen years old, who lived with his grandmother. He was so poor that he had no bow. When enemies came, however, he chased them with the other Sioux. Two of the enemies took their stand under a cutbank and bluffed the Sioux warriors, but Charred-Face picked up a stick, rushed in, and struck them both. When he returned, his grandmother was singing a song:

> My grandson struck the enemy;
> Yet he had no bow.

From that day his tribe of Sioux took the name Itazipdro, Sans Arc.

1818 *Smallpox Epidemic.*

1819 *They Brought Them Home with Horseshoes on.* The Sioux captured horses with iron shoes for the first time.

1820 *They Brought Home Curly Horses.* Curly horses were greatly admired by the Sioux because of their rarity. The hair on these animals was curly all over. Some say Indians would try to make a horse curly by singeing his coat.

1821 *They Used Hair at a Ceremony.* The explanation of this item seems to have been lost. (*Alowanpi?*)

1822 *Eight Scouts were Killed.*

1823 *Eagle-Hunter Killed.* This man, Eagle-Hunter, got his name because he was always hunting eagles. One day when he was lying in the eagle pit on the hill, enemies found and killed him.

1824 *People Drowned.* At the mouth of the Cheyenne River, there was a camp of Sioux. It was spring, and the ice was going out. A visitor to the camp heard the ice 'crying' and advised the people to move up on the tableland. Those who failed to take his advice were drowned when the water backed up in the mouth of Cheyenne River.

1825 *The Whistlers Die After They Come Home.* A hungry war-party killed a sick buffalo and ate its flesh. Buffalo afflicted by this disease were known as 'whistlers.' According to some, this has reference to the belching of gas from the stomach.

Makes-Room, White Bull's father, was born.

1826 *They Burn a Small Beaver Lodge.*

1827 *Fighting Over a Woman.* Several young men were wooing the same girl, waiting their turns to talk with her. Those waiting became impatient, and a fight resulted.

1828 *Those Digging Holes were Killed.* A Sioux reported he had seen three enemies near the camp. The Sioux could not find them, though there seemed to be no place where they could hide. Finally one of the Sioux, passing up a ravine, was fired at, but not hit. All the Sioux came running, and killed three enemies found lying in a shallow hole covered with brush.

1829 *Little-Bear was Killed.*

1830 *Six Rees were Killed.* They came to steal horses, but the Sioux killed them all.

1831 *'We-Ta-Pa-Hato' Fought Among Themselves.* This was a feud in one band (Wuh'-ta-piu?) of the Cheyenne nation.

In this year, Sitting Bull, White Bull's uncle, was born.

1832 *The Sans Arc First Live in Log Houses.* This was near the Missouri River. The fireplaces were built in the corners of the houses.

1833 *The Stars Move.* This was the great meteor shower of November of that year.

1834 *Lame Deer Pulled His Arrow Out.* The Sioux were afoot on the warpath and encountered enemies on foot. The enemies ran. The Sioux pursued. Lame Deer was ahead and shot an enemy. The enemy kept on running, but Lame Deer overtook him, jerked out his arrow, and used it again. This enemy died.

1835 *Fighting Over the Ice.* A Minniconjou war-party saw Crow enemies crossing the river ice on foot. When the Crows were in the middle of the river, the Sioux rushed them. They knocked one Crow over, and, though he took cover in the timber, they followed him and killed him.

1836 *Many Elk were Killed.*

1837 *They Came Home Without Body.* Body was shot in two places (the stomach and the ribs) in a fight with the Crows. The Sioux left him for dead. Some days after they reached home, they saw a man walking back and forth on a near-by hilltop. It was Body, come back to life. Hence they still call that hill Body Butte. This butte is some three miles above the mouth of White Bark Creek in the Black Hills.

1838 *Grass Killed Himself.* He had trouble with his folks and hanged himself. Though Sioux women generally used this method of committing suicide, the men preferred other methods as a rule.

1839 *Three Hohe (Assiniboin) were Killed.* The Sioux saw them coming and killed them. Perhaps they were scouts.

1840 *They Brought Home Many Spotted Horses.* These were captured from a Crow camp west of the headwaters of Arrow (Pryor) Creek.

1841 *One Feather Prayed.* In an attack on the Crow camp, some of the Sioux relatives of One Feather were killed. A year later, he called a meeting and collected one arrow from every man present. He then gave one arrow to every good warrior and begged them all to fight. They agreed, but could not find the Crows.

1842 *Keeping a Buffalo Head Inside.* That winter a medicine man kept the head of a buffalo in his lodge.

1843 *They Fenced with Pine.* The Minniconjou built fences around their camp.

1844 *Plenty Food in Ash Trees.* Camping in an ash grove, they hung meat to dry on the branches.

In this year Crazy Horse was born, and thirty Oglala were killed.

1845 *They Reached Them from Behind and Killed Some.* Returning from a fight, the Sioux got strung out. The enemy crept up and killed three who were in the rear.

This year Sitting Bull counted his first *coup*.

This year Chief Four Horns (Sitting Bull's uncle) was left for dead on the battlefield. After his relatives had given away all their property in mourning, Four Horns turned up again.

1846 *They Came Home Without Two-Herd.* Two-Herd was shot in battle. They brought him some distance and then left him, at his own request. Later he came in alone.

1847 *Hole-Creek Froze to Death.* He went hunting and was caught in a blizzard. His parents found his horse and his body.

1848 *No-Grass Winter.* Apparently a drouth prevented the growth of grass the previous summer.

1849 *Enemies Came to the Hunting Ground.* Two Sioux hunters became separated from their comrades and were killed near Slim Buttes.

This year Chief Joseph White Bull was born.

1850 *Calf-Woman was Born.* See Chapter IV,. above. White Bull heard this story from Young Bird, who killed the cow. See also, Clark, *The Indian Sign Language*, Philadelphia, 1885, page 88.

1851 *First Big Issue was Made.* This was the great treaty council at Fort Laramie.

1852 *Plenty Snow Winter.*

1853 *They Brought Navajo Blankets Over the Mountains.* This same year they killed a Crow Indian wearing a bonnet with four horns.

1854 *Brave Bear was Killed.* A Sioux war-party tracked some Hohe into some rocks northwest of Slim Buttes. Brave Bear, armed with a spear, advanced, and was shot. Also another Sioux was killed there.

1855 *White-Beard is Holding.* White Beard (General William S. Harney) held prisoner the Sioux women and children captured in the attack on Little Thunder's Camp.

1856 *Four-Horns Came to Make the Alo Wanpi Ceremony.* The Hunkpapa chief, Four-Horns, Sitting Bull's uncle, thus adopted Noisy-Walking-Elk as his son. An account of such a ceremony is given in Bulletin 61, Bureau of American Ethnology.

1857 *Ten Crows Killed at Captive Butte.* This is the fight described earlier in this book (Chaxter XI).

1858 *One-Horn Prepares for Spirit-Keeping Ceremony.* This ceremony is described in Bulletin 61, Bureau of American Ethnology.

1859 *Big Crow and His Brother were Killed.* These two boys went hunting. Their father has a premonition of disaster, followed them, and found them killed by enemies.

1860 *Surrounding a Red Tipi.* Little Bear led a party against the Crows. They found Crows in a lone red tipi with a horse-corral alongside. They killed several Crows.

In this year there was a big battle between the Sioux and the Crows on the Red Water. The Sioux leaders were

Sans Arcs. The Crows captured two hundred head of horses, more than they ever captured again.

1861 *Plenty Buffalo.*

1862 *Red Feather, a Hohe, was Killed.* At the mouth of Red Water the Sioux saw a Hohe, horseback, coming. He dismounted to fight with his gun. The leading Sioux sheered off. The Hohe chased him, but stumbled and fell. In the fall his gun was accidentally discharged. Red Thunder, Iron Hail, Iron Plume, counted their *coups* on him. Brown Buffalo rode up, drew his knife and stabbed the Hohe on the cheek, chin, chest, and shoulder. The Hohe pulled Brown Buffalo off his horse. Then Big Skirt shot the Hohe. They gave Brown Buffalo the fourth *coup* because the enemy had touched him. One-Dreamed-About was leader of the Sioux. This was above the mouth of Red Water

The same day the Sioux surprised two young men building a fire some distance from the Hohe camp. These young men were all dressed up and had no weapons. They were going to see their girls and were waiting outside the camp until dark. The Sioux killed them. The last Sioux to count *coup* almost dropped his *coup*-stick as he struck at the Hohe. The Hohe boy pulled the brass arm-let from his upper arm and hurled it at his antagonist. This futile gesture made the Sioux laugh.

1863 *Eight were Killed.* An account of this fight is given earlier in this book (Chapter IV).

1864 *Four Crow Indians were Killed.*

1865 *Chasing-Crow Died.* He died of sickness.

1866 *One Hundred White Men Killed.* This was the celebrated Fetterman fight or 'massacre' at Fort Phil Kearny, December 21, 1866 (see Chapter VI, above).

1867 *Icy Winter.* A heavy snow was followed by a heavy rain and a week's thaw. Cold weather then returned, snow followed, and the whole country was covered with a coat of ice. The following spring a woman, felling cottonwood trees to feed her horses, cut down one tree, leaving a stump three feet high. As the tree fell against another tree, the trunk slid down and smashed her thigh, shattering the bone. The Sioux could not set a broken thigh-bone; she died. Because of this, the name of Spring Creek was changed to the Creek-Where-the-Woman-Broke-Her-Leg.

1868 *Fifteen Persons were Killed.* A large war-party of Sioux went against the Crow Indians. Half the men were mounted, half afoot. They found the Crow camp in a valley. The Sioux footmen halted on the bluff just above the timber, beyond which lay the Crow camp. The horsemen advanced towards the camp, riding to the north. Meanwhile the men on foot built a corral or 'fort' of logs.

However, the Crows soon discovered their enemies, and swarmed out of their camp in such numbers that the Sioux had to run for their lives. The men on foot could not save themselves. Fifteen were killed: of the Minniconjou, Black Elk; of the Brulé, Red Dog and Heart-Take-Heed; of the Oglala, Black Bird; and of the Sans Arc Sioux, Eagle Man, Cloud Man, Chasing Hawk, Walks-with-His-Pipe, Long Fish, Runs-Against, Little Bear, Charging-First, Brave Thunder, Running Hawk. This disaster occurred on the headwaters of Arrow Creek.

Luckily, White Bull was away on a visit when this war party started out, and only heard of their failure on his return home. However, had he gone with them, it is unlikely that he would have been among the slain. For in all his life he never once went to war on foot.

1869 *Thirty Crows were Killed.* An account of this fight is given in my biography of Sitting Bull (Chapter XVI).

In this year the Hunkpapa fought the Hohe and Rees; the Oglala, Sans Arc, and Minniconjou fought the Crows; and the great battle with the Flatheads took place. See elsewhere in this book (Chapter XI).

1870 *High Hump was Killed.* They were fighting the Shoshoni in the White (Big Horn) Mountains. The Sioux were retreating. High Hump was hit while defending the rear. He rode up to his friend, Chief Crazy Horse, gave him his six-shooter, and fell from his horse, dead.

1871 *Long Forelock was Killed with Three Others.* This affair is narrated elsewhere in this volume (Chapter XIII).

1872 *A Crow Riding a White Horse was Killed.* Crows raided the Sioux camp, but were driven back. One brave Crow on a white horse stood off the Sioux. One of the Sioux,

Poor Elk, shot the Crow's horse. It began to pitch, and bucked the Crow off. For a while he fought with his bow until Red Eagle fired and killed him. Short Bull, a Brulé, counted *coup*. This was on the headwaters of the Little Big Horn River.

White Bull's first son was born.

1873 *Little and His Wife Died*. They died the same day. White Bull's cousin saw this and told him of it. Little and his wife were very old. When she died of sickness, her husband said: 'I have lived with this woman many years. I do not care to live without her. I am going to die too. But before I die there is something in my body which will come out of my body. I wish to be buried beside my wife.'

Little was a shaman. Sitting in his lodge, he placed a buffalo chip before him, and made some gestures. Then a small bird flew out of his mouth. This bird settled on the buffalo chip and grew larger. It was a prairie-owl, like those that live in prairie-dog holes. The man said: 'After I die, let the bird fly away.' Then the old man lay down in his bed and died the same day.

That same year the Sioux fought the Slota on Rosebud River, as narrated in this book (Chapter XV).

1874 *Killed in his Lodge*. A Crow Indian shot a Sioux in the Sioux's own lodge. This happened on the Big Dry. It was at night. The Sioux hunters were straggling in from a buffalo surround. At the end of the camp there was a big lodge with a fire inside, which threw the shadows of those inside on the wall of the tent. A Crow slipped up and shot one of these men.

1875 *One-Horn Died*. He was one of the six hereditary chiefs or Scalp-Shirt-Men of the Minniconjou.

In this year some of the Sioux were given whiskey, and signed a treaty ceding the Black Hills. One-Horn came home from this treaty council and died of shame.

This year is sometimes remembered as the *Winter When White-Deer was Killed and Came Alive*. White Bull rescued this man, as narrated elsewhere (Chapter XXI).

1876 *Long Hair is Killed*. General Custer was killed on the Little Big Horn River, June 25, 1876.

This year is also remembered because horses were taken

away from the Indians at the Agencies, and because there was a second treaty with regard to the Black Hills.

1877 *Crazy Horse was Killed.* Crazy Horse had surrendered and was invited to the fort to talk. They tried to put him in the guardhouse. He resisted and was stabbed in the back with a bayonet.

1878 *Running-Hawk Killed.* He was a scout for a war-party. He was climbing a hill when his enemies crept up the coulees on either side and killed him. He was Minniconjou.

1879 *Shoots-Bear-Running was Killed.* A Sioux party on foot captured horses from the Crows, but were overtaken between the mouth of Tongue River and Powder River. Only one Sioux was killed, though three were shot.

1880 *Camped on Tongue River for the Winter.* The people were on foot at the mouth of Tongue River. Their horses had all been taken by the soldiers.

1881 *They Stop at Standing Rock to Camp for the Winter.* These are the same Sioux referred to under 1880.
White Bull is made Chief in place of his father.

1882 *Crazy Heart Died.* This man, a son of Chief Lame Deer, died of despair because his father had been killed by the soldiers and all his horses had been taken away.

1883 *Bull Eagle was Punished.* That summer, in the last great buffalo hunt, the Sioux had captured three white buffalo hunters for poaching. They let these men go unharmed, but white officers came from the Black Hills, took Bull Eagle, and put him in prison (see Chapter XXIII).

1884 *Crow King Died.* This Hunkpapa had been a friend of Sitting Bull's and was a good warrior and a member of the Indian Police at Standing Rock.

1885 *Flying-By Died.* This famous man was one of the six hereditary chiefs of the Minniconjou.

1886 *Plenty-Snow Winter.*

1887 *Dish Face (Concave Face) Died.* This same year Chief Four-Horns of the Hunkpapa died. Four-Horns was Sitting Bull's uncle, a quiet man, well liked, tall and slim, with a light complexion. He had a bullet in his body from the fight at Killdeer Mountain (1864), which was believed to be the cause of his death.

1888 *Measles Epidemic.* White Bull lost a daughter and had the disease himself.

That same winter, Black Moon, Sitting Bull's uncle, died. He was always loquacious and fond of joking.

1889 *'Three Stars' Came to Buy Land.* General George 'Three Stars' Crook, came to the Agency to secure a cession of Sioux lands.

1890 *Sitting Bull was Killed; also Spotted Elk.* An account of Sitting Bull's death will be found in my biography of that chief (Chapter XXXVIII). Spotted Elk, a Minniconjou, was killed by soldiers at Pine Ridge.

1891 *They Made a Big Steal at the Agency.* The Indians say that the Agent was caught in a fraud.

1892 *Owns-the-Boat was Killed.* This white man was interpreter for General Crook in 1889. He was a squaw-man named Fielder and was killed when resisting the Agency Indian Police.

1893 *They Got Payment for Horses.* The Sioux were paid in part for the horses taken away in 1876.

1894 *No-Grass Winter.* Gall died that year of sickness. Some say he died of an overdose of Anti-Fat, others from a fall from a wagon. However, it is more credible that Gall died from the bayonet wounds received in the winter of 1866–67. In his delirium on his deathbed, he is said to have repented his friendship for the whites, and to have asked for his gun in order to shoot some of them.

1895 *Straight (Buffalo) Gut Died.*

1896 *Many Old Men Died.*

1897 *The Sacred Pipe was Taken by the Agent.* The sacred pipe given to the Sioux long before by the White Buffalo Maiden was taken from its Keeper by some of the Indian Police. White Bull, with the help of the Agent, was able to recover it. All the policemen involved in this affair died soon after.

1898 *Spotted Eagle Died.*

1899 *The Crows Came.* Some Crow Indians visited the Sioux.

1900 *White Swan Died.* White Swan was the son of one of the six hereditary chiefs of the Minniconjou.

The same year many died of smallpox.

1901 *White Bull was Punished.* He was put in the guardhouse by the Indian Agent for insisting upon better terms in the leasing of Indian land (see Chapter XXIII).

1902 *Many Eagles were Killed.* In Fall and Spring, eagles flying from and to the Black Hills are numerous on the Cheyenne River Reservation. That year the Sioux killed an unusual number.

1903   *Celebration at Rapid City, South Dakota.*

1904   *Many Horses were Winter-Killed.*

1905   *Makes-Room Died.* Makes-Room, or *Kiyukan'pi* (Make-Way-for-Him), White Bull's father, died, at the age of eighty.

1906   *White Bull Captured the Ute Indians.* The United States Government sent White Bull to persuade the Utes to keep the peace at the time of a threatened uprising, as narrated elsewhere in this book (Chapter XXIV).

1907   *The Utes Camp Here Until Winter, Then Move to Thunder Butte* (see Chapter XXIV).

1908   *Chief Hump Died.* Chief Hump was a celebrated leader, who is said to have captured a Thunder Bird. He was blind in his old age.

       That year they opened part of the Cheyenne River Reservation to white settlement.

1909   *Yellow Owl Died.*

1910   *Black Hills Council at Cherry Creek.* This meeting at White Bull's camp was attended by representatives from nine reservations. The object of it was to recover damages for the Black Hills, taken from the Sioux by force.

1911   *Wood-Pile Died.* Wood-Pile was one of White Bull's close friends and relatives, and one of the best fighters of his generation. He was tall, slim, had a light complexion, and a gay, jolly disposition.

1912   *Fair at Bear Creek.*

1913   *Flag-Raising at Eagle Butte.*

1914   *Elk Head Died.* Elk Head was Keeper of the Sacred Pipe. No-Heart died the same winter.

1915   *Short Log Died.*

1916   *Council Bear Died.*

1917   *Owns-Bobtail Died.*

1918   *Many are Sick and Die.* Influenza epidemic.

1919   *Runs-After Died.*

1920   *Bad Black Hills Meeting at Crow Creek.*

1921   *Electing Representatives.* At this time the Sioux chose their attorney in the suit for damages for the Black Hills.

1922   *The Commissioner of Indian Affairs Comes to Eagle Butte.*

1923 *Black Hills Matter was Judged*. Proof of damages was offered.

1924 *All the People Voting*. American citizenship for the Sioux.

1925 *They are Getting Paunches*. One hundred buffalo were killed at Pierre, South Dakota. White Bull and other Indians were given the paunches of these buffalo.

1926 *White Bull Visits the Custer Battlefield*. This was at the time of the Custer Semi-Centennial Ceremonies, June 25–26, 1926 (see Chapter XXV).
      That year the Sioux sold oil leases.

1927 *Fast Horse Died*.

1928 *Eagle Claws Died*.

1929 *Indian Council at Rapid City*. Before this, during the visit of President Coolidge to the Black Hills. White Bull was chosen from all the Indians to make the speech of welcome.

1930 *The Investigator was Here*. The senatorial investigation of the Indian Bureau is referred to.

1931 *Hard Winter*. There was no grass. The Indians depended upon the Red Cross.

1932 '*Famous*' (*Stanley Vestal*) *Wrote Down the Story of White Bull's Life*. White Bull conferred the name 'Famous' (literally, His-Name-is-Everywhere) upon the author. The Chief's own great fame gives him the right to confer such a name.

BIBLIOGRAPHY

Bourke, John C., *On the Border with Crook*. New York, 1891.

Byrne, P. E., *Soldiers of the Plains*. New York, 1926.

Clark, W. P., *The Indian Sign Language*. Philadelphia, 1885.

DeBarthe, Joe, *Life and Adventures of Frank Grouard*. St. Joseph, Missouri, 1894.

DeLand, Charles E., *The Sioux Wars*. In South Dakota Historical Collections, vol. xv. Department of History, Pierre, South Dakota, 1930.

Engagements with Hostile Indians, 1868–1882. Official compilation.

Finerty, John F., *War-Path and Bivouac*. Chicago, 1890.

Grinnell, George Bird, *The Fighting Cheyennes*. New York, 1915.

Hebard, Grace Raymond, *Washakie*. Cleveland, Ohio, 1930.

McLaughlin, James, *My Friend the Indian*. Boston, 1910.

Miles, General Nelson A., *Personal Recollections of General Nelson A. Miles*. Chicago, 1897.

Standing Bear, Chief, *Land of the Spotted Eagle*. Boston, 1933.

Vestal, Stanley, *Sitting Bull, Champion of the Sioux*. Boston, 1932.

INDEX

Topics connected with Indian warfare and related subjects are indexed in heavy-face type, and references to the same subjects appearing in Stanley Vestal's *Sitting Bull* are included, following the initials *SB*. Where the same name applies to two different Indians, they are distinguished by (a) and (b) when not otherwise identified.

Afraid-of-the-Enemy (Enemy-Fears-Him), 150
'A-Good-Job-Well-Done-While-They-Slept,' a horse-stealing incident, 207
Alamo, 50
Alex, white man on buffalo hunt with Indians, 239
All-Against-Him (At Bay), *see* Spotted Breast
Alone-on-One-Side, joins bullet-proof Order, 133; is shot, but unhurt, 137
Ambush, prepared for soldiers of Fort Phil Kearny, 56, 59, 72; for Flatheads, 118, 119, 121; feared, 177. *SB* 54, 59, 122, 123, 181, 210
Appah, Ute leader, 243
Archery, feats of, 63. *SB* 34
Arms and equipment, 61–66, 73, 79, 178, 199, 219, 240. *SB* 28, 30, 35, 45, 47, 48–54, 60–62, 76, 116, 135, 148, 149, 165 *ff.*, 178, 188
Army Camps, *see* Forts and army camps
Arrow (Pryor) Creek, 48, 117; Chief Blackfoot quoted, 131, 137, 138, 149, 237
Ash Creek, *see* Reno Creek
Attack, 11, 43, 60, 71, 73–79, 119, 149, 177, 187, 192, 220, 223. *SB* 29, 36, 45, 58, 59, 62, 115–17, 137, 210, 212

Bad Hair, son killed in fight with soldiers, 221
Bad Lake, 186; kills white man who wounds friend, 213
Bad Lands, 161
Bad-Light-Hair, killed in Custer Battle, 203. *SB* 182
Bad Soup (Bad Juice), found Gen. Custer's body lying naked, 203, 253. *SB* 135, 174
Bag Butte, 48
Baker, Major E.M., *n.* 137, *n.* 150

Barefoot, strikes *coup* on U.S. scout, 45
Battle of Kildeer Mountain, *n.* 35. *SB* 54–59, 64, 66, 75, 234
Battles — Rees and Hunkpapa fight over horse-race, 20, 21; Fetterman Fight, 60–66; Wagon-Box Fight, 70–79; Fight-Over-the-White-Buffalo-Hide, 101; with Flatheads, 119–23; with Crows, 148, 169–71; with Slota, 156–59; 177, 178; Three Stars, 187–89; Custer, 192 *ff.*; in snow, 211–13; Miles, 223. *SB* 6, 13, 29–31, 35–37, 45–49, 51–64, 76, 78, 115 *ff.*, 120–26, 127–31, 137, 138, 142, 155 *ff.*, 162 *ff.*, 177 *ff.*, 188 *ff.*, 196 *ff.*, 207, 300
Bay, Indian scout, 234
Bear Butte, 93, 132, 161, 183, 233
Bear-Chasing, in Wagon-Box Fight, 71, 72
Bearded Man, Cheyenne, killed in Custer Battle, scalped by mistake, 199, 203
Bear Ears, killed in Fort Phil Kearny Battle, 67
Bear-Grabs, gets insignia from Fox Soldiers, 52
Bear Hail, 102
Bear Lice, counts *coup* in Custer Battle, 197; in rough-and-tumble fight with soldier to help White Bull, 199
Bear-Loves (Bear Pities), 11; smokes war-pipe with raiding-party, 39; with war-party against U.S. soldiers, 43; gets insignia from Fox Soldiers, 52; in attack on Wagon-Box corral, is wounded, 72, 78; begins Sun Dance, 95; organizes war-party, 114, 115; joins bullet-proof Order, 133; withstands shock of bullet, 136; with horse-stealing party, 170; 227
Bear's Heart, killed by Crows while stealing horses, 34